28

The heart of Jazz

William L. Grossman and Jack W. Farr

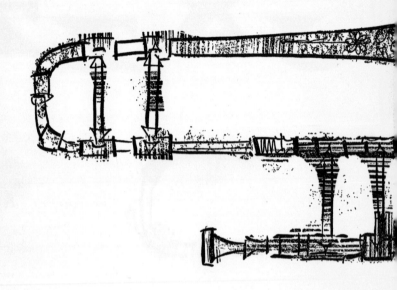

line drawings by Lamartine Le Goul

Washington Square, New Yo

THE HEART OF

JAZZ

York University Press · 1956

Acknowledgments

We have learned a great deal from our talks with jazz musicians. Especially helpful were Paul Barbarin, Danny Barker, Sharkey Bonano, John Brunious, Eddie Edwards, Bud Freeman, Frank Gillis, Richard Hadlock, Jim Heanue, Bob Helm, Avery Howard, Willie Humphrey, John LaPorta, John Lewis, Joe Muranyi, Turk Murphy, Tony Parenti, Sammy Price, Alton Purnell, Jim Robinson, Wally Rose, Lester Santiago, Harry Shields, Edmond Souchon, and Bob Thomas. Mr. Hadlock, whose record reviews and criticisms appear in *The Record Changer*, provided searching analyses of the several types of jazz, reflecting both his experience as a musician and his perspicuity as a critic. Bob Helm and his wife, Kay, generously supplied tapes and other private recordings of immeasurable historical and musicological value. Turk Murphy not only gave freely of his time in several interviews but also made available his large collection of jazz data and memorabilia. Dr. Edmond Souchon, an eminent physician who, like Mr. Hadlock, Mr. Helm, and Mr. Murphy, is a jazz scholar as well as a musician, provided much valuable literature and other material.

Professor Martin L. Bernstein, Chairman of the Department of Music of Washington Square College (New York University), pro-

5

vided invaluable criticism of some of our ideas with respect to both jazz and "serious" music. In connection with the little statistical study on musical preferences, expert advice was graciously given by Professor Frederick R. Ottman, Director of Gallatin House. Other members of the New York University faculty who provided generous help and to whom we wish to express our thanks are William L. Berliner, Professor Joseph Bram, Professor Lawrence D. Brennan, Professor Fred E. Crossland, Professor Herbert B. Dorau, Herbert W. Edwards, Professor Vincent F. Hopper, Professor Milton K. Kalb, Dr. Fredric Kurzweil, Professor Mildred E. Marcett, and Father Andrew J. O'Reilly. Thanks are due also to Richard D. McClure, Director of the New York University Christian Association, for his gracious help.

We are deeply indebted to Frank Driggs, writer and lecturer at Sarah Lawrence College, for data concerning little-known facets of jazz; to Dr. Maurice Green for the draft of an unfinished article; to Eileen Nuccio, economist and music scholar, for elaborating her unusual critical approach to jazz; to Boris Rose, recording engineer and jazz scholar, for the use of his immense and extraordinary record collection and for his constant readiness to provide or check information; to Ted Sack, producer of *Look Up and Live* (CBS-TV), for furnishing copies of some of the scripts of that fine program; and to Professor Marshall Stearns, executive director of the Institute of Jazz Studies, for information and for making available the Institute's collection of jazz literature.

For informative and stimulating discussions of various aspects of jazz, we are beholden to Aram Avakian, Joseph C. Berkwit, Jr., A. Harold Drob, Stephen M. Goldman, John Graziano, John P. Griffin, Orrin Keepnews, Carl Kendziora, Richard Krasuski, Louis Levy, Al Meyers, Mrs. Gerry Mulligan, Robert Lewis Shayon, Terry Southern, Irving W. Stone, Robert F. Tannenbaum, and Neil Walden.

For valuable material, information, or leads to sources of information, we wish to express our gratitude also to Professor William R. Bascom of Northwestern University, Michael Bregman of the Village Music Shop, Anatole Broyard, Leonard Chase and Gerald Silverman of the Electronic Workshop, Rosalind Cherry, Dr. Aaron H. Esman, Professor Joseph H. Greenberg of Columbia University, Langston Hughes, Deborah Ishlon, Professor Alan P. Merriam of the University of Wisconsin, Professor Hans Nathan of Michigan State University, Norman Orleck of *The Cash Box*, Professor Wil-

6

lard Rhodes of Columbia University, Winthrop Sargeant, and Joseph Sweeney.

Parts of the manuscript were read by Dr. Herman Kantor, by Chauncey Korten, and by Margo Rieman. Their valuable comments are reflected in the final text. Betty Melder provided expert editorial assistance.

Thanks are due also to Dr. Edmond Souchon, Lamartine Le Goullon, Bud Weil, W. T. O'Dogherty, Arthur Kramer, the Audio-Visual Center of Indiana University, R.C.A. Victor, and Good Time Jazz, Inc., for furnishing photographs used in the book.

A special debt of gratitude is owed to Mrs. E. M. Farrell and to Mignon, Ruth, and Elizabeth Grossman, who helped in many ways.

The reader should not infer that the persons, or any of them, named in these acknowledgments necessarily agree with statements of fact or opinion set forth in the book.

JACK W. FARRELL
WILLIAM L. GROSSMAN

7

Preface | *by Turk Murphy*

I am very pleased to have been asked to write a preface to this book on jazz. The music that I have been making for the past fifteen years has been the subject of a concerted critical animosity, almost unanimous, in the music "trade" press. To be given the opportunity to present my views in print is something for which I'm very grateful to Mr. Farrell and Dr. Grossman.

There are those who will wonder why I've been asked to do this; there are also those who will wonder why I haven't written a book myself. In answer to both, I can do no better than to quote from an earlier source: *Steps to Parnassus, the Study of Counterpoint,* by Johann Joseph Fux. This book, written in Latin in 1725, has been studied by every great composer-musician from Bach on down to the present time. And the words that Fux wrote, over two hundred years ago, as *his* preface say what I want to say:

"Some people will perhaps wonder why I have undertaken to write about music, there being so many works by outstanding men who have treated this subject most thoroughly and learnedly; and more especially, why I should be doing so just at this time when music has become most arbitrary and composers refuse to be bound by any rules and principles, detesting the very name of school and law like death itself.

9

"To such, I want to make my purpose clear. There have certainly been many authors famous for their teaching and competence, who have left an abundance of works on the theory of music. . . . [But] I shall not be deterred by the most ardent haters of school, nor by the corruptness of the times. . . .

"However, my efforts do not tend—nor do I credit myself with the strength—to stem the course of a torrent rushing precipitously beyond its bounds. I do not believe that I can call back composers from the unrestrained insanity of their writing to normal standards. Let each follow his own counsel." *

Musical history has a curious way of repeating itself. And what is scorned in one period (witness both Brahms and Beethoven, to name only two) can become eventually respected in another. In view of the often scathing trade reviews of my work, I can scarcely deny that I'm what might be called a "controversial figure." So I can only repeat, along with Johann Joseph Fux: "I shall not be deterred by the most ardent haters . . . nor by the corruptness of the times."

In San Francisco, in the late 1930's, we knew a kind of recorded music that we liked. It had for us, and for many other record collectors, life and interest. And it was happy. When we began playing our own interpretations of this music, we found that we weren't alone in liking it as "live" music. Traditional jazz, when played in the spirit originally intended, is basically dance music played by obviously happy musicians for the purpose of instilling a pleasant mood in the listener, thereby, as things come about in a Rube Goldberg cartoon, causing the listener to dance. (If the musician is not happy with his music, he should either examine the music he is playing or check with his doctor for ulcers.)

"We want New, Fresh Music!" cry the commercial critics. I cannot deny that to the modernists our traditional jazz is completely static. Of course, new tunes added to the traditional repertory are quickly ignored by them. Only progressive jazz, in all its stages, is supposed to move. It's always moving, apparently. Could this be reason to believe that it moves because it so quickly becomes boring to the performers? If progressive jazz stood still, might one wonder if it could stand the scrutiny given, over the years, to traditional jazz?

And what is new? Our music is called either "traditional" or

---

* Alfred Mann, ed. and tr., *Steps to Parnassus*, by Johann Joseph Fux (New York: W. W. Norton, 1943).

"New Orleans revival" because we went back in time for the sources of some of the things we play. What, then, should we call the progressives who are attempting the techniques and harmonies of Schoenberg, Richard Strauss, Debussy, and Bach? *New* and *Fresh?*

Basically, however, I have no quarrel with the modernists. As Fux said, "Let each follow his own counsel." I do find myself at variance, however, with some of the attitudes, particularly the one involving undanceable music played for the rigid and vacuous listener by an uncommunicative group of stony-faced musicians. At one time we had with us one of the best of the modern musicians who had free time between engagements for his own group. When time came for him to leave us, he very nearly didn't. He departed shouting: "Why do I have to go back to those stony faces? I was made to be happy! Now I have to go back and strike an attitude!"

Without serious critical evaluation no art can be healthy. I have been criticized many times along the musically dangerous color line by critics who have said nothing more constructive than that I was of the wrong race. There seems to be no such segregational criticism of progressive jazz. This leads me to believe that critics with no musical ground on which to criticize us use this as a club to put down a form of music not to their individual liking. But serious criticism, to any serious musician, is both helpful and valuable. I should hate to be forced to play traditional jazz for a crowd of Strauss waltz devotees, but I would think twice before attacking their lack of understanding of my music.

However, the more serious evaluations there are made of jazz, evaluations such as this book, the more understanding there will be among the listeners. And I wish Mr. Farrell and Dr. Grossman every success in their venture into serious criticism.

TURK MURPHY

New York
January 12, 1956

Contents

13

14

The heart of Jazz

Introduction

1   The writing of still another book on jazz requires justification, which must come from inadequacies in the already voluminous literature on the subject. The preoccupation of most of this literature with history, biography, technical analysis, and merely laudatory or depreciative characterizations of performers and performances has left certain other significant areas largely neglected. Most conspicuously neglected are the ascertainment and evaluation of the content of jazz. There have been many condemnations of jazz for its supposed aphrodisiac effect or lack of emotional restraint; but these come from persons who know little about the music. Knowledgeable critics such as Roger Pryor Dodge, Wilder Hobson, and Charles Edward Smith have provided insight and balanced judgments within important areas, but even the best writers on jazz have dealt only sporadically with the exposition and critical evaluation of jazz content.

Yet jazz cries for such evaluation. For one thing, its appeal is immensely strong and widespread. If its content is harmful, the harm must be devastating; if its content is salutary, the benefit is inestimable; if, as appears most likely, the content of some of it

Notes to this chapter begin on page 301.

is harmful and the content of some is beneficial, there is a desperate need to distinguish accurately the former from the latter.

It may be objected at this point that music and its content cannot be harmful or beneficial but only pleasant or unpleasant. Against this contention, weighty authority may be cited. "Music," said Aristotle, "has the power of producing a certain effect on the moral character of the soul,"[1] for, as he pointed out, different kinds of music represent different human attributes and emotions. The modern mind, however, will be persuaded less by authority, even the authority of so acute an observer as Aristotle, than by up-to-date scientific demonstration. Recent psychiatric studies[2] indicate clearly the power of music to change the mood of the listeners and, if the music is heard with sufficient frequency and regularity, to contribute to permanent changes in their emotional attitudes. The content of the music, it need hardly be added, has been found to be closely associated with the emotional attitude that the music tends to establish. Only on the assumption that all emotional attitudes are equally desirable can one avoid the conclusion that listening to music of a given description may contribute to the improvement or deterioration of the listener.

Jazz is not merely popular. Some of it has an intense emotional and intellectual interest for men of scholarly inclination or attainment. Of the seven musicians in a certain traditional-jazz band playing recently in New York, four had received graduate academic degrees. Writers and lecturers on jazz include at least five college professors who teach subjects other than music, as well as a psychiatrist, an economics researcher, a consulting optician, a surgeon, an experimental psychologist, several lawyers, and several clergymen. When many men of the caliber suggested by such professions devote themselves to the intimate study of a contemporary art product, one suspects that the product's content is valuable and elsewhere uncommon. It is surprising that critics have not been goaded into more persistent and conscientious efforts to assay it.

Evaluations having some reference to jazz content are continually being made, but they are, for the most part, curiously superficial. For example, many writers on jazz—like some of our literary critics —use "exciting" as a term of approbation. They rarely tell us, however, precisely what emotion or feeling it is so desirable to excite. Very obviously, excitement is not necessarily good or even enjoyable. The critics' uncritical use of "exciting" suggests the possibility that they have capitulated to the popular scheme of values in which the highest good is the conventional desideratum known as "kicks," i.e. thrills, laughs, and other vivid or stimulating experiences. Perhaps what is needed is an American Julien Benda to remind these intellectuals of their obligation to remain detached from the current of popular criteria and passions. It is hardly necessary to add that one cannot avoid essential vulgarity of outlook by a virtually mechanical approval of the novel and the esoteric.

Most jazz writers manifest only a passing interest in the nature of the content of the music. In this connection, something may be learned from the comments made by the participants in the annual jazz critics' poll, conducted by the magazine *Down Beat,* for the selection of the best performers and combinations of the year.[3] Of the fourteen critics who submitted comments with their 1955 votes, only five said anything about the specific content of the music of any of the performer-composers or groups for which they voted. (The terms, used by one or another of these five, that might be thought to denote specific content were: exciting, touching, dynamic, fresh, virility, warmth, great heart, passion, and feeling.) Interest turned more to expressive power and originality than to the nature of that which was expressed or originated.

Some critics appear to judge the value of the content of a performance by its relation to the "mainstream" or "cumulative creative center of jazz." The concept requires identification of this center, and there's the rub. The assumption of the more stylish critics that jazz has been continually advancing—in 1955 it was, according to Barry Ulanov, "bigger and better than ever" [4]—tends to obtrude itself in the mainstream idea. Although the mainstream advocate rejects the newest-is-best theory in its literal application, he tends to conceive the creative center historically rather than critically, and the concept is therefore essentially uncritical. He does not seriously entertain the possibility that time-honored accretions may constitute retrogressions in quality of content. But a critic who is worth his salt will assay and evaluate the content of the art products that he is criticizing, and will use the most authoritative principles of evaluation that he can find. He will not accept certain content as valid or valuable merely because many performers have expressed it in the jazz idiom.

The critic who regards jazz prior to the development of Louis Armstrong's individual style (circa 1925) primarily as the archaic origin of a mainstream that was to lead to better things—a mainstream traced through Armstrong, Roy Eldridge, etc., and held up as a developmental norm from which jazz creators ought not radically to diverge—may miss the mark as widely as the "modernists" of the Hellenistic age (circa 320–31 B.C.) who took the same attitude toward the "archaic" art and literature of the fifth and fourth centuries B.C. We now recognize the earlier Greek product as classic and immortal, and most authorities consider the Hellenistic product inferior to it. The tendency of post-Hellenistic literature, in the Imperial age, to resume what came to be accepted as the real mainstream, i.e. the classical tendency, gave the Imperial age literature greater vitality than that of the intermediate period. The writers of the present volume believe (for reasons that will be indicated in the course of the book) that the current renaissance of New Orleans jazz and of other traditional jazz represents a similar revitalization, and that the most valuable recent development in American popular music is the one that derives not from the end product of a continuous mainstream but from a reversion to early models and ideals.

II   The writers who are the most specific about jazz content are, as a rule, devoted to a Rousseauistic or primitivistic point of view that distorts their perception of the content and makes their evaluations dependent upon the validity of a most questionable set of principles. "The Negro dance music," says Darius Milhaud, "still has a savage and African character" [5]—and the context indicates that he considers this a fine sort of character to have. Rudi Blesh observes admiringly that a certain drum solo played by Baby Dodds "was produced in a state that definitely resembled possession." [6] Hugues Panassié maintains that jazz presents "the characteristics of primitive music" and defends it on the ground (among others) that "in music primitive man generally has greater talent than civilized man." [7] Robert Goffin takes much the same line. "Jazz," he says, "is a return to primitive instinct," [8] and he considers such a return wholly desirable. There is no dearth of statements by additional writers on jazz indicating their perception and approval of a primitive or savage character in jazz.

As suggested in the foregoing paragraph, the dangers in this critical point of view are two. First, the critic may fail to perceive, or to grasp the full significance of, elements and values in the music that tend to contradict or to depreciate his highly prized primitivism. Second, the point of view leads to judgments based on false principles of value. If anything has been established by history since

20

the triumph of Rousseauism, it is that the naturalistic way of life leads at best to frustration and at worst to utter destruction. Rousseauistic criticism of jazz will be adverted to again, because the present writers believe it has seriously handicapped the efforts of many persons to understand and to evaluate jazz. With false principles for major premises and false concepts of the nature of jazz for minor premises, the Rousseauistic writer, although some of his observations may indicate great sensibility and feeling for the music, has been a source of endless confusion. One may say of such a writer as Mr. Blesh what Irving Babbitt said of Croce, that "he combines numerous peripheral merits with a central wrongness. . . ." [9] At least, however, there is something at the center. For the currently more stylish critics (both amateur and professional) who exhaust themselves in praise of the latest jazz ephemera, one is tempted to complete Babbitt's sentence: ". . . and at times with something that seems uncomfortably like a central void."

An objective examination and evaluation of the content of the several types of jazz has been discouraged also by the jazz-booster attitude of certain writers, who bring to mind George F. Babbitt rather than Irving. These writers love all types of jazz. They consider the rejection of any large category of jazz as "cultism" or disloyalty to the great cause, i.e. the promotion of jazz; in this way they make a cult of jazz itself. One notes with reluctance that some of the jazz boosters are also jazz entrepreneurs of one sort or another, whose livelihood or prestige depends upon the support of patrons who like different kinds of jazz.

Naturally, the boosters are reluctant to examine closely the content of the heterogeneous music that they are boosting. One of the participants in the 1955 critics' poll, for example, split some of his votes between "modern" and traditional performers or groups because "I refuse to call either of the two very different current jazz directions 'better' than the other," but said nothing about the content of either type of jazz. An examination of content might have indicated the superiority of one over the other. It would be indeed curious if, upon careful critical examination, two very different directions in a creative art were found equally desirable.

There is reason to believe that much "modern" jazz represents an attitude toward life almost directly antagonistic to that expressed in most New Orleans jazz. If this is true, the critic who embraces both is in need of Socratic interrogation on fundamentals extending far beyond the realm of jazz. Indeed, the very effort to evaluate

21

music without considering its content is Socratically questionable. Socrates himself, it will be recalled, thought that the purpose of the art of music was the improvement of the soul.[10]

III   The critic of jazz, if he is really a critic and not merely a reviewer, uses principles of evaluation in which some ideals and emotional attitudes are placed above others, and in which some are rejected as false or harmful. For he is considering not the commercial value but the human value of the music. Although such criticism has moral implications, it does not make the critic a moralist in the usual sense. He does not expect music to teach a lesson, moral or other. But his approval or disapproval, or degree of approval, of a piece of music will depend upon its relationship to the good inner life. If the music is wild, and the critic thinks wildness to be destructive of human values, he cannot avoid disapproval of the music. The more perfect the expression of wildness, the more harmful the music. (It is assumed here that the wildness is in the attitude expressed by the music, not merely in its subject matter—a distinction discussed in Chapter 3.)

Thus, given the nature of the content of various types of jazz or of various jazz performances, the genuine critic will place a higher value on the jazz that eloquently expresses superior attitudes than upon the jazz that, with equal eloquence, expresses inferior attitudes. It is not enough for a jazz performance to be brilliant or original or expressive: if its fundamental attitude is bad, it is a poor thing or a dangerous one, like a fine piece of rhetoric inspiring abject despondence in the listeners, or like a "good" gun. Art for art's sake, jazz for jazz's sake, is part of the rubble of a provincial ivory tower. Neither art in general nor jazz in particular has any sake; but people have.

These premises appear almost axiomatic to the authors. Obviously, they require the most careful ascertainment of content for purposes of criticism. But even the uncritical student or listener may find his understanding and enjoyment of the music enhanced by study of its content. If nothing else, such study may help him find new "kicks" or excitement in the music. There is at least a possibility, however, that his recognition of those elements in the content of the music which provide him with such great satisfaction will lead to a firmer sense of values in relation to the music and of the underlying relationship between jazz-listening and other aesthetic or spiritual experiences. What is profoundly valuable in the best

22

jazz and what is profoundly valuable in other music and in other forms of creative art are essentially the same. For the profound is universal; it is the superficial, the mode of expression, that is unique.

Accordingly, a substantial part of the present volume represents an effort to stimulate thought concerning the nature of the content of jazz and the effects of this nature on the evaluation of the music. The book does not purport to provide the last word on the subject. Such a task would be beyond the capacity of the writers or, probably, of any writers.

IV   The content of a musical performance, it may be contended, cannot be ascertained, because it is wholly subjective and varies from one listener to the next. This contention is untenable, for both critical literature and empirical studies indicate a fair degree of accord on the content of musical performances. In an especially valuable study,[11] made in 1948 by Dr. Alexander Capurso, then head of the Music Department of the University of Kentucky and more recently appointed director of the School of Music of Syracuse University, each of 105 selections was played for large numbers of nonmusical students. After the playing of each selection, the students indicated which of six stated categories best described the effects of the composition. In general, the categories represented kinds of content. One, for example, was "Happy, Gay, Joyous, Stimulating, Triumphant." With respect to 61 of the 105 compositions, at least half of the students indicated the same category, and in each of the other cases no more than two categories were indicated by a majority of the students.

In ascertaining the typical content of various types of jazz, the present writers have sought to use every available source, including the literature on jazz, historical data not reported in that literature, and innumerable conversations with listeners and musicians, as well as the authors' own perceptions of content. With respect to both the ascertainment of jazz content and its evaluation, they have derived some guidance from study of the triple parallel of the development of jazz, the development of "serious" music,* and the development of basic points of view in human thought. As everyone knows, changes in the ideals and attitudes of artistic creators

---

* Except where the context indicates otherwise, "serious" or "classical" music, with inverted commas, will be used broadly in the present volume to denote art music in the European tradition. No implication that jazz is not serious, without inverted commas, is intended.

23

and, perhaps even more, of the public that patronizes the creators, tend to be reflected in changes in the content of all art products, including musical compositions. "We know," says A. Clutton Brock, "that it [art] is a symptom of something right or wrong with the whole mind of man and with the circumstances that affect that mind." [12] It is therefore to be expected that the romanticism, the secularization of thought, and the hegemony of mass-man that have characterized the history of human attitudes in the past two hundred years will be found to have influenced jazz as well as "serious" music. It will be seen that classic, New Orleans jazz began at a point comparable to that attained by "serious" music in the eighteenth century and subsequently suffered the effects of those major developments in Western thought. Jazz provides, therefore, a sort of musical or cultural microcosm and a curiously accurate reflection of the development of modern man.

The drawing of the jazz-"serious" music parallel, or acceptance of it as drawn by someone else, may require a person to overcome certain prejudices. When he looks for, or determines whether or not to accept someone's allegation of, a common element in the content of a type of jazz or specific jazz performance and in the content of certain European art music, he must exercise care not to be diverted by differences in idiom and manner or by his opinion of the merits of the respective media. The more elaborate and detailed craftsmanship of a schooled composer need not prevent his expressing very much the same faith or joy in life—or the same trite, warmed-over substitutes for deep feeling—as a comparatively unlearned performer-composer. So far as the effects of formal or technical limitations are concerned, his range of possible content may certainly include a substantial part of that of the comparatively unschooled musician. Therefore, there is no a priori reason why (say) Haydn and New Orleans jazzmen should not express much the same sort of humor, vitality, and good will. Unfortunately, any near-identity in expressed content between a type of jazz and certain European art music will be recognized only by the few listeners who are thoroughly familiar with both idioms and who are, at the same time, receptive to the content at issue.

Although the triple parallel applies to almost the entire field of jazz, and although an effort will be made in the present volume to indicate at least the outlines of such application, the major part of the book is devoted to New Orleans jazz or, more broadly, to traditional jazz—a term meaning New Orleans jazz and other types of

24

jazz very similar to it. For this, there are three reasons. First, New Orleans jazz, as the classic type of jazz, occupies a sort of nuclear or normative position. Second, because of the comparatively long period during which it has been performed, New Orleans jazz permits study with greater perspective and more secure judgments than other types of jazz. Third and most important, the study of successfully expressed attitudes in the content of the several types of jazz strongly suggests the superiority of New Orleans jazz—and again, more broadly, of traditional jazz—over other types. There is reason to believe that New Orleans jazz or traditional jazz at its best deserves consideration as an important contribution to the music of the Western world.

v   However much one may desiderate a serious study of jazz content, such a study by itself is likely to appear somewhat unsubstantial. It requires enrichment by a study of aesthetic practices and objectives. Therefore, the book pursues two lines of inquiry, which some readers will doubtless regard as an "abstract" approach dealing with the "philosophy" of jazz and a "concrete" approach dealing with the practices and problems of specific performers and bands. It is believed that these lines of inquiry complement each other and that both are necessary if the book is to serve as a reasonably adequate introduction to the study of traditional jazz. One's understanding of content will be more secure for a knowledge of the "concrete" material, and the significance of specific performers, bands, and schools rests largely upon the emotional attitudes expressed in their music. In conjunction, the two approaches may provide some notion of the rich and varied experiences to be found in traditional jazz.

For the *aficionado* rather than for the neophyte, the authors, in some of the "concrete" chapters, have made a point of noting the importance of certain jazzmen who, because of the paucity of their recordings, have received little or no attention in prior works on jazz. Emphasis, however, is placed upon comparatively well-known figures. At the same time, traditional-jazz lovers may find some of their (and the present writers') favorite jazzmen omitted from these chapters, for no attempt at encyclopedic coverage has been made. Especially conspicuous is the omission of singers. Little attention is devoted to vocal jazz, because its tendency on the one hand to revert to folk origins and on the other to borrow the style of nonjazz popular ballad singing would complicate the study of content and form. The writers do not mean to disparage vocal jazz, which might well be made the subject of a special study.

VI   Two small matters relative to the text itself may be noted. Where the term "Christian" appears, the authors originally wrote "Judeo-Christian." They shortened it because the full term is too cumbersome for such frequent use and because, in any case, the reader knows that the spiritual and moral essence of Judaism is subsumed in Christianity.

Although the authors accept joint responsibility for the entire book, the pen was pushed by Grossman in the Introduction, the first twelve chapters, Chapter 31, and the Conclusion, and by Farrell in Chapters 13 through 30 and Chapter 32.

1. Can jazz be defined?

1   Efforts to define jazz have sometimes been thwarted by the use of a wholly unnecessary premise: that jazz is a superior sort of music. By this premise a great deal of music commonly called jazz is not jazz at all. The definer is especially likely to draw a bead on "the commercial product," which he regards as a sort of counterfeit that does not deserve to be called jazz.[1] Jazz thus becomes an evaluation concept. The definer is really an appraiser. But jazz is a kind of music, not a kind of good. Its definition must be, above all, a useful tool to a person who is reading, writing, studying, thinking, or talking about music that might or might not be called jazz. His determination of the value of the music is another matter, although a good definition will help him in the analyses preliminary to careful evaluation. Accordingly, what is needed is a pragmatic definition.

A fairly serviceable, although by no means unexceptionable, indication of the actual use of the word "jazz" at the time (1944) the definition was published is provided by Lloyd Hibberd in the *Harvard Dictionary of Music:* "A generic name for twentieth-century styles in the music usually associated with American popular danc-

Notes to this chapter begin on page 301.

ing; more properly, that branch thereof which came to be distinguished in some respects from its predecessors Ragtime and Blues as well as, by some enthusiasts, from the more recent Swing." But usage has so changed in the few intervening years that a great deal of music wholly dissociated from dancing is now called jazz. Such a definition as Mr. Hibberd's, i.e. one that seeks to state usage, must be changed frequently and, in any case, really comprises two or more definitions that seek in vain to represent the myriad differences in usage at a given time.

A pragmatic definition, especially one that will be useful in serious studies of the music, must be more than an indication of usage. Without doing violence to usage, it must provide an orientation that will help to direct usage into rational and consistent channels. Can jazz be defined in this way? An apparent difficulty lies in the fact that musical compositions or performances cannot be strictly compartmentalized. For example, jaded European composers of "serious" music,* in quest of the exotic, sometimes write what they maintain to be jazz, although few American listeners would readily recognize it as such. If our definition must either include or exclude this music—no middle ground—the definition will have failed. It will be misleading, for the music is and is not jazz.

Insistence on a definition that places precise bounds on the field of jazz is seen, then, to be based on a misapplication of the premise that every given musical composition or performance either is or is not jazz. Such a premise can be as misleading as the proposition that a piece of music is or is not classical. In the narrow, most precise sense of "classical music," the propriety of its use as a predicate depends upon the degree to which the characteristics of the music in question approach those of a certain norm, usually identified with the symphonies, quartets, and sonatas of Haydn, Mozart, and Beethoven in his early period. Is Tschaikowsky's *Fifth Symphony* classical? In basic structural outline, very much so but not completely; in content or emotional attitude, hardly at all. Are Bach's *Brandenburg Concertos* classical? In general structure, no, except that successive movements generally have contrasting tempos; in substantive content or feeling, however, these concertos are fairly classical, for, like many of the works that represent the classical norm, they contain pensiveness and restrained gaiety, both of

* For the sense in which the term "serious" music is used in the present book, see footnote on page 23.

which are felt optimistically (i.e., the pensiveness is not depressing and the gaiety is not frantic or desperate) and with an undertone of profound seriousness. They are far closer to that norm in content than many works written in strictly classical form—e.g., Prokofieff's cute, brittle *Classical Symphony*.

The analogy to classical music will serve to bring out two points. First, a musical composition * may be more or less jazzy,† just as it may be more or less classical. At the center there is a norm, comprising actual music as thoroughly and obviously jazz as Haydn's *Surprise Symphony* is classical. At shorter or longer distances from the norm are the various musical performances to which the term "jazz" may be applied. The distance in each case—i.e., the degree of propriety in the use of the term as predicate—will be proportionate to the degree of resemblance between the significant characteristics of the performance and those of the norm. The definer's task is to identify the norm and to ascertain its significant characteristics.

The futility of attempting to define jazz without reference to specific music as the norm may be illustrated by the definition promulgated by Barry Ulanov, a well-known jazz critic and historian. A perusal of Mr. Ulanov's writings and the fact that he teaches English literature in a university show clearly that, if his definition is faulty, it is not for want of articulateness. Jazz, he says, might be defined as "a new music of a certain distinct rhythmic and melodic character, one that constantly involves improvisation—of a minor sort in adjusting accents and phrases of the tune at hand, of a major sort in creating music extemporaneously, on the spot." [2] This definition hardly serves to identify jazz, even with the help of Mr. Ulanov's explanatory statements that in jazz "a melody or its underlying chords may be altered"; that "the rhythmic valuations of notes may be lengthened or shortened" either schematically or without pattern; that the beat or rhythmic base is "usually four quarter-notes to the bar"; and that the improvisers play "eight or twelve measures or some multiple or dividend thereof." A musical performance may conform to all these requirements and yet be unrecognizable as the type of music called jazz.

* "Composition" is here used broadly to include an improvised performance.

† "Jazzy" is sometimes used by musicians to mean "corny," i.e., trite and obsolete. We are not using the term in this sense but are using it merely to mean "having characteristics of jazz."

29

Among the various characteristics that he might have selected as indispensable to all music properly called jazz, Mr. Ulanov has chosen—apart from his reference to an unspecified "rhythmic and melodic character"—an aspect not of the music itself (although it certainly affects the music) but of the manner in which the music is composed. He tells us, by his definition, that only improvised music is jazz. Undoubtedly the absence of improvisation is one factor tending to make a musical performance relatively remote from the norm of jazz. But if the performance closely resembles the norm in all other respects, most informed persons would call it jazz, however much they might deplore the absence of improvisation. Syncopation, too, is generally characteristic of jazz, but Mr. Ulanov says, and correctly, that music can be jazz without being syncopated. By the same token, it need not possess another specific characteristic of the norm, such as improvisation, although, *so far as it lacks such characteristics*, it is less jazzy. Use of the adjective "jazzy," rather than the noun "jazz," serves as a reminder that music is not divided into two mutually exclusive categories—jazz and not-jazz—and that a musical performance is more or less jazzy according to the degree of its resemblance to the norm.

The analogy to classical music brings out also the fact that the norm by which a type of music may be fruitfully defined has two aspects or sets of characteristics: form and substance or content. Certain forms or elements of form and certain types of content may be well or ill suited to each other: form and content are therefore not mutually independent. But neither are they wholly interdependent. After his definition Mr. Ulanov states, in substance, that the expressed content of jazz permits no limitation; with respect to expression, he says, the ends of jazz are the ends of all art, which he describes with the utmost breadth.[3] Thus he insists on a definition of jazz in terms of form only. Such a definition is merely technical, and its usefulness in a study of the meaning and significance of jazz is therefore narrowly confined. Reference to actual music as a norm permits one's definition to relate to the content of the music as well as to its form.

Omission of a relation to substance or content is, indeed, more serious than omission of a relation to form—although there is no need to omit either. Even a musicologist is likely to grant that the popular extension of the term "classical music" to cover Tschaikowsky is more scandalous than its extension to cover Bach; for, however much the baroque * may differ from the classical, the romantic is the *opposite* of the classical *in substance,* even when there is a clear resemblance in form.

II   We may proceed, then, to search for the music that will constitute the most useful norm for purposes of the definition of jazz. The most obvious condition that such music must fulfill is that it be undeniably jazz—a music that every informed person will recognize as jazz. It must, therefore, come within Mr. Ulanov's definition of jazz and within every other definition framed with thoughtfulness and knowledge, however inadequate the definition may be. Popular dance music, as played by (say) Guy Lombardo's orchestra or Les Brown's, would not qualify as the norm because it lacks the improvisatory quality required by some definitions (including Mr. Ulanov's). For the same reason, symphonic jazz, such as Gershwin's *Concerto in F,* must be rejected as a candidate. Some knowledgeable *aficionados* maintain that all or a great deal of "modern" or "progressive" jazz is not jazz at all but merely experimental music along the general lines of more or less recent developments in European music.† Whether or not we agree, and whether or not we think this music is "good," their refusal to accept it as jazz discourages us from using it as the norm, or from including it in the norm, by which we define jazz.

With each successive rejection of a type of music that cannot fulfill the basic requirement for adoption as a norm, we are pushed a little farther in the direction of traditional hot jazz. One may consider much of this music inferior or obsolete, but no one who knows anything about jazz would seriously deny that it is jazz. The chief objections to its adoption might be that it is too vague as a class of music and insufficiently homogeneous to be serviceable as a norm. One is impelled, therefore, to look for a fairly uniform and readily recognizable nucleus within the category of hot jazz.

The analogy to the norm in classical music indicates that our jazz norm should consist of music that has served as a model or as a

---

* Baroque music is the music of which J. S. Bach is generally regarded as the greatest and culminating composer. Its development preceded that of the classical norm.

† Rudi Blesh has maintained that Duke Ellington's music is not jazz. *Shining Trumpets,* pp. 229, 281. He does not even regard swing music as jazz. *Ibid.,* p. 6.

31

source, direct or indirect, for all or at least a large part of the music (other than the norm music itself) to which the term "jazz" is customarily applied. It suggests also that only music that is still vital, still studied, and still performed by jazzmen ought to be considered.

Only two types of jazz can survive these requirements. One of them is called New Orleans jazz. This jazz was initiated and developed by Negroes. Its antecedents comprised spirituals, work songs, blues, marches, minstrel songs, classical overtures, Creole songs, neo-African rhythm music—indeed, virtually all the music heard by New Orleans Negroes of the 1880's and the 1890's. The present writers believe that, among all the antecedents, the spirituals and the marches probably exercised the most significant influences on traditional jazz. The inception of New Orleans jazz or of any kind of jazz as a clearly differentiated type of music is associated by some * with the activities of Buddy Bolden (1868–1931), a barber, cornetist, and band leader who flourished in New Orleans from about 1894 to 1907, when insanity cut short his career. There is good reason, however, to believe that music which would be recognizable as jazz was played even earlier. Indeed, recent researches (unpublished at the present writing) by Professor Hans Nathan of Michigan State University indicate that distinctly jazzy banjo music was played as early as 1840 or 1850.

The other candidate for election as norm is a type of music developed chiefly by white musicians in New Orleans. Generally called Dixieland jazz or white New Orleans jazz, it is nearly as old as (Negro) New Orleans jazz. The term "Dixieland" is often employed more broadly to denote not only the music in question but also the types of hot jazz developed subsequently by white musicians elsewhere and strongly resembling New Orleans jazz and/or white New Orleans jazz. In the present book, "Dixieland" will be used in the narrower sense indicated. A handy term, already noted, to cover New Orleans jazz and types of jazz, such as Dixieland, closely related to it, is "traditional jazz."

The antecedents of Dixieland were virtually all the types of music, including New Orleans jazz, heard by white men in New Orleans in the last decade of the nineteenth century. Accordingly, spirituals, blues, and other kinds of prejazz Negro folk music were less directly significant in relation to Dixieland than in relation to New Orleans jazz, and music in which the nominal time value of

* See Chapter 4, Section III.

Jelly Roll Morton.

Bunk Johnson.

notes was more strictly observed probably exercised a proportionately greater influence on Dixieland than on New Orleans jazz.

Nevertheless, the resemblances between the two types of jazz are more striking than the differences. Both New Orleans jazz and Dixieland are thoroughly and indisputably jazz—*echt* jazz, so to speak. Both have had immense effects on the development of jazz. Classic performances of both types of jazz on records are still studied and imitated. Perhaps the norm should be made broad enough to include both. Certainly each influenced the other. New Orleans jazz, however, appears to enjoy a certain primacy. Most old New Orleans and Dixieland jazzmen believe that, as one of them said, jazz "probably came from the Negroes." [4] It appears also that there were more Negro jazzmen than white jazzmen in New Orleans during the 1890's, so that by mere force of numbers the preponderant direction of influence in the very early days was probably from New Orleans jazz to Dixieland rather than the reverse.

III   The jazz norm—i.e. New Orleans jazz—cannot be identified with the works of two or three composers, as can be done for the classical music norm. A "work" in New Orleans jazz band music is generally not a written score but a performance, and the composers of the performance include the members of the band (see Chapter 2). With every change in the personnel of the band, a new collective composer comes into existence. In place, then, of the works of two or three composers with which the norm can be identified, we must be content with band performances that exemplify the norm and to which some special importance is attached. And only the comparatively few performances that have been recorded can be regarded as candidates. The others are lost forever.

Among the earliest New Orleans jazz recordings, those made by cornetist King Oliver's Creole Jazz Band in 1923 and those made by pianist Jelly Roll Morton and His Red Hot Peppers in 1926 may be taken as outstanding examples of the music. Although the records were made in Chicago, which by then had become a center of hot jazz, the leaders of the bands and most of their fellow musicians came from New Orleans. These records constitute models of traditional jazz still studied and imitated by hot-jazz musicians.

Morton (1885–1941) is distinguished as one of the foremost composers of jazz music, whether we think of composition in the conventional sense or in the sense of improvised performance. The importance of Oliver (1885–1938) flows not only from his records but

33

also from the influence of his live band-leading and cornet improvisations, notably on Louis Armstrong, who in 1922 came to Chicago from New Orleans to play second cornet in Oliver's band. From 1920 to 1924 the Oliver band, playing chiefly in Chicago, was considered by many to be the best traditional-jazz band in that city, where the most important developments in hot jazz were taking place. In brief, Oliver and Morton are outstanding for the quality and influence of their live work within the norm and for the vitality of the recorded models that they left behind. In a sense—the analogy must not be pushed too far—their position in jazz is roughly comparable to that of Mozart and Haydn in classical music.

If the indicated norm is accepted, a musical performance will be considered more or less jazzy according to the degree of proximity of its significant characteristics to those of New Orleans jazz. Consequently, an inquiry into the nature of New Orleans jazz must be undertaken.

2. *Formal characteristics of New Orleans jazz*

I   The usual basic structure of New Orleans jazz performances is variations on a theme (or themes). It is not exactly theme and variations, however, for in most cases no statement of the theme in its pure, unembellished form is provided. Omission of a literally accurate statement may be confusing to a listener not already familiar with the piece.

A piece may contain more strains or melodies than one. The conventional popular-song form consists of an introductory "verse" of sixteen measures and a "chorus" of thirty-two. In some performances only variations of the chorus are played. If the verse is included, it may or may not be played as frequently as the chorus, according to the judgment of the band leader with respect to the comparative interest of each.

Many jazz pieces, including most of the classic New Orleans pieces, are not in popular-song form. Some have only one strain, as in the simplest blues, exemplified by *Careless Love*. Others, including many of the compositions of Jelly Roll Morton, have three, four, or even more strains; in most such pieces, there is at least one melody in a key other than the initial key, and in some of them a

Notes to this chapter begin on page 302.

35

transitional passage of two or four measures, which may or may not contain a modulation, connects two of the melodies. Except in twelve-measure blues, most of the strains and melodies consist of eight, sixteen, or thirty-two measures.

Some pieces or performances are introduced and/or terminated by short passages, typically two or four measures in length. A terminating passage of this sort is little more than an additional cadence; it is called a "tag." In some pieces, such as the classic *Sister Kate* (more fully, *I Wish I Could Shimmy Like My Sister Kate*), an added cadence is part of the piece itself and is played at the end of each chorus.

New Orleans jazz is in common (four-quarter) time, with offbeat accents that in some performances are sufficiently pronounced to create a sort of duple rhythm. There is abundant use of syncopation. Also, an effect similar to that of syncopation is provided by the playing of a note slightly offbeat. It is sometimes hard to draw a definite distinction between such playing and clear-cut syncopation in the music.

In New Orleans jazz the major mode or scale is used almost exclusively. Sometimes, however, a note is played intentionally a little below the customary pitch. On the conventional piano, because the notes are fixed in pitch, an approximation of such off-pitch playing is sometimes achieved by the use of a note one half-tone below the note from which a deviation is intended; the two notes may even be played together. The third note in the scale is subjected to off-pitch flatting with especial frequency, but no note in the scale is wholly immune.

The chief reason for this practice is expressiveness. Unhampered by academic concepts of inviolable pitch, the New Orleans jazzmen found that by playing a note slightly below conventional pitch they could achieve an ironic, quasi-melancholy effect. Indeed, the off-pitch notes are sometimes referred to as "blue" (i.e., melancholy) notes and are especially common in the performance of blues. It should be noted also that the disregard of exact pitch is a logical corollary of the effort of New Orleans jazzmen to make their music "talk"; this effort has been frequently remarked and will be adverted to again in the present volume.

Jazz Africanists have promulgated the theory that in the blue notes the jazzmen are expressing an unconscious nostalgia for African scales. For the reasons indicated in the foregoing paragraph, this theory is wholly gratuitous. Indeed, yearnings for some-

36

thing associated by the theorists with Africa can account for the theory more readily than the theory can account for the music. New Orleans jazz conspicuously expresses a robust acceptance of life, profoundly alien to the nostalgia for African antecedents on which the theorists rely.

Efforts are made to apply the theory especially to the flatted third and to the flatted seventh. In the latter case, the inadequacy of the theory becomes apparent, for the note is not used in place of the unflatted seventh. More often than not, it is the minor seventh, played off pitch or on pitch, merely as part of a conventional modulation to subdominant harmony.

With respect to tone or timbre, it should be noted that the speechlike quality of many jazz instrumental performances necessitates a tone far from the pure tone that a performer in the European tradition generally seeks to achieve. New Orleans jazzmen vary considerably in the degree to which their training and aesthetic ideals lead them to adhere to the European concept of acceptable tone and, accordingly, vary considerably in their degree of departure from it.

A New Orleans jazz band consists typically, but by no means invariably, of one or (much less frequently) two cornets or trumpets, a clarinet, a trombone, and a "rhythm section" of two or more of the following four instruments: piano, banjo (or guitar), double bass (or tuba), and drums. On most of the 1923 Creole Jazz Band recordings and 1926 Red Hot Peppers recordings, referred to in Chapter 1 as good examples of New Orleans Jazz, the band consists of seven pieces: cornet—in the Creole Jazz Band, two cornets—clarinet, trombone, and all four rhythm instruments, except that Oliver used no bass or tuba (he did use bass or tuba in most of his live music). Oliver used banjo, not guitar; Morton used sometimes one, sometimes the other, and varied also between tuba and bass.

The leader of the band is always one of the performers—often and most logically the cornetist. He does not conduct the band, but he may give signals from time to time if certain procedures in the performance are not predetermined, indicating, perhaps, that a certain performer is to take a solo or that the next chorus is to be the last. It may be noted that the nominal leader is not in every case the actual leader. One well-known Dixieland (white New Orleans) trombonist is the *de facto* leader of virtually every band in which he plays.

In the ensemble or *tutti* parts of the performance (they may con-

37

stitute the entire performance), the trumpet or cornet generally plays an approximation of the basic melody, while the clarinet and trombone follow their own respective lines in what often amounts to a sort of counterpoint. This counterpoint is not usually imitative; in other words, one instrument does not usually repeat a phrase just rendered by another. Rather, the trombone plays a free sort of bass, which often assumes distinct melodic significance, with occasional use of *glissandi* (slides from one note to another), and the clarinet combines runs, arpeggios, and genuinely melodic phrases into a line of its own.

The rhythm section supplies both the basic rhythm and the harmony, which is generally simple. In some cases, as in the traditional twelve-bar blues form, it consists wholly of three or four elementary chords. As a rule, the harmonic progressions are not changed from variation to variation, nor is the tempo or the basic rhythm. Variation is, therefore, wholly a matter of melody and internal rhythm. Because of the harmonic "rigidity," it has been maintained that the ensemble choruses in New Orleans jazz are primarily "vertical" rather than "horizontal," essentially harmonic or homophonic rather than polyphonic or contrapuntal. Most writers who have dealt with the subject, however, lean rather in the opposite direction.

In addition to the ensembles, a performance may include one or more solo variations, generally by one of the wind instruments. During the solo, the rhythm section continues to supply the harmony and basic rhythm. The other wind instruments are sometimes silent during a solo, but in many cases one or both of them play softly and polyphonically behind it. Indeed, it is sometimes difficult to distinguish a trombone or clarinet solo from a shift of the melody lead from the cornet to such instrument. In New Orleans jazz, as distinguished from some of its progeny, ensemble choruses, rather than solos, usually predominate.

A formal device characteristic of New Orleans jazz is the *break*. This is a passage interpolated during a rest at the end of a phrase. It is generally played by one instrument alone and serves as a sort of reminder of the vitality and independence of the individual in what is essentially a group performance. Jelly Roll Morton was insistent upon its indispensability to good jazz. Characterizing a break as "a musical surprise," he maintained that "without breaks and without clean breaks and without beautiful ideas in breaks, you don't even need to think about doing anything else, you haven't got a jazz band and you can't play jazz. Even if a tune haven't got a break in it, it's always necessary to arrange some kind of a spot to make a break." [1] In many jazz tunes, such "spots" are readily available—e.g., *Sister Kate* (seventh and eighth measures) and *Tiger Rag* (many places).

II   The curious method of composition of New Orleans jazz is closely related to both its form and its substance. One must distinguish between (1) the composition of the basic melody or melodies of a piece, (2) the composition of the piece as published for piano, (3) the composition of arrangements and patterns at rehearsals, (4) the acquisition by a performer, through listening to others and still more through the process of trial and error in prior improvisations of his own, of habitual ways of playing certain pieces, and (5) improvisation during a performance. The relative importance of these several acts of composition has been beclouded by persistent exaggeration on the part of writers and lecturers—an exaggeration sometimes encouraged, for obvious reasons, by the musicians themselves—on the last of the five, i.e. on the role of improvisation and spontaneity in the public performances of New Orleans jazz.

Persons who wish to believe, or to have others believe, that jazz is an utterly spontaneous creation during performance tend to belittle the importance of the basic melody. It is, they say, merely the raw material of jazz. Any melody, they point out, can be jazzed, for jazz is a way of playing. Here we are in the region of half-truths, in which the very substance of jazz is ignored. Any series of notes may be made the subject of a fugue, any musical subjects may be stated and developed in sonata form, and any melody may be jazzed, but this does not mean that the musical product will be equally good no matter what subject or melody is utilized. Jazz is no more a way of playing than any other type of music; it is, like all other music, compounded of melody, timbre, rhythm, and harmony. The melody or melodies played are important in every musical performance (it is questionable whether mere drumbeats on the same tone can properly be called music), and in New Orleans jazz, as we have seen, the underlying theme or themes of the piece are usually approximated—played with embellishments, freedom of emphasis and of note value, and even occasional moderate departures from the theme without violation of its basic structure—in the cornet melody lines of one or more of the ensembles; they are reflected indirectly in the other parts and in solos. If the under-

39

lying melody is insipid, as in many popular songs, the chance that the performers will achieve a first-rate musical product is small. If, however, the basic melody, with its customary harmonies, is genuinely expressive of something that people like to hear expressed, it may well become a classic, loved for itself and for the comparatively pleasing performances that it has engendered and is likely to engender—pleasing by comparison with performances even by the same band using less fruitful thematic material. Audiences often applaud as soon as they hear the opening notes of *Tiger Rag, Basin Street Blues, When the Saints Go Marching In,* or any of various other New Orleans jazz pieces. Frequently members of the audience request a band to play a certain piece, even if they have never heard the band play it before. They would not do these things if the selection of a basic melody (the "raw material") were unimportant. Apparently a very significant element in the ultimate, performed composition is contributed by that melody.

The underlying melody or melodies of a performance—the subject of the variations—may be a Negro spiritual, a folk blues, a Creole song, a rag, a popular song, any melody at all. But if it is uninteresting and inexpressive, or if it does not lend itself to jazz treatment, even a very competent New Orleans band cannot process it into a first-class musical product.

Once in a while, a band uses as the subject of its variations no preselected theme at all but merely the traditional harmonic progression and phrasing of the twelve-measure blues, usually played in B-flat major. Given this harmonic progression, the division into three phrases of four measures each, and the general spirit of blues, a jazz band can render a coherent performance without a predetermined melody.

The piece may never be printed for publication and may, indeed, never be reduced to writing at all. Or it may be written and published *after* it has been performed by one band or by many. Even if a piece has been published, the performers may play it without reference to the printed version. Many of them were and are unable to read music and some others never learned to read fluently. It should be noted also that if a piece is performed frequently before it is reduced to writing, it acquires the aspect of a folk tune. The specific version of the melody ultimately printed and published may be nothing more than an arbitrary selection among many possible versions, all based on the same underlying melodic structure; even the original composer, at least after a few renditions of his piece, may have in mind no definitive passing notes or beats to be syncopated.

For several reasons, then, the publication of a piece in printed form is generally not an event of very great importance with regard to New Orleans jazz performances. Partial exceptions exist when a New Orleans band leader consults a printed copy of a popular song that he may have heard once or twice and is considering for use; or if the composer is a New Orleans jazzman who himself provides the printed version either directly or by transcription of a performance that he has rendered, as in the case of several Morton compositions. Such a printed version may be, apart from the almost unrepresentable (in writing) little departures from note values, virtually a representation of part or all of a New Orleans jazz composition, i.e. of one performance of the piece in New Orleans jazz style.

At its rehearsals, a band is likely to take important steps in the molding of the final composition. In some cases, the pieces themselves have been created at rehearsals. Even in the more usual case, in which a pre-existing piece is rehearsed, the band at its rehearsals may work out some passages in full detail. Because the musicians perform without written music, they commit the fully arranged parts to memory. Unwritten arrangements are called "head" arrangements. At the rehearsals, decisions may also be made about breaks, ways of playing certain choruses together, etc., apart from specifically arranged passages.

Ultimate decisions, at the rehearsals, are ordinarily within the prerogative of the band leader. The extent to which he actually prescribes the details of the performance—which is the completed composition—depends largely on his temperament and on the degree of his confidence in the other members of the band. Morton generally circumscribed the freedom of his musicians much more strictly than Oliver, and Oliver planned parts of his band's performances more carefully and thoroughly than various other New Orleans jazz band leaders. In some cases, Morton actually wrote out some of the passages to be played, a procedure rarely followed by others, because, as we have seen, many of the musicians could not read fluently.

Thus the band leader may be, in a sense, a composer of his band's rehearsed performances. He is not, however, the sole composer, even in cases in which he wrote the piece that his band is playing. For to some extent—and it may be a very great extent—he permits

41

the members of the band to develop and determine their own parts, or works out aspects of the performance with them, making and receiving suggestions. As a rule, more nearly complete freedom is permitted in solos than in ensembles, for obvious reasons, but even in solos the band leader may give instructions of a general nature. (In a case, for example, where a trombonist was playing a solo too sweetly and softly, the leader told him to "rough it up a little.")

The arrangements and patterns prescribed at rehearsals still leave room for extemporization in the public performances. However, a musician does not necessarily extemporize to the full extent permitted. Probably he has played the piece many times, both at rehearsals and at prior performances, and has heard it played by others. By a process of perhaps unconscious selection from his own and other performers' extemporizations, he may have developed certain phrases which he uses in the piece habitually or from time to time. He may even have developed whole choruses, at least in general melodic line. Even in a "jam session"—i.e., an unrehearsed performance by a group of musicians—some or all of the performers may be following very closely the customary lines of their past performances of the selections being played. "After all," Duke Ellington is reported to have said, "there is so little that's really improvised at a jam session" [2]—a proposition not universally applicable but certainly true of many jam-session performances.

Certain phrases and solos have become traditional. For example, a high-spirited virtuoso clarinet solo, composed-performed more than half a century ago by a New Orleans Creole named Picou on the basis of the piccolo part of the march arrangement (the piece was originally a march), is still played, with minor deviations, by the clarinet in almost every performance of *High Society* by a traditional-jazz band. In *Dippermouth Blues* (also called *Sugarfoot Stomp*), it is customary for the cornet or trumpet to play a solo similar to a certain chorus played, and doubtless composed, by Oliver. Highly traditional also are certain clarinet breaks in *Tiger Rag*, played and possibly originated by Larry Shields of the Original Dixieland Jazz Band at least as early as 1918. Several other examples can be given.

It is seen, then, that compositions as performed in traditional jazz are, as a rule, neither wholly worked out in advance nor wholly created in the course of performance. The importance of prearrangement, habitual residue, specific traditional material, and extemporization, respectively, varies from band to band and from performer to performer within a band. Accordingly, the oft repeated statement that traditional jazz is improvised or extemporized music is seen to be only a half truth. One wonders why writers on jazz who have access to the facts nevertheless promulgate the proposition which the facts controvert. In at least some cases the reason for this curious inconsistency appears to be a desire to buttress another proposition, which is less than a half truth, viz. that jazz is a sort of rebellion against old ideas and impediments to freedom, both aesthetic and social or political. In other cases the reason may well be the desperate need of some jazz lovers to participate vividly in an act of creation.

III   So much for the general features of form and method of composition in New Orleans jazz. They are readily verifiable and present no great difficulty to the unbiased inquirer. With respect to the substantive content of the music, however, the case is less simple. Almost all informed persons who have considered the matter agree that New Orleans jazz, or traditional jazz in general, has great vitality, that it is friendly music, that it is usually happy or "good-time" music, that it is sometimes sad (chiefly in the blues), and that it is often humorous. With these obviously true propositions—which serve to show, at any rate, that there is a specific, ascertainable content in New Orleans or traditional jazz—unanimity of opinion ends. One or another writer has maintained that the music is sexual to the point of aphrodisia, that it is savage or primitive, that it is part of the modern movement in art away from traditional concepts, that it is primarily an expression of social and political protest, and that it utterly lacks profundity. An effort will be made in later chapters to show that these propositions are wide of the mark. An effort will be made also to show that New Orleans jazz contains Christian feeling and aspiration. In the writers' opinion, the synthesis of this religious element with the music's robust vitality lies at the very heart of New Orleans jazz.

Finally, it may be observed that in New Orleans jazz, as in all other music, form is related to content. The smallness of the band discourages turgidity. The instrumentation invites an expression of vigor, not of languor. The simple harmonies encourage straightforwardness and make it hard to express decadence. A man who studied under Percy Goetschius recalls that Goetschius referred to the simple triad, which dominates traditional-jazz harmony but is virtually a last resort in some of the ultramodern jazz, as "God's own chord." The polyphony of New Orleans jazz introduces the intellectual-emotional factor of the subordination and integration of several coexisting diverse parts. Such integration, as the history of music shows, lends itself to (although it does not demand) religious content and is somewhat inimical to romantic expression.

3. Can music be Christian?

1   The evidence of the existence of a strong Christian element in New Orleans jazz is overwhelmingly persuasive. Before turning our attention to it, however, we shall try to anticipate and to answer three objections that might prevent unbiased consideration of the evidence. The first of the three, based on the contention that music cannot express Christian feeling, requires extended consideration, which is given it in the present chapter. The other two are considered in Chapter 4.

Common sense (not always the most reliable guide) tells us that there is such a thing as religious music, i.e., music that expresses religious feeling or religious emotional attitudes. The music may be sung with words, which make the meaning explicit, but, apart from the words and even if there are none, a religious feeling is thought to be expressed in the music itself. Musicians of religious sensitivity, as well as laymen, generally accept this belief. The great French organist Widor, for example, accepted it or he would not have said of Bach: "What speaks through his works is pure religious emotion."[1] Many learned and respected writers have recognized religious expression in music. Philip Hale recognized

Notes to this chapter begin on page 302.

it in Bruckner's *Eighth Symphony;* [2] Cecil Gray, in early Christian music and in Palestrina; [3] George Grove, in the final movement of Beethoven's *Ninth Symphony;* [4] Max Graf, in Mahler's symphonies; [5] and no end of additional examples can be supplied. Theodore M. Greene, a leading American authority on the theory of criticism, indicates his belief that art, including music, can express religious experience, and he specifically attributes to Bach's *Mass in B minor* the expression of the meaning of the words of the mass. [6]

There are musicologists, however, who deny the existence of religious music as something inherently distinguishable from all other music. They concede, of course, that some music is repeatedly played for religious purposes, but they maintain that this use of a composition does not show that the music itself is different from music not so used. "Fundamentally," they maintain, "there is no distinction between sacred and secular music." [7]

Music in which expression of a distinctly religious feeling predominated would presumably be religious music. It must be assumed, therefore, that the existence of such expression in music is denied by persons who contend that there is no inherently religious music. But if music can express other feelings—and virtually everyone agrees that it can and does—its inability to express religious feelings requires one or the other of two premises: (1) the special quality of religious feeling makes its expression in music impossible, or (2) religious feeling, as something distinct from other experiences, does not exist and therefore cannot be expressed. From the limited literature on the subject and from an oral statement made by one of the musicologists, it appears that the second premise is the one generally implied. The contention seems to be that all the specific feelings associated with religion—reverence, awe, calmness, ecstasy, etc.—can be experienced without religion. Therefore religious feeling is not conceived as a really distinct type of emotional experience; hence, music expressing it is not a distinct type of music. Everything here turns on a question of fact concerning the nature of religious experience.

Many persons, of course, maintain that their religious experience has a distinct quality, presumably a consequence of its primary orientation toward God rather than toward nature, society, or self. For this reason, if not simply on common-sense grounds, some readers will be inclined to reject as patently absurd the proposition that religious music is not inherently different from secular music. The evidence supporting it, however, cannot be lightly dismissed.

46

Professor Martin Bernstein, an experienced and expert educator in music, maintains (and he is doubtless right) that many pieces of music composed to sacred texts could easily be palmed off on an average listener who did not know what the words meant as music written for, and aptly expressing, secular texts. Such a listener, for example, might readily accept the Hallelujah Chorus from Handel's *Messiah* as a triumphal chorus celebrating the return to Rome of an emperor or great general after a successful military campaign. From this it may be argued that the religion was in the text, not in the music.

It is, indeed, not unusual for a melody to be sung to both sacred and profane words. For example, the thirteenth-century canon, *Sumer Is Icumen In,* was given a set of sacred words (Latin) as well as its original secular ones. The tune for which the religious poem *Battle Hymn of the Republic* was written had previously been *John Brown's Body,* a march song of the Union troops, and, still earlier, had been a hymn, the words of which began, "Say, brothers, will you meet us [sung three times] on Canaan's happy shore?" More recently, it has been used as the melody of a labor movement song. Along the same line is the use of certain music in both secular works and ostensibly religious ones. The first movement of Bach's *Brandenburg Concerto in G major* (No. 3) is used, with additional orchestration, as the sinfonia of his cantata *Ich liebe den Höchsten* (No. 174), and the first movement of his *Clavier Concerto in D minor* becomes the sinfonia of his cantata *Wir müssen durch viel Trübsal* (No. 146). Many additional examples might be given.

ii The first thing for one to note, in connection with this apparent versatility of pieces of music, is that the performance of a piece for secular purposes may be different from its performance as religious music. There may be differences in tempo, in phrasing, in dynamics (contrast of, and variations in, loudness and softness), in rhythmic emphasis, in the timbre (sound quality) of the instruments and/or human voices, and, if permitted, in instrumentation and in harmonic or polyphonic arrangement. An ultimate musical product, a piece of music in the most intelligible sense of the term, is a composition as performed, either actually or in the composer's concept. In this sense, what is said to be one composition or piece may be two or more very different musical products or pieces of music, because of some or all of the types of difference indicated.

47

Consequently, one of them may express something that another does not express; one may have religious content and another not, or one may have a more intensely religious content than another.

Let us suppose, however, that a composition is played as substantially the same piece of music for both religious and secular purposes. It does not follow that both uses make the same demand with respect to the content of the piece. Nor does it follow that the piece is really appropriate to both uses; nor that there are not additional pieces (some of Palestrina's, for example) that almost every sensitive listener would recognize as predominantly religious in nature.

Most interesting, in the light of the ultimate application of our conclusions to New Orleans jazz, is music that (like much of Bach's music) seems, to a qualified listener, to have both religious and secular content. Only a bigot (secular or religious) would maintain that the existence of one necessarily excludes the other from the same piece of music. If religious precepts and feelings ought to guide us in secular activities—and we are told repeatedly on high authority that they ought—it would seem to follow that music expressing a Christian emotional attitude but dealing also with secular feelings is precisely what is needed. Such music is appropriate in both a sacred and a profane setting, and its successful use in both would not suggest a lack of religious content but rather the presence of both secular and religious content.

In connection with scholars who deny the existence of religious music, one is reminded of the clergyman who asked an atheist, "What precisely is this God whose existence you deny?"—suspecting that definition would show it not to be the God whose existence he himself affirmed. One would like to ask the scholars to describe the religious music whose existence they deny. It appears, in at least some cases, to be not the sort of music we have just indicated, but rather a music containing only pure religious feeling wholly alien to mundane emotions and activities. A person at once musically and spiritually perceptive may affirm that such music, or something very close to it, exists—in Gregorian chant, for example. But even if it did not, its nonexistence would be consistent with the existence of music that has, in varying proportion, both religious and secular content.

In any case, the concept of religious music as comprising nothing but purely religious music is tenable only on a very narrow view of the relationship between the sacred and the secular. Not only are religious attitudes and insight utilized in secular activities and in the governance of emotions associated with such activities, but spiritual experience itself is thought generally to integrate religion with other elements, in varying proportion. Professor Greene's statement on this subject is worth quoting:

Man's spiritual experience is, indeed, seldom if ever exclusively religious, social, or introspectively self-conscous. No religion is completely divorced from social intent and conduct; man's social relations frequently assume religious character and value; and a consciousness of self not only pervades all conscious awareness but is itself, in turn, conditioned by a consciousness of other-than-self. Yet our spiritual experiences are often *predominantly* religious, social, or introspective in character. . . .[8]

Perhaps the matter can be disposed of most simply and most accurately through the distinction between the subject matter and the content of a piece of music (or of any art product). The *subject matter* may include a specific program, such as the death throes of a swan; or it may consist solely of certain emotional states or other subjective experiences. The *content* of a piece of music is a broader concept: it is, indeed, everything expressed in the music. It includes not only the subject matter but also, so far as relevant, the emotional attitude, understanding, and personal point of view of the composer—his *insight,* let us call it. For he is not composing music merely *about* something: he is also composing *with* something, which, in this connection, is his insight into the subject matter and into the world of which it is a part. Different composers, like different painters doing portraits of the same person, see a given subject matter through different "eyes," i.e. different ideas or feelings with respect to its real nature or significant aspects—in short, with differences of insight. The intrusion of the composer's insight affects the subject matter as presented in the musical product. For example, a musical expression of sorrow—let us say the sorrow of the Virgin at the Cross—may or may not include, or may include in varying degrees, despondence, love, bitterness, puzzlement, anguish, humility, a sort of calmness or elevation, and so on, according to the spiritual understanding (insight) of the composer.

Subject matter and content are often confused by persons who talk and write about art (including music), but the distinction between them is basic to systematic criticism.[9] The distinction may be illustrated by Albert Schweitzer's discussion of the content of Bach's *Well-tempered Clavichord.* Dr. Schweitzer indicates that what fascinates us in this work is the composer's insight rather than the subject matter or the form. "Joy, sorrow, tears, lamentation, laughter—to all these it gives voice, but in such a way that we are transported from the world of unrest to a world of peace, and *see reality in a new way. . . .*" [10] Bach depicts "the reality of life felt by . . . a spirit in which the most contradictory emotions, wildest grief and exuberant cheerfulness, are simply phases of a fundamental superiority of soul. It is this that gives the same transfigured air to" a certain "sorrow-laden" prelude and a certain "care-free, volatile" prelude.[11] In short, Bach's expression of his own spirit, the source of his insight, was the essential and valuable element in the content of his music, far more important than the subject matter, which was, indeed, "transfigured" by the composer's way of seeing or feeling it.

Because religion entails a certain emotional attitude or spiritual insight, it may enter into the content of music as that by which the subject matter is understood, not merely as the subject matter. Indeed, the raw subject matter may be secular, but religious insight will nevertheless color it or transfigure it, as in the case of Bach's music. The music may be *about* triumph, joy, sorrow, etc., but these emotions will be present as a religious spirit feels them (assuming full power in the composer to express his own experience). By the same token, a mass or hymn may be composed by one whose point of view or emotional attitude is so alien to profound religious insight that the piece of music is only faintly, or not at all, religious in content.

One sees, then, that there is some truth in the contention that no real difference exists between religious music and secular music. For religious and secular subject matter, solely as raw material unilluminated by spiritual insight, may be remarkably similar. The joy of a person whose love for another human being is reciprocated and the joy of a person who feels sure of God's love are approximately the same emotion to one who understands neither of them. After passing through the creative and censorial spirit of the composer, they are again likely to be similar, at least to a substantial degree, but with a new similarity bestowed upon them by the identity of that spirit. If the composer's insight is wholly secular, he is likely to assimilate the sacred love to the profane; if his insight is sufficiently religious, he will either assimilate the secular to the sacred or will represent it with a benignity and optimism that suggest the pervasive presence of God's love. Widor, it may be noted, did not say that Bach's sacred music expressed religious emotion: he said that Bach's music did so. All Bach's music is religious in the sense that it expresses the composer's religious way of feeling and understanding. Accordingly, his use of a concerto movement in a church cantata is wholly appropriate.

In the same way, it may be appropriate for a hymn or a Negro spiritual to be performed in New Orleans jazz or for this type of jazz to be used as the accompaniment of a gospel singer. The reason why these common uses of New Orleans jazz are not offensive to a qualified listener is that the music's religious element lies not in its subject matter but in a traditional way of looking at things, a way that includes a conspicuously religious orientation.

III From the fact that music can have religious content, it does not necessarily follow that it can have specifically Christian content. If, however, one accepts also the premise that different religions present, to some extent, different emotional attitudes or different kinds and degrees of spiritual insight, one will conclude that a sufficiently skilled composer who shares the special attitude or insight of a given religion can express it—or perhaps cannot help expressing it—in his music.

There is plenty of authority for the existence of specifically Christian content in art in general and music in particular. Professor Greene maintains that "the best examples of religious art should express not religion in general . . . but some particular religion such as Christianity." [12] In his classic work, *The Evolution of the Art of Music,* Sir Hubert Parry states: "From the very first the spirit of the religion [Christianity] was most perfectly and completely reproduced in its music. . . ." [13] Cecil Gray writes that "music is the art in which the early Christian values are best expressed and embodied. . . ." [14] Frazer, in *The Golden Bough,* maintains that "every faith has its appropriate music," and illustrates by reference to the difference between certain pagan religious music and Christian music.[15]

It will henceforth be assumed, therefore, that music can be Christian, i.e. that it can have specifically Christian content.

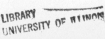

4. The Christian element in New Orleans jazz

1   One of the two remaining objections which might prevent unbiased consideration of the evidence of a strong Christian element in New Orleans jazz rests upon the fact that New Orleans jazz is conspicuously kinetic, is indeed a sort of dance music. In various pagan religions, dancing plays a part in ritual. In Christianity, however, dancing has lost its overt religious significance. Can dance music, music that swings, nevertheless bear the Lord's word?

The aria *Merke, mein Herze,* from Bach's cantata *So du mit deinem Munde* (No. 145) has been aptly characterized as "full of swing and almost dance-like." [1] Listening to it, the British music scholar William S. Hannam sees "happy figures dancing." [2] But probably no one who accepts the possibility of Christian content in music will deny that this aria expresses Christian feeling. Mr. Hannam finds also that the instrumental part of *Zion hört,* in Bach's cantata *Wachet auf* (No. 140)—the "theme" music of a popular radio program—suggests "a dance tune." [3] Dance rhythm or dance-like music is found also in specifically religious works by Handel,

Notes to this chapter begin on page 302.

52

Mendelssohn, and other composers. Apparently there is no inherent incompatibility between dance music and Christian content.

The last of the anticipated objections is an *argumentum ad hominem.* How, it may be asked, can music of genuinely Christian content be composed by the sort of men who play hot jazz? The first fact to be noted in connection with this objection is that most New Orleans jazzmen are serious, dignified citizens. They must not be confused with the offensively superficial "showmen" of sweet dance music and swing, or with the Broadway-saturated characters of Tin Pan Alley, or with the perverse individuals among modern jazzmen. Even on the rare occasions when a New Orleans jazzman clowns professionally, his innate dignity is not hard to perceive through the clowning. If the reader saw the second edition of Cinerama, he will doubtless recall the mock vocal growling of the late Oscar "Papa" Celestin in *Tiger Rag.* In this performance Celestin maintained his customary benevolent dignity without permitting it to interfere in any way with the fun; in fact, it created a superior sort of fun, in which, by a sort of miracle, boisterousness and gentle graciousness were blended. Miracles, even small ones, are a Christian specialty.

Most New Orleans jazzmen believe in the basic truths of Christianity and more than a few are deeply religious. Some of the correspondence of King Oliver and of Jelly Roll Morton provides an indication of the religious feeling of these men. The letters containing the following passages were written by Oliver to his sister at a time when poor health and professional misfortune challenged the power of his Christian gratitude and optimism:

> I'm still out of work. Since the road house close I haven't hit a note. But I've got a lot to thank God for. Because I eat and sleep. . . . Look like every time one door close the Good Lord open another.[4]
> We are still having nice weather here. The Lord is sure good to me here without an overcoat.[5]

The following passage follows an account of a seriously adverse turn in Oliver's physical condition and of the virtual impossibility of his obtaining medical treatment (he died two months later):

> Don't think I'm afraid because I wrote what I did. I am trying to live near to the Lord than ever before. So I feel the Good Lord will take care of me. Good night, dear. . . .[6]

The passages quoted, which might serve as textbook illustrations of the eloquence that profound sentiment sometimes lends to the

53

pen of even a semiliterate man, provide ample proof of Oliver's faith, humility, and Christian cheerfulness.

From what we are able to learn about Oliver from people who knew him, he appears to have been a kind, honest, upright man. During most of Jelly Roll Morton's life, his character, unlike Oliver's, was far from exemplary. Nevertheless, the following passage from a letter written by Morton to his wife in 1940 indicates that by then he had attained intense religiousness:

I slid off the road in Wyoming in a sleet storm and damaged the car a little. The blessed mother was with me and I did not get hurt. I had to leave one of the cars * in Montpelier, Idaho, on account of the weather was too dangerous. And the next couple of nights I was caught up on a mountain in Oregon near the town of John Day. The snow was very slippery and deep. The police car had to pull me out and I was not hurt. Yes, the blessed mother really taken care of me in a-many ways in all the storms and danger I had to confront me. I did not get a chance to make many novenas on the road on account of driving all the time, but I said lots of prayers just the same.

I am trying to find some kind of good climate and will soon or I will keep roaming till I do.

I cannot go home [New Orleans] at this time without money, but I will send you there as soon as I can. Give the priests and all my friends my best regards and will always remember you in my prayers. May God bless you and keep you.[7]

One of the leading figures in the renaissance of traditional jazz was the New Orleans trumpeter Willie G. "Bunk" Johnson (1879–1949). Johnson was active in a Negro Masonic lodge, which, like all Masonic lodges, admitted only religious believers. Convincing evidence of Johnson's religious feeling in relation to music may be found in his love for spirituals. In 1945, he was brought to New York to lead a band of New Orleans musicians in a series of concerts at the Stuyvesant Casino. It was not his practice to announce his selections, but he rose to announce the opening number in the first of these concerts. The occasion was memorable because it was the first time that young New Yorkers had heard live New Orleans jazz as it had been performed during its classic period. The selection chosen and announced by Johnson was not a rag or a stomp or a popular song but a spiritual, *Down by the Riverside*. Johnson made two recordings of this number, which

---

* Morton owned two cars. He had been driving one of them, with the other in tow.

appears to have been his favorite. On one of the recordings, Johnson, no vocalist, was moved to sing the words:

Down by the riverside, I'm going to lay my weapons down. I ain't going to study war no more.

Johnson made band recordings of at least eleven spirituals, some of them more than once—at least fourteen recordings in all. In addition, he accompanied a gospel singer, Ernestine Washington, in four recordings of hymns and spirituals. It is interesting to note that the most famous of all blues singers, Bessie Smith, sang in a church choir, and that Sister Washington also enjoys a reputation as a blues singer.

Louis Armstrong, the best known of all traditional jazzmen, writes as follows about a period during his boyhood in New Orleans:

I was going to church regularly for both grandma and my great-grandmother were Christian women, and between them they kept me in school, church and Sunday school. In church and Sunday school I did a whole lot of singing. That, I guess, is how I acquired my singing tactics.
. . . At church my heart went into every hymn I sang. I am still a great believer and I go to church whenever I get the chance.[8]

Oliver, Morton, Johnson, and Armstrong have been selected as examples because of the great influence they have exerted and because the facts related about them are matters of public knowledge. Their religious feelings are representative of those of many other New Orleans jazzmen.

II   Every historian of jazz recognizes the obvious fact that Negro folk songs exercised a strong influence on New Orleans jazz. Some of the songs, the spirituals, were religious. Others—of which the work songs and blues are thought to have exerted an important effect on jazz—were secular. The blues, in turn, are regarded as derived from both the work songs and the spirituals. Jazz historians have chosen, however, to ignore the discovery, made by the musicologist H. E. Krehbiel, that there was a "paucity of *secular* working songs" in Negro music and that to a great extent "the American Negro's spirituals were also his working songs."[9] If Krehbiel is right—and we have seen no refutation of his contention—the influence of the spirituals on New Orleans jazz has been even greater than is generally supposed.

Additional evidence of the strength of this influence has recently been made public. A Folkways record, *Country Brass Bands*, containing music by two rural Southern Negro brass bands believed to represent music from which jazz largely developed, has been issued. The two bands, recorded *in loco* by Frederic Ramsey, Jr., show similarities to early jazz groups. According to John S. Wilson, jazz record reviewer of *The New York Times*, they have maintained "a continuity of existence from the nineteenth century and, presumably, a continuity of style and material." The two following facts, taken in conjunction, are therefore of the utmost significance. First (again quoting Mr. Wilson), "the style and repertory of the New Orleans brass bands were determined largely by country brass men who moved into New Orleans." Second, most of the selections played by the two bands "come from the church, originally the sole source of material for these brass bands, although secular songs have been added over the years."

It may be concluded, then, that the influence of the spirituals on New Orleans jazz was strong and fundamental. To understand the nature of this influence on the content of the music, one must first recognize the spirituals as an expression of Judeo-Christian values and aspirations. The error into which several writers have fallen, of finding in the spirituals little more than an Americanization of African attitudes and musical devices, makes it impossible for these writers to grasp the nature not only of the spirituals themselves but also of New Orleans jazz.

The effort to disregard or to depreciate the Christianity of the spirituals sometimes attains a desperate intensity that leads to ludicrous consequences. In a well-known book [10] on Negro folk songs, for example, the author, Dorothy Scarborough, devotes no chapter to spirituals but manages to cover a few of them, such as *The Gospel Train*, under railroad songs! The word "train" occurs in one stanza of *Reborn Again* and of *Every Time I Feel the Spirit;* there is no reference to railroads in any other stanza or in the chorus of either of these spirituals. To Miss Scarborough, however, they are railroad songs rather than religious songs. Even in spirituals in which the train as the vehicle to heaven plays a much larger role, the concept is of course metaphorical.[11]

Miss Scarborough's judgment may be contrasted with that of the late Negro writer James Weldon Johnson. Although he recognized an African element in the spirituals, he also perceived the dominance of Christianity in the emotional content of these songs. The spirituals, said Johnson, were

a body of songs voicing all the cardinal virtues of Christianity—patience—forbearance—love—faith—and hope—through a necessarily modified form of primitive African music. The Negro took complete refuge in Christianity, and the Spirituals were literally forged of sorrow in the heat of religious fervor. They exhibited, moreover, a reversion to the simple principles of primitive, communal Christianity.

The thought that the Negro might have refused or failed to adopt Christianity—and there were several good reasons for such an outcome, one being the vast gulf between the Christianity that was preached to him and the Christianity practiced by those who preached it—leads to some curious speculations. One thing is certain, there would have been no Negro Spirituals.[12]

When one bears in mind the supramundane nature of Christianity, it becomes evident that what the Negroes did in their spirituals was to turn away from the inadequacy of the mundane toward the glory of the other life. Slavery made the inadequacy vivid and immediate. But the composers of the spirituals perceived the broader implications of their misery and therefore were able to attain a valid concept of Christian salvation. The words of many of the spirituals make abundantly clear the Christian aspiration that the songs express: "You may have all this world, give me Jesus." "King Jesus shall be mine." "O, some say give me silver, some say give me gold, but I say give me Jesus." "I want to go to heaven when I die." "I'm going to fly all over God's heaven." And so on.

It is, then, inaccurate and unfair to Negro music to maintain that the slaves who sang the spirituals were merely expressing their desire for the emancipation which was granted them in 1865. Slavery and the hope for emancipation colored the spirituals but did not reduce their Christian content; on the contrary, they enhanced the religious intensity of the songs, for slavery and emancipation have profound spiritual significance to persons who have absorbed the Judeo-Christian tradition. They represent the bondage imposed by the prince of this world and the freedom bestowed by the Prince of the other. This is why the analogy which the Negroes found between their own plight and that of the Jews in Egyptian bondage—an analogy reflected in some of the spirituals—must be understood from a religious rather than an ethnic or sociological point of view. It is also why the emancipation of the Negroes was seen by men of imagination as essentially a religious event—witness

Whittier's "Laus Deo." It was the Negroes' creative imagination, inspired by religious insight, that saved the spirituals from what would otherwise have been a wholly justifiable but aesthetically and spiritually arid music of protest against slavery.

In their eagerness to emphasize the African origins of American Negro thought and music, some persons have maintained that the heaven sought by the composers and singers of the spirituals was really the Africa that their ancestors had known. Here again the desire to deny or to depreciate the obvious Christianity of these songs takes on the aspect of a phobia and leads to absurdity—in this case, the premise that the spirit of the slaves was dominated by inherited nostalgia.

III   In some cases, failure to recognize the genuineness and profundity of the Christian element in Negro spirituals appears to result from the exuberance of the music as sometimes performed, an exuberance manifested at times by the singers' spontaneous interjections. This characteristic is said to be African and not Christian. The difficulty may be quickly dissipated, however, if one bears in mind the effects of Christianity on groups who have recently discovered it.

The creation of spirituals reached its peak in the three decades immediately prior to the Civil War. To the American Negroes of that period Christianity was still new. They were therefore affected by it in much the same way as the Christians of the early centuries A.D. James Weldon Johnson, in the passage quoted, recognized this fact, which, if not obvious, can be established by ample evidence. For example, like the early Christians the Negroes (neo-early Christians, one is tempted to call them) found sculpture and painting inadequate for the expression of their intense Christianity. Only music could even begin to express the spirituality they had discovered. The following explanation by Cecil Gray, relating to the early Christian's preference for musical expression, is equally applicable to the similar preference on the part of the American Negro:

> The other arts can speak only of the pomp and splendour of transient things, of mortal desires and earthly passions; music, free from the tyranny of the concrete and the material, can alone hymn the glories of the Kingdom of Heaven. . . .[13]

The early Christians, in their intense need for spiritual expression, created plainsong, which, we are led to believe, excelled all prior music as an expression of spirituality. The American slaves performed a similar, if lesser, miracle in creating the Negro spiritual, an eloquent expression of intense Christian aspiration, out of vastly inferior musical material.

Interjected exclamations and even glossolaly ("outburst of in-' articulate sounds" [14]) were not uncommon in early Christian worship. The good news of the Lord's resurrection, ascension, and future return and of the kingdom of heaven, if genuinely believed, naturally leads to extraordinary jubilation. In the text of the final choral of Bach's cantata *Wachet auf* (No. 140), this joy is described as beyond anything that eye has perceived or ear has heard, and indeed becomes so intense that language is abandoned and the singers become bacchantes gleefully chanting "i-o! i-o!" In the expression of such joy, the Negroes' shouts, interjections, and general euphoria in singing religious songs cannot be called excessive or indicative of a failure to understand the message of Christianity.

With special reference to the relationship between Christian worship and shouting or the making of inarticulate sounds, we may turn to St. Augustine for an authoritative statement. The following passage is taken from his commentary on the Thirty-second Psalm:

And for whom has this "jubilatio" more propriety than for God, the unspeakable? Language is too poor to speak of God. And if language cannot help you and yet you do not like to be silent, what is left for you but to shout in jubilant strains, so that your heart may be glad without uttering words? The boundless width of joy cannot be comprised within the narrow limits of syllables.[15]

And again, in his commentary on the Twenty-second Psalm:

One who is jubilant does not utter words but sounds of joy without words. The voice of the soul overflowing with joy tries as much as possible to express its emotion, though without giving it a clear sense. A person full of great joy at first utters in his exultation a few inarticulate sounds, not words with a special meaning; afterwards, however, he proceeds to jubilant sounds without words, so that he appears to express joy with his voice, a joy so excessive that he cannot find words for it.[16]

Perhaps, if his voice is inadequate, he will make jubilant sounds, something like those of a voice, on a trumpet or on a trombone. We shall see, in Chapter 5, that these instruments in New Orleans jazz are, in a very direct way, substitutes for the human voice.

The listener's interpretation of exuberance in ostensibly religious music will depend, of course, on the listener's own religious attitude.

59

An eighteenth-century critic, imbued with French rationalism, condemned Bach's music for being too passionate. A passionate believer, on the contrary, would welcome passion in the expression of his faith. Again, the tendency of many individuals to think of religion romantically—to embrace Wagner's "new religion"—may lead them not to recognize fully the Christian element in the spirituals. The makers of the spirituals were devoted to no Wagnerian romanticism but to what they themselves called, in one of the best-known spirituals, "that old-time religion."

Krehbiel observed that Negro songs, including spirituals, were written chiefly in the major mode. From this and other evidence (one need only listen to the songs!) he concluded that, even when apparently sorrowful, the music was essentially patient and optimistic in mood. A nineteenth-century writer on spirituals had, according to Krehbiel, sounded "the keynote of the emotional stimulus of the songs" when he had written: "Nothing but patience for this life—nothing but triumph in the next." [17] Krehbiel vehemently denied that, as some other writers seemed to think, the Negro folk songs had been "conceived in sorrow and born in heaviness of heart by a people walking in darkness." [18] With great acumen he linked the underlying cheerfulness of the songs with their Judeo-Christian subject matter:

"They could not sing of the New Jerusalem, toward which they were journeying, in terms of grief. The Biblical tales and imagery . . . also called for celebration in jubilant rather than lugubrious accent." [19]

New Orleans jazz inherited this jubilation from the spirituals, which in turn, as we have seen, derived it from Christian faith—not from the freedom attained in 1865, for almost all the spirituals had been created before then. To suppose that the Negro needed emancipation in order to be exuberant in spirit and in music is to fly in the face of the known facts.

If, then, the spiritual is the father of the conspicuous cheerfulness of New Orleans jazz, Christianity is its grandfather; and the heritage can be traced in both history and lineament. Most striking (and it is a matter to which we shall have occasion to advert again) is the insight with which New Orleans jazz treats human sorrow. Here one may trace a clear line of descent from Christianity, through the spirituals, to the alchemy by which the blues are converted to expressions of comfort and sometimes of exultation. The blues are, initially, expressions of grief, in some cases expressions of intense

60

and seemingly hopeless grief. Such grief is at the heart of the basic story of Christianity. It is true, of course, that the several causes of grief represent descending levels of spirituality. We do not contend that the sadness in the blues achieves the significance or the elevation of the sorrow of the *mater dolorosa*. Some of the spirituals, however, sing the passion of Christ in musical and poetic terms humbly close to the ineffable subject matter. Others deal with the misery of the bondage of this world, a subject by no means remote from the passion. An additional step toward the commonplace brings us to the loneliness, unrequited love, etc., which are the immediate causes of the grief expressed in the blues. But properly understood, are they not parts of the congeries of inadequacies that make up the human bondage from which the singer of the spirituals is seeking emancipation, and from which, indeed, his faith emancipates him?

The significant thing is that, just as the spirituals maintain a Christian cheerfulness while dealing with intense misery and thus transform the misery, so New Orleans jazz maintains its cheerfulness when it expresses the sorrow of the blues,[20] which is similarly transformed. This creative magic can be explained only as a humble example of the power of the insight by which sorrow, even the greatest sorrow, is known to be transient, a prelude to a still greater joy.

5. The Christian element in New Orleans jazz (concluded)

1   Many Negro jazzmen have played church music, either in services or on other occasions. It has always been one of the functions of New Orleans jazzmen to play spirituals and hymns in funeral processions. In the early years, however, these selections were not played in dance halls. Negroes of the old school throughout the South drew a sharp line between Christian music and frivolous music. Not many would have gone so far as W. C. Handy's father, who was willing to pay for organ lessons but forbade his son to play the guitar because it was "one of the devil's playthings." [1] Many, however, would have considered it improper to bring sacred music into the honky-tonk. Besides, there was no need to do so; the profane repertoire was ample and sufficiently attractive.

The playing of Negro religious songs by jazz bands in dance halls and other places of entertainment appears to have begun in the North during the second half of the 1920's. It has been going on ever since. In many performances these selections are played "straight," with little or no apparent adaptation to the secularity of the occasion. This is especially likely to be the case if the band is a regular New Orleans jazz band, not only because in such a

Notes to this chapter begin on page 303.

band the old religious tradition is still strong enough to make mistreatment of a religious song appear sacrilegious but also because such a band performs most of its pieces in a style very similar to the style in which sacred songs are sung and played on religious occasions. The difference between the sacred and the profane in Negro music is not always musically or spiritually significant. Indeed, the two are in some cases so similar that one is obliged to suppose either that the secular music has a strong religious element or that the sacred music is not genuinely sacred. For reasons indicated in Chapter 4, the latter supposition is untenable.

In other cases, jazz bands play religious selections with adjustments intended to make them more "entertaining." This occurs especially in performances by bands not strictly within the realm of New Orleans jazz. Such adjustments may take the form of comedy —spoken or played—and/or a beat, tempo, or type of arrangement not customary in the playing of religious music on sacred occasions. As a rule, such adjustments involve departures from the norm, i.e. from New Orleans jazz.

But whether the religious songs are played "straight" or not, the demand for them in traditional jazz has risen sharply in recent years. Obviously there is a special content in these songs that an audience is seeking *when it comes to hear traditional jazz.* The nature of the special content is indicated by the nature of the songs. At the close of the final performance of an engagement by Turk Murphy's band in Philadelphia in October 1954, a substantial part of the audience begged for a rendition of *Just a Closer Walk with Thee,* a song whose gentle, devoutly lyrical mood is deeply alien to the pagan or Dionysiac spirit that many persons associate with jazz. It is hard to escape the conclusion that members of the audience were seeking a specifically Christian experience.

Undoubtedly the most popular traditional-jazz number, sacred or profane, during the past few years has been *When the Saints Go Marching In* or, more briefly, *The Saints.* Where traditional jazz is played, audible demands for this old song—which Louis Armstrong, in a slightly doctored version, popularized as jazz in 1939 * and which Bunk Johnson, playing it "straight," repopularized in 1945 with lasting effect—far exceed those for any of the traditional-jazz numbers of secular origin. A Dixieland band, in what is apparently an effort to benefit by the song's vogue, calls itself Preacher

* Negro clergymen protested against Louis' 1939 record of *The Saints.*

Rollo and the Saints. Most of the listeners are familiar with the words, which express the singer's fervent hope that he will be "of that number" when the saints enter heaven and the "sun begins to shine." Commonly, members of the audience sing or mumble this fundamental Christian aspiration along with the band performance, which in many cases includes a vocal rendition.

It is true of spirituals and religious songs in general, not only of *The Saints*, that their lyrics, more often than those of other selections played by traditional-jazz bands, are sung during the performances by one or more members of the band and are known by the listeners. Clearly the subject matter of the spirituals, set forth in their words, has a special interest for the audiences, an interest enhanced by the music, which gives parallel expression to the sentiment.

In this connection, it is significant that the revival of traditional jazz and especially of New Orleans jazz in the forties coincided with an increase in religious interest and church attendance. Many young persons, imbued with the popular tradition of unbelief and of independence from spiritual authority, find themselves impelled toward religious acceptance. The need to scoff and the need to believe come into head-on conflict, a conflict to which the jazz rendition of spirituals offers a convenient solution. The apparent reduction of religious belief to the level of the dance hall, the beer palace, and the hot beat lends support and expression to the scoffer's aggressiveness toward spiritual values and to his denial of suprarational discipline. At the same time, the genuine Christian aspiration in the spirituals and hymns permits him a surreptitious religious experience, for which he obviously feels an intense need.

The curious mock-religious attitude in some jazz (not New Orleans jazz) performances tends to support the dual hypothesis of a religious content in jazz and of an impediment to its full acceptance. The listeners whose demands such performances are designed to gratify are persons obviously not uninterested in religion. They are at least suspect of trying to sneak a Christian experience past a censor imposed by social or personal resistance to overt Christianity.

II   In his recording of *Lonesome Road*,[2] made in 1931 or 1932, trumpeter Louis Armstrong says, "Now, sisters and brothers, this is Reverend Satchelmouth Armstrong going to speak to you. . . ." During a large part of the record he continues his comedy preacher

64

Oscar "Papa" Celestin (d. 1954), famous New Orleans jazzman.

Marching band at Celestin's funeral. Trombonist at right is Bill Matthews.

talk, the high point of which appears to be his remark that if the collection were larger he would be able to get his shoes out of pawn. The music, except for Mr. Armstrong's solo, is in the sweet, large-band, saxophone-dominated style. Therefore it is by no means "straight" sacred music. But it is the spoken burlesque that makes the record a peculiarly explicit example of the mock-religious attitude referred to in the preceding section of this chapter. It also exemplifies the significant identification of the trumpeter or cornetist in traditional jazz with a Negro preacher.

Armstrong's "reverend" comedy talk began in Chicago in 1925, just when he was beginning to establish his independence from the strictly New Orleans way of looking at jazz—a point of view, however, which he has never completely abandoned. The New Orleans jazz tradition was not alien to humor but it was inconsistent with irreverence.

Even more explicit on the subject of trumpeter-preacher identification than his *Lonesome Road* talk is Armstrong's introduction of himself in his 1939 recording of *The Saints*: [3] "Sisters and brothers, this is Reverend Satchmo getting ready to beat out this mellow sermon for you. My text this evening is *When the Saints Go Marching In*." In short, the trumpeter is a preacher and his playing is a sermon. The trumpet is the preacher's voice. There is, indeed, a jazz selection entitled *Preachin' the Blues*.

There is additional evidence of the trumpeter-preacher identification. King Oliver is described as "holding his cornet with the fervor of a preacher holding the Bible." [4] Banjoist-guitarist Danny Barker says that the New Orleans trumpeter Chris Kelly "should have been a preacher. But he preached so melodiously with his horn that it was like somebody singing a song. . . ." [5] Here again the playing itself is heard as preaching.

The identification is promoted by the well-known ability of many jazz cornetists and trumpeters—among them Oliver, Armstrong, and Muggsy Spanier—to make the instrument "talk." But the jazz trumpet goes beyond mimicry. As one writer aptly expresses it, "the relation between voice and instrument takes place on a higher level than that of mere imitation. Rather, the trumpet becomes an extension of the human voice, and translates the accents of speech, the staccato consonants and long drawn vowels, into trumpet timbre." [6]

The symbolic significance of the trumpet as a call to judgment is found in several of the spirituals and is no doubt reflected in

65

the significance of the instrument in traditional jazz. It will be remembered that the trumpet or cornet generally plays the "lead," i.e. the principal melody line representing the basic theme, in a traditional-jazz ensemble. The following passages from spirituals indicate the Christian implications of the trumpet:

> The trumpet sounds within my soul,
> I ain't got long to stay here.
> > (*Steal Away to Jesus*)
> Where shall I be when the first trumpet sounds,
> When it sounds so loud till it wakes up the dead?
> > (*Where Shall I Be When the First Trumpet Sounds*)
> You'll hear the trumpet sound
> To wake the nations underground.
> > (*My Lord, What a Morning*)
> Blow that trumpet, Gabriel, blow that trumpet,
> And I hope that trump will blow me home to my New Jerusalem.
> > (*Blow That Trumpet, Gabriel*)
> When the trumpet sounds its call
> I want to be in that number.
> > (*When the Saints Go Marching In*)

The trombone, too, which plays a fundamental role as the lowest of the three contrapuntal voices in a typical traditional-jazz band, is associated with religion and specifically with the voice of a preacher. James Weldon Johnson, in explaining why he named his book of Negro sermons in verse *God's Trombones,* said that he had found the trombone "of just the tone and timbre to represent the old-time Negro preacher's voice." [7] He had previously considered the titles "Trumpets of the Lord" and "Trumpeters of the Lord." Although less frequently than trumpeters, jazz trombonists are sometimes expressly associated with preachers.[8]

Thus it is seen that two of the three instruments in traditional-jazz counterpoint have strong Christian implications for the Negroes who created (and are still creating) the New Orleans jazz that is behind all traditional jazz. It is seen also that these implications extend specifically to the playing of the instruments in jazz bands. The inference that the music itself, as performed, has strong Christian content is inescapable.

III   "When you come right down to it," said the late Mutt Carey, a prominent New Orleans trumpeter, "the man who started the big noise in jazz was Buddy Bolden. . . . I guess he deserves credit

66

for starting it all." [9] Bunk Johnson, who played in Bolden's band, reported to the same effect: "King Buddy Bolden was the first man that began playing jazz in the city of New Orleans, and his band had the whole of New Orleans real crazy and running wild behind it." [10] Even if jazz in some recognizable form existed a little earlier, these statements by New Orleans contemporaries of Bolden's make it clear that, more than any other individual, he gave New Orleans jazz its definitive style and direction.

Therefore it is of the utmost importance for us to ask where Bolden derived his concepts. Another New Orleans musician, Bud Scott, provides an answer: "Each Sunday, Bolden went to church and that's where he got his idea of jazz music." [11]

Perhaps, in the light of the foregoing, one can understand the colloquial characterization of New Orleans jazz as "righteous"— e.g., "that righteous New Orleans stuff." [12] This persistent use of an adjective associated with religion, and especially with Judaism and Christianity, can be explained most naturally as a reflection of a conspicuously religious character in the music, a character apparently recognized by jazzmen even if some of them, like Bolden in his day, do not themselves always follow the path of righteousness.

But one need not confine oneself to inferences about the feelings on this question of jazzmen who are qualified to speak authoritatively. For example, Sam Price, a well-known pianist who divides his career between Negro church music and jazz, maintains that there is a strong religious element in Negro jazz and that it is inevitable because of the strong religious element in the nature of the men who created and are creating the music. He believes that even Negroes who talk cynicism in relation to religion are likely to have a deep-seated religious belief out of reach of the cynicism. When Negroes play jazz, says Mr. Price, they do not "turn off" their Christian feeling. He cites two cases, which he witnessed, of prominent Negro jazzmen openly weeping just after the completion of recording performances in which they participated. In one case the piece was *Yield Not to Temptation,* sung by Myrtle Jackson, and the emotion felt by the late drummer Sidney "Big Sid" Catlett was clearly religious in nature. In the other, it was the piece *How Long Blues,* which vocalist Jimmy Rushing associated with the recent passing of the trumpeter "Hot Lips" Page; but Mr. Price, who knew well both the music and the men, believes that the emotions aroused in the two cases were essentially similar.

Unlike some other white Dixieland performer-composers, clarinetist Tony Parenti, who spent his boyhood in New Orleans during the classic period when Oliver, Ory, and Armstrong were still there, can play fine New Orleans jazz. This is because he understands the music emotionally as well as technically. Therefore he was asked what he thought the music expressed, apart from the fact that much of it was "happy" music. "You have to understand," he began, "that New Orleans was a place where religion and the churches were very important and the music shows it." Although their statements would vary in scope, detail, and emphasis, few persons as well qualified as Mr. Price and Mr. Parenti to have an opinion on the subject would not affirm the existence of a pronounced religious factor in New Orleans jazz.

In summary: The Christian content of the spirituals and their great influence on New Orleans jazz, the Christian attitude toward sorrow in New Orleans jazz, the popularity of sacred songs in the jazz repertoire, the identification of the traditional-jazz trumpet and trombone with the voice of a preacher, and reports by jazzmen qualified to express an opinion, all point to the existence of a strong Christian element in New Orleans jazz. A listener who is both familiar with the idiom and genuinely receptive to the communication of Christian feeling needs no evidence beyond the music itself, provided of course that he has an open mind on the subject. The evidence may be helpful in opening his mind.

Writers on jazz have sometimes done lip service to a religious element in the music but, almost uniformly, have failed to recognize its strength and its profound Christianity. Proper recognition of this element would inevitably affect their critical approach. Perhaps the orientation of many of the writers—socioethnic, anthropological, Rousseauistic, Afro-mystical, everything except Christian and humanistic—prevents proper recognition of the Christian element. No amount of learning in African drumbeats, anti-Negro discrimination, or the managerial policies of New Orleans brothels at the turn of the century can enable a listener to receive a Christian message preached by a trumpet and a trombone if he would be wholly unreceptive to it in the sermons of the preachers for whom the instruments are substituting. True, he might be able to receive it more fully, more authentically, through the music. As St. Augustine said, "Language is too poor to speak of God."

6. *Secular elements in New Orleans jazz*

I   Virtually everyone familiar with New Orleans jazz agrees that the music is "warm" and "friendly." If the word "love" had not been cheapened, in connection with popular music, by its free use in sentimental ballads, New Orleans jazz might well be called loving. It breathes affection and good will to men. This is hardly surprising in Christian music intended for social purposes.

On the question of its sexual-love content, however, the inquirer may run into difficulty. One reason for this is the human but uncritical reluctance of some of our jazz historians to tear themselves away from the sporting houses of pre-World War I New Orleans. Thanks to their researches, we have the names of several of the old houses and of their madams, the address and telephone number of one, the number of chambers in another, and a great deal more such information apparently considered indispensable to the earnest student of jazz. The repute of these long-abandoned houses may still be ill, but it has a fair chance of permanence.

If this emphasis on brothels merely amused or titillated the readers and thus made the books more marketable, no comment would be called for. But there is an additional effect: the unwary

Notes to this chapter begin on page 303.

reader may come away with an impression that New Orleans jazz underwent an important part of its early development in brothels. This is an old and persistent error. There has been so much talking and writing about the houses in connection with jazz that even the guitarist, band leader, and jazz concert impresario Eddie Condon lends support to it, saying in his autobiography that in Chicago "Al Capone and his lieutenants replaced the madams of Storyville as sponsors for the new music."[1] (Storyville is the district in New Orleans to which the houses were confined by the provisions of an 1897 ordinance.) It is fairly clear that Mr. Condon knows better, for elsewhere in his book he states that the jazz bands—it must be remembered that New Orleans jazz was chiefly band music—"were too loud and distracting for the bordellos; the madams preferred string ensembles and piano players."[2]

In truth, very few New Orleans jazzmen ever played in a brothel. Most of them were willing to play wherever someone would pay them to play, but with rare exceptions the sporting houses did not want them. The closest most New Orleans jazzmen ever came to playing in a brothel was to play in a cabaret. They played and still play also in parades and at dances and funerals. They played at lawn parties and picnics. One may be forgiven for asking why some historians dwell more upon the brothels than upon all these other institutions and occasions together—and, indeed, why they devote more attention to them than to the churches, where, according to a man in a position to have firsthand knowledge, Buddy Bolden derived the concept of jazz.[3]

The tenuousness of the relationship between the sporting houses and jazz is indicated also by the fact that a good deal of music other than jazz was played there. Jelly Roll Morton said that Tony Jackson was the best of the pianists who played in the houses and that his repertoire included opera arias, which he sang to his own accompaniment.[4] Morton himself served an extensive apprenticeship as a pianist in brothels, but most of his music is extremely chaste.

It may be asked, then, whether New Orleans jazz never contains a pronounced sexual element. It does. The titles of a few of the songs strongly suggest such an element. Persons familiar, for example, with the original names of the pieces now known as *I Wish I Could Shimmy Like My Sister Kate* and (among other aliases) *The Girls Go Crazy About the Way I Walk*, respectively, will find in them a clue to the nature of the sexual element in the music: it is direct, earthy, and unsentimental. The atmosphere of the jazz band

70

hardly suggests dalliance in the boudoir. In most New Orleans jazz performances, indeed, the sexual element is indistinguishable from the general vitality of the music.

Although undiscriminating writers on jazz frequently speak of its sexual excitement, *aficionados* of traditional jazz generally know better and, if they write on the subject at all, are likely to indicate that this music is not aphrodisiac. Thus, referring to "honest-to-God hot jazz" (which in the context appears to cover little more than traditional jazz), Ralph de Toledano says that it was "governed by an inclusive set of criteria, none of which took in . . . the cheers of an undisciplined generation excited by the effects of rhythm on the urino-genital system." [5] Another lover of this music writes, with respect to it: ". . . don't speak to me of a 'sexual art.' Exactly the opposite is true. A devotee of jazz does not slacken the rein which checks his lower passions. On the contrary. . . ." [6]

II   The unromantic, sometimes earthy vitality of New Orleans jazz is broader than its sexual content and is, indeed, fundamentally characteristic of the music. New Orleans jazz is hearty and, at its best, full of good-humored inventiveness. Although sometimes complicated, it is not sophisticated within the usual connotation of that unhappy term. All this is generally recognized. Generally unobserved, however, is the trap that it sets for the traditional-jazz *aficionado*. If, like some of our Rousseauistic jazz critics, he places a high value on naturalistic expansiveness, he is likely to see in this earthy music a product of the man of nature who scorns the artificial restraints of civilization. When this concept joins forces with his justifiable sympathy for the oppressed Negro race, he may find that salvation, musical and other, lies in the adoption of African spontaneity and vitality and in the rejection of white Americo-European formalism and effeteness. And there he will be, head over heels in the trap and quite unable to accept New Orleans jazz as it is. For, to maintain consistency, he will have to deny two undeniable essential characteristics of the music: first, that it is hemmed in by restraints with respect to both form and substance,[7] restraints more narrow and rigid than those imposed upon art music in the European tradition; second, that it contains a strong Christian element,[8] which is of course profoundly inimical to naturalistic emotional expansiveness.

In conjunction with the Christian element, the immense secular vitality of New Orleans jazz colors almost all its other characteristics. Again and again one reads that this jazz is "happy" music. But happiness plus abounding vitality equals exuberance, and the music is indeed exuberant. When New Orleans jazz expresses sadness, as it often does in the blues, its vitality saves it from wistfulness, just as its Christianity saves it from despondence. The consequence is a rich sadness, implying a source of comfort. In this respect it may be compared with the sadness sometimes found in Hebrew religious music. It is perhaps significant that Ethel Waters, a fine blues singer, has been celebrated also for her rendition of *Eli, Eli.*

The presence of humor in jazz has been frequently remarked. At least in New Orleans jazz, this humor is not the product of an occasional special effort. It is inherent. Although a few of the musicians clown now and then to please their audience, the music is not slapstick. Neither is it witty. Occasionally there is a suggestion of comedy, as in some of Kid Ory's trombone playing. Most of the time, the music hovers close to the tenuous line between humor and good humor or general high spirits. The smile it induces is the smile of a man whose abundant vitality and profound (Christian) optimism would make any other facial expression inapposite.

The hypothesis of a causal relationship between those more profound elements in the music and the inherent good humor is reinforced by the existence of the same characteristic in works of those European composers who, like the New Orleans jazzmen, were able to infuse into their music a combination of abundant vitality and Christian spiritual insight. One finds it in many of the works of Bach—the *Bourrée* from the Third Suite for 'Cello and the *Preambule* from the Sixth Violin Sonata, to select examples almost at random. It is present in much of Beethoven's *Eighth Symphony.* Curiously, the first two movements of this symphony conspicuously utilize some of the devices of jazz. The second subject of the first movement is heavily syncopated, and the syncopation produces a sort of gracious humor. The second movement has what jazzmen would call a "solid beat"—quite naturally, for its first theme was improvised as a humorous tribute to the inventor of the chronometer, the predecessor of the metronome. A jazzlike humor may be found in the *scherzo* of Beethoven's string quartet, Opus 18, No. 6; indeed, a Beethoven scholar maintains that this *scherzo* was "the first piece of jazz." [9] Many of Haydn's works also might be cited.

Some years ago, a study was made of the effects of ten phonograph records—one of them a sweet fox trot, the others all nonjazz—

on a number of listeners. The reported feelings of the listeners were correlated with each of the four elemental musical qualities: rhythm, melody, harmony, and timbre (quality of the sound of a voice or instrument), predominant in the several pieces. The results with regard to the feeling of "amusement" (the closest to humor) were "not wholly conclusive" but were thought to show that this feeling was aroused through rhythm and timbre rather than melody or harmony.[10] Rhythm in New Orleans jazz comprises not only a strong, regular beat, explicit or implied (and sometimes stronger when implied), but also syncopation and other more subtle departures from the regular beat. Because of its great importance in this music, and in the light of the results of the afore-mentioned study, one may reasonably assume—and perhaps the reader's examination of his own experience as listener will confirm the assumption—that part of the humor of New Orleans jazz is dependent upon rhythm.

Although the causal connection between jazz rhythm and jazz humor cannot be ascertained with certainty, a well-known theory of the nature of laughter may be thought to provide a clue. By this theory, we laugh at mechanical conduct where there ought to be the flexibility and adjustability that we expect of a human being. For example: Groucho Marx, as the president of a small European republic, offends the ambassador of a foreign power. When the ambassador calls Groucho a cad, Groucho slaps his face with a glove. Later the two become very friendly, and Groucho remarks laughingly that he can't even remember the word that made him angry. Reminded that it was "cad," he immediately becomes furious and again slaps the ambassador. We laugh because Groucho is acting like a machine, always responding in the same inflexible way to a given force or stimulus, whether his response suits the circumstances or not. Chaplin's conduct in the factory sequence of *Modern Times* provides an even more obvious instance of a laughable combination of the human and the mechanical.

Seeking to apply this theory to the humor derived from the rhythm of New Orleans jazz, one may repeat the common observation that the regular beat of music corresponds to the regular rhythm of life processes, including physiological processes. A jazz beat is often said to be "alive." Nevertheless, so far as men are subject to regular, automatic processes, they are human machines—and that is laughable. Perhaps, therefore, enjoyment of the beat in New Orleans jazz and other good-humored jazz takes two forms: experience of the fundamental vitality represented by the beat and amuse-

73

ment at the mechanical aspects of man which it also represents. The syncopation and other irregularities of rhythm in the melodic lines playfully defy the mechanical pattern of the regular beat and resist control by it, almost as if they were asserting man's flexibility and his independence of the natural order represented by the beat.

If this suggestion of possible meaning in the humor of New Orleans jazz comes close to the truth, it provides an additional reason (Christianity is the other) for the lack of bitterness in that humor. The regular beat, like the fundamental mechanical vitality that it represents, is not merely a limitation; properly conceived and utilized, it is the indispensable foundation on which the whole jazz (or human) structure rests. That is why it has to be a "solid" beat. Provided it be kept firmly in its place, it is no enemy but an ally. Therefore the laughter at it is friendly laughter.

III   The philosophical-religious problem of the One and the Many has a counterpart in the balance between unity and diversity in musical pattern. This balance may be presented through successive elements, as in the sequence of variation after variation, all different yet all based on the same theme and (in New Orleans jazz) on the same harmony. Or it may be presented through different but simultaneous elements that continually form part of a whole, as in polyphony or counterpoint. A New Orleans jazz performance presents unity and diversity in both ways, for it consists of polyphony in variations form.

In contemplation, whether religious or philosophical, of the universe, many men recognize a single unifying spirit or principle (the One) manifested in the varied phenomena (the Many) of the world. Some identify the One with God. (On a lower level and within a narrower scope, the same sort of concept is applied to limited fields of experience, as when one seeks a unifying explanatory principle behind a number of related historical developments.) Thinking of the diverse and resistant Many as subject always to the One and, if the inquiry is religious, as existing for the sake of the One, a man is likely to feel a certain emotion, in which tension and satisfaction are combined. The tension reflects the balance between unity and diversity, and the satisfaction results from the triumph of unity, from recognition of the fact that the existence of the Many which he experiences is quite consistent with domination by the One that he trusts or to which he thinks he has access. For want of

74

a better term, we shall speak of the indicated emotion as the feeling of unity-in-diversity.

Music can stimulate this feeling. It can induce the listener to perceive unity and diversity in the course of a performance as a whole. Through polyphony it can induce him to perceive them at every moment during the performance. If he has to be alert, and has to make an effort, in order clearly to perceive both, and to see how the Many are at once diverse and unified and how the unity is expressed through the diversity, the music gives him a microcosmic workout in world contemplation. By its three-part polyphony, New Orleans jazz provides the competent listener with such a workout. His successful effort to perceive the One-Many relationship in the music exhilarates him and thus enhances the element of satisfaction in his feeling of unity-in-diversity.

In polyphony there are different degrees of contrast and mutual independence among the several voices or instruments carrying the melodic lines. The more contrast and independence, the greater the emphasis on individual differences. A great deal of polyphony is canonic or imitative; in such music, as a rule, one voice begins alone and, as it continues, a second voice comes in, performing what the first voice did prior to the second voice's entry; additional voices in similar imitation may subsequently come in. If the imitation persists throughout the piece or throughout an extended passage, the piece or passage is called a canon. If it is intermittent and in accordance with certain principles, the piece is a fugue. A piece may be neither a canon nor a fugue and still have snatches of imitative counterpoint. Some polyphony is nonimitative, with varying degrees of contrast between the simultaneous melody lines. European art music abounds in both imitative and nonimitative polyphony.

In New Orleans jazz, voices (instruments) rarely imitate each other, and the melodic lines are noted for their mutual contrast and independence. Thus there is greater emphasis on diversity than in most polyphony. It has been suggested that in this diversity, together with whatever freedom to improvise exists, there is an expression of democracy. The thought appears to be that democracy grants to individuals as much independence and freedom as possible but utilizes the distinct mind and capacity of each for achievement of a common goal; and that a New Orleans jazz performance democratically recognizes the independence and individuality of each of the three wind instruments but utilizes them for a common purpose.

75

This theory is not wholly without foundation. It should be remembered, however, that contrast between melody lines long antedated the rise of modern democracy; that in the singing of spirituals in churches, which goes back to the days of slavery, considerable freedom is and was permitted to individuals, although the Negroes were not part of a democratic society; and, perhaps most important, that any emphasis on freedom as a clue to the content of New Orleans jazz must reckon with the fact that, as will be indicated in the following chapter, this is a highly traditional music in which freedom of expression is severely circumscribed. The musicians may be independent of each other to an important extent, but they are all subject to a very exacting over-all unity, which perhaps suggests oneness in God at least as much as it suggests oneness in democracy.

7. Secular elements in New Orleans jazz (concluded)

1   We have arrived at a crucial point in jazz criticism, a point at which the critic chooses the orientation and principles by which he will try to understand jazz and to evaluate it. The problem of basic critical orientation and adoption of principles is not essentially different when the object is jazz from when it is, say, French classical drama or nonobjective painting. Applications vary, but valid principles do not. The fatuous notion of some jazz *aficionados* that in jazz they have something wonderfully new, requiring new principles of criticism and virtually a new attitude toward creative art, does not merit refutation.

Winthrop Sargeant, who, although hardly an *aficionado,* wrote a valuable book on jazz, maintains that jazz and serious music in the European art tradition present totally different problems to the critic. "When you try to approach jazz from a critical point of view," he writes, "you are immediately struck by a curious split which divides almost every aspect of jazz from any real correspondence with so-called 'classical' music. . . . Even the impartial critic is at a loss for any similar scale of standards in the two arts. Though many a jazz aesthete has tried to, you can't compare a Louis Arm-

Notes to this chapter begin on page 303.

strong solo to a Josef Szigeti sonata performance, or a Bessie Smith blues to an aria from *Rigoletto*. There isn't any common ground." [1]

In cases where the jazzman's known or assumed purpose is different from the "classical" musician's, and within the area in which the critic seeks to determine whether a composer or performer has succeeded in accomplishing such purpose, Mr. Sargeant's contention is certainly sound. One of his illustrative examples indicates this application. He says that a solo by Louis Armstrong must not be compared to a Josef Szigeti sonata performance; by disregarding the identity of the sonata, he leads us to believe that he is thinking here only of the performer's success in attaining his established goal with respect to any sonata in his repertory. Mr. Szigeti means, presumably, to convey fully and correctly that which another musician (the composer) intended; Armstrong generally does not, for he himself is, in substantial part, the composer of that which he performs. It is foolish, then, to maintain that Armstrong's recorded performance of (i.e., based on) *Wild Man Blues* is necessarily worthless because he has substituted a new emotional content for that of the original piece. But we may validly reject a performance by Mr. Szigeti of Beethoven's violin sonata in F major if he fails to convey the healthful freshness and good humor of the work. Here we are concerned with an executant's success or failure in realizing the purpose of a performance. Within this limited area of criticism, again, we cannot apply the same criteria to a traditional-jazz performance as to a "classical" performance in matters of tone quality and intonation, so far as the performers have mutually different goals in these matters. Even in relation to the composition of music, if the critic is interested only in the composer's skill and not in the value of the composition, the differences between the limiting conditions of jazz and those of "classical" music may cause the critic to adopt two separate frames of reference.

But there is another, and far more important, field of criticism: the evaluation of a complete musical product. This may be a written composition as one believes its composer intended it to be performed. Or it may be a composition as performed on a specific occasion, criticized with regard to the value of the whole, not merely with regard to the executants' success in their limited function. Or, in the case of an improvised performance, it will be the composition resulting from the combination of improvisation and underlying material.

Genuine criticism of a musical product will be addressed in part to the evaluation of the content of the music, not merely to the adequacy of the means, including the composer's musical articulateness and the executants' skill, by which the content is conveyed. For it is the ordinary purpose and achievement of a listener to *experience* something—feelings, ideas, aspirations, attitudes, or other substantive elements in the content of the music—but *not all experiences are equally valuable.* Indeed, even so modern a music critic as Bernard Shaw knew that mankind is better without certain types of experience at all.[2] To suppose that music criticism is concerned only with the success of the composer, performer, or composer-performer in expressing something effectively, in giving his listeners a full or vivid experience, is as nonsensical as to suppose that criticism of human endeavor in general is concerned only with a man's success in attaining his goal, not with the excellence of the goal itself. Some things are not worth attaining, not worth expressing, not worth experiencing.

Even critics who adopt a "liberal" attitude (which has long been the fashion) toward the content of music and who are willing, musically, to enjoy both divine aspiration and savage sensuality, are likely to reject excessively sentimental music and thus to indicate that they have not really abandoned criticism of content. There is no reason why such rejection should be confined to music in a certain idiom. We may disapprove a composition, whether jazz or "classical"—even if it is composed and performed with great skill—because what it expresses is sheer, cheap sentimentality. We may applaud New Orleans jazz because, unlike sweet dance music, it avoids such emotional content, and we may applaud a composition by Bach *for the same reason.* Thus, criticism of jazz and criticism of "classical" music meet on common ground when they are concerned with the evaluation of the substantive content of music. Music critics who do little more than review concerts of "classical" music may be forgiven for failure to recognize this common ground, for they spend the major part of their professional lives in a less important field of criticism, i.e. evaluation of the success of executants in the performance of established compositions which are not being evaluated.

In criticism of the expressed content of jazz, one meets the same problems as in such criticism of European art music, because sentimentality, humor, romantic love, earthy vitality, savagery, sensuality, frenzy, Christian aspiration, and every other nameable and nameless type of content, with the infinite variations of each, are good, bad, or indifferent, in varying degrees, no matter what the creative medium. The medium itself is subject to criticism only with respect to its adequacy as medium. If the only things expressible in jazz were not worth expressing, jazz would have to be condemned, but a piece of "classical" music expressing the same worthless things would have to be condemned for the same reason.

It may be asked, on what basis a critic can evaluate the content of a piece of music. Here we are carried beyond the realm of music in itself to the field of human attitudes and points of view, especially with respect to the evaluation of experiences. Points of view are not all equally valid, and their validity or invalidity is reflected in the success or failure of human lives. If music criticism is to be something more than an esoteric exercise of specialists, if it is to be a part of the evaluation of ways of life—and otherwise it will be a trivial thing indeed—the criticism of jazz and of European art music will be one discipline. And this discipline is seen to be inextricably bound up with points of view applicable to all fields of creative art and beyond.

It is not surprising, therefore, that one of the most valuable pieces of music criticism by an American writer was produced by Irving Babbitt,[3] no musicologist but an extraordinarily well-equipped student of the history of human thought. Babbitt showed, among other things, that Rousseauism is at the root of the modernist movement in music as well as in other fields of creative art. Although Lord Acton doubtless was guilty of exaggeration when he said that Jean-Jacques Rousseau "produced more effect with his pen than Aristotle, or Cicero, or Saint Augustine, or Saint Thomas Aquinas, or any other man who ever lived," one may confidently affirm that the attitude or point of view popularized by Rousseau in the second half of the eighteenth century has profoundly affected the course both of artistic effort and of art (including music) criticism ever since. It has strongly affected the development of jazz and of jazz criticism. We may do well, then, to examine this attitude before continuing.

II   Rousseau made war upon the formal, the traditional, and the civilized. He advocated freshness, spontaneity, and emotional expansiveness, all of which he associated with man in a state of nature. In the enjoyment of every form of art he sought primarily to be enchanted, even at the expense of rationality. "The man who thinks," he said, "is a depraved animal." Some of Rousseau's creative followers wrote novels glorifying the "noble savage," notably the American Indian, and one suspects that the glorification of African music and African attitudes by some recent writers is essentially Rousseauistic in motivation.

In the Western world, persons who find the Rousseauistic point of view unsatisfactory are likely to follow either the Judeo-Christian tradition or the humanistic tradition, each of which has its aspirations and its restraints. The watchwords of humanism are reason, reasonableness, and moderation.

The Rousseauist talks so much of freedom that one is tempted to define the difference between the three points of view in terms of their respective concepts of freedom. The Christian seeks freedom from whatever prevents him from following the course prescribed by the Lord; he is therefore especially eager to subordinate his own mundane drives to the Godward drive. The humanist, in quest of the moderate and the reasonable, seeks freedom from excess of every kind and from domination by passion or other forces of unreason. The Rousseauist seeks freedom from prescribed forms, institutions, and anything else that impairs his spontaneity, his expansiveness, and his capacity to be enchanted.

More often than not, the Christian and the humanistic points of view lead to the same broad judgments in matters of art, judgments frequently antithetic to those inspired by the Rousseauistic point of view. For example, some jazz performances have been said to indicate a state of trance in the performer or performers and/or to produce a state of trance in qualified listeners; the jazz trance is associated with the state of "possession" induced with the help of music, or at least of drumbeats, in African rituals and in derivative rituals in the Americas. A Rousseauist is likely to seek jazz that will enchant him in this way and, as critic, to eulogize the performers. In such a state of possession, to the Rousseauist's delight, one experiences a release from reasonableness and decorum. But for that very reason, the humanist will eschew it; and because the departure is not Godward, the Christian, too, will reject it.

Heard with unbiased understanding, New Orleans jazz ought to be odious to a listener whose orientation is essentially Rousseauistic. It is extremely conventional music, closely bound by tradition. In structure and harmony, this is most obviously true; in rhythm, there is variety only within the limits of a general style—not the broad variety of rhythmic choice available to a composer in the European tradition, who may compose in, say, five-quarter time, or employ

81

Slavic folk rhythms, or use any of a hundred devices to give his work rhythmic interest. Perhaps the only thing he has been unable to do very successfully in this connection is to utilize jazz rhythm.

In expressed content, New Orleans jazz is traditionally limited. Romantic love, for example, which the Rousseauist ought to and usually does champion—for it is supposed to defy conventional restraint and dull reasonableness—is outside the scope of the New Orleans tradition. Also, the Christian element in the music inevitably implies certain restraints.

How can a Rousseauist, with his love of freedom, his hatred of convention, and his advocacy of enchantment-at-any-price, approve a type of music so fettered and so conventional? For one thing, the Rousseauist naturally feels a strong bond of sympathy for oppressed groups, groups that have been denied freedom. His point of view may lead him unwittingly to do harm to their cause, but his sympathy is nonetheless intense. Just as Communists found all sorts of excellence in Chaplin's pictures, even the poorest of them, as soon as he was officially suspected of being a fellow traveler, so the Rousseauists love the art of an oppressed people. This does not mean that the art is undeserving of their affection, but merely that they love it for the wrong reason.

Again, a Rousseauist's rebellion from authority may be directed so intensely against specific conventions and traditions that he finds irksome that he will ignore other artificial limitations and will embrace an art which, although laden with such other limitations, is at least free from the ones against which he is rebelling. New Orleans jazz is free of the convention of completely prescribed, written composition. This freedom may so affect the Rousseauistic critic's imagination that he will blind himself to the music's own severe traditions. He may also blind himself to the fact that Rousseauism has itself become a tradition and that its advocates are as dully predictable in their reactions as any of the neoclassicists whom Rousseau detested.

Finally, it should be observed that a person whose ostensible critical principles are Rousseauistic may nevertheless evidence a sort of artistic taste that suggests the existence, underneath, of hidden, perhaps unconscious standards of a different nature. In any case, whatever the true reason for his devotion to New Orleans jazz, he feels he must justify this devotion on Rousseauistic grounds. This means that he must impute to the music characteristics that can be approved under such principles. One of these characteristics, extemporization—with its freedom and spontaneity—has already been shown to play a less important role in New Orleans jazz than some would lead us to believe. We turn now to certain other imputed characteristics.

III   Some writers maintain that the inducement of trance or of a state of something like possession is characteristic of New Orleans jazz.[4] We have seen why such inducement would please a critic whose point of view is essentially Rousseauistic and why he might be impelled to attribute it to music that he likes. One may describe the corresponding element in the content of the music as a sort of mystical, African-type enchantment. It is associated especially with the drums; indeed, drums alone are considered adequate to produce the trance.

But in New Orleans jazz the drums are only one of several instruments and, as a rule, their position is far from dominant. If any instrument may be said to dominate, it is the cornet or trumpet. Some traditional-jazz bands fairly close to the New Orleans norm, notably Turk Murphy's band, Clarence Williams' Blue Five, and the Dixieland Rhythm Kings, have dispensed with drums altogether. In some of the first records made by Louis Armstrong as leader of a combination (Louis Armstrong and His Hot Five), no drums were used.

In the best New Orleans jazz, care is exercised to keep the drums subordinate. Bunk Johnson refused to re-engage for his band a certain very popular drummer because this musician played his drums too loudly and too elaborately, making them a major element in the combination and thus "muddying" the polyphony of the brasses and clarinet. A well-known traditional-jazz trombonist, faced with a similar problem, removed from the bandstand most of an offending drummer's equipment, leaving him unable to play more than his appropriate role in a Dixieland or New Orleans combination. This role is succinctly described in an obituary of the late Abbie Brunies, a New Orleans drummer: ". . . he was never given to loud clanging of the cymbals or 'drum solos' . . . Abbie's idea was a solid beat—never lagging, and with just enough 'push' to drive his front line to a rousing finish."[5] His playing, says the obituary, in summary, was in "good taste," the highest and ultimate praise for a New Orleans jazz drummer. In short, a New Orleans jazz drummer is expected to avoid excess and thus to satisfy a humanistic, not a Rousseauistic, criterion; and, as we have seen, nothing could be more antithetical to African ritualistic possession than the humanistic insistence upon moderation and reason.

Also associated with the inducement of trance is the continued repetition, sometimes crescendo, of a figure or short phrase ("riff"). However, although fairly common in large-band swing music, such repetition is heard only occasionally in New Orleans jazz. In the comparatively infrequent instances in which riffs are employed in New Orleans jazz, they are generally performed with subtle changes in accent and intonation that avoid the trancelike monotony of swing-band riffing.

Although the reader may think the attribute somewhat incompatible with trance-inducement, jazz is said also to be "a music of protest against discrimination and Jim Crow." [6] The blues in particular, it is maintained, sing "a continuing slavery against which the Thirteenth and Fourteenth Amendments stand as empty and mocking gestures." [7] Before categorizing the blues as an expression of social protest, however, one would do well to study the words of the songs. The words are undoubtedly our safest guide to the causes of the melancholy expressed by the music. By far the most common cause appears to be "trouble in love." Protest is frequently made not against social discrimination but against a lover's absence or infidelity, or both. Staple in blues lyrics are such complaints, threats, and forebodings as "My baby he done left this town," "I'm going to stop my man from running around," "Don't know how I'll make it, baby, if I don't have you," "If you want to keep your baby, better get yourself a lock and key, because too many men have been stealing my baby from me," "I ain't seen my baby since I don't know when," "Going to lay my head on the railroad track because my baby she won't take me back," "Oh, the Mississippi River is so deep and wide, and my gal lives on the other side," and "If I had wings, like Noah's faithful dove, I would fly away to the man I love." Among the many other themes found in the words of blues are homesickness, loneliness, wanderlust, and the death of a loved one. Express or clearly implied protest against discrimination is not unknown in the blues, but it is rare. Poverty, which of course is in part a result of discrimination, expressly contributes to the melancholy in a few instances, but to bewail poverty and to protest against a specific social cause of poverty are of course two different things.

By singing about general or universal human experience instead of about the causes of his special social and economic plight, the

Negro has complied with at least the first requirement of permanence in artistic creation. Writers who attribute to him a merely ethnocentric insight into human misery are suspect of projecting their own spiritual provincialism. Through the Negro's creative insight and broad humanity, his blues, like his spirituals, have thus escaped the shallowness and aesthetic aridity of the many songs of social protest composed within the past fifty or sixty years. These songs have gained little or no currency beyond the groups interested directly in the narrow protests that they voiced, while Negro spirituals and blues—and the jazz to which they contributed—not only have persisted but have attracted a continually larger audience among artistically sensitive persons throughout the civilized world.

IV   Persons not so familiar with New Orleans jazz as they might be sometimes characterize jazz in general as agitated, restless, or even frenzied music. It is, they point out, appropriate to the civilization that nurtured it. "Jazz," says the British writer R. W. S. Mendl, "is the product of a restless age." [8] According to Winthrop Sargeant, it is "a rip-snorting stimulant to the social life of a restless, energetic people." [9] But lovers of New Orleans jazz know that this music, although energetic, is rarely restless. They often describe performances of it as "relaxed."

Efforts to account for an art product in terms of the specific environment in which it was created may entail something worse, however, than a misleading generalization: by exaggerating the uniqueness of the surroundings in which the product was created, they may obscure the art product's relationship to permanent factors in the human spirit. This has surely happened in the case of New Orleans jazz. A prominent authority expresses the usual approach to historical criticism of jazz when he writes that jazz "grew up in response to the immediate needs of people in a new environment." But the environmental factors most important to New Orleans jazz were age-old.

One of these factors was a society in which straightforward artistic expression of robust, secular vitality was encouraged or at least not repressed. A society of this sort must have existed in England in the late Middle Ages, or *The Canterbury Tales* and the exuberant, earth-scented canon, *Sumer Is Icumen In,* would not have been produced. Art products characterized by such vitality are found in many times and places, each of which must have provided the requisite environmental factor.

85

When and where music containing a pronounced Christian element is demanded and composed, or is composed and eagerly accepted, the environment very obviously is friendly to Christian experience and encourages its artistic expression. One must conclude also that the mundane satisfactions offered by the environment have been found an inadequate substitute for spiritual gratification. This must have been the case in New Orleans during the early development of jazz and must have been the case in one or another part of Western Europe most of the time since the creation of plain song; for otherwise music containing a strong Christian element would not have been desired and composed.

No two environments are wholly alike. To some extent, therefore, the environment in which jazz developed was different from all other environments. Nevertheless, one may ask what was so very unusual about it that its newness should be emphasized in writings on jazz. If one were to assume, with the afore-quoted writer, that jazz developed as a response to needs growing out of a new environment, an indication of the new, unique quality of the environment should be discernible in the expressed content of the music. Something significantly unique in the content would suggest the presence of something significantly unique in the environment that gave rise to the special needs to which the music was a response.

We have seen the major elements in the content of New Orleans jazz. They are far from new. Exuberant vitality, earthiness, humor, Christian sentiment, did not come into music for the first time with the development of jazz.* Nor did the feeling of unity-in-diversity, whether created through successive or through simultaneous mu-

---

* The appropriate use of a term, such as "good humor," to describe a characteristic of various art products does not mean that the designated characteristic is wholly identical in all the art products. If genuinely appropriate, however, it indicates an area of significant similarity. For example, the good humor of one New Orleans jazz performance may not be exactly identical with that of another, and neither may be quite the same as the good humor of the *scherzo* in Beethoven's string quartet Opus 18, No. 6, to which reference has been made, but it is believed that the commonness here is more significant and more striking (to a listener familiar with both idioms and receptive to the type of humor) than the diversity. It is true, of course, that the elements of content in an art product present themselves as an integrated whole, not as discrete characteristics. This, however, need not vitiate an analysis of the elements, provided that the analysis relates them to the synthesis upon which they depend.

86

sical experiences. Perhaps, after all, it is nothing new in the environment but something old in the human spirit that explains the need to which New Orleans jazz appositely responds.

Only critics and *aficionados* who have gone wrong on first principles would try to justify their enjoyment or approval of a type of jazz primarily on the grounds of its novelty. The glory of New Orleans jazz does not lie in the newness of its idiom but in the fact that it provided and provides a lucid, living experience of wholesome old profundities. The newness has worn off long since, and the shallower jazz lovers and critics—among the critics, at least, they constitute a majority—have turned away to embrace the successively current novelties in jazz. But the old profundities remain. Music that effectively conveys them is likely to survive generation after generation of the latest thing.

8. Jazz as synthesis

I   There is a widespread belief that jazz was born of a creative synthesis and that from this synthesis it derives its strength and essential nature. The belief evidences sound critical intuition, although no satisfactory statement of the nature of the synthesis appears in the literature on jazz.

Most commonly, jazz is said to be the product of a synthesis of Negro and white elements, or of African and American (or Western European in a broad sense) elements. The distinction between these two syntheses, although often ignored, is of the utmost significance. If the Negroes who created and developed New Orleans jazz had still been Africans, with an African religion and a specifically African point of view, the distinction would be unimportant, for Negro and African would be identical. It has been shown, however, that American Negroes created in their spirituals a music that was essentially and intensely Christian.* They could not have done this

Notes to this chapter begin on page 304.

  * See Chapter 4. It has been established also that the Negro spirituals were derived principally from European-American, rather than African, sources. George Pullen Jackson, *White and Negro Spirituals*, pp. 292–93 and *passim*.

88

if they had not adopted what was ostensibly the Western European and American religious tradition. Evidencing the fervor that is characteristic of new Christians, they may be said to have become more passionately Christian than most of their white brothers, even if, in many American Negroes, vestiges of superstition persisted (as they did, indeed, in many of the early Christians).

In a devout Christian, white or black, his Christianity colors and dominates his entire point of view and creative activity. In the light of this faith, and of the Christian attitude and feeling in the spirituals and in New Orleans jazz, one cannot accept Rudi Blesh's proposition that "Afro-American music," including the spirituals and New Orleans jazz, is African in its "determining character." [1] The inconsistency of this proposition with the Christianity of the music may be exemplified by the freedom from feelings of vindictiveness that characterizes almost all American Negro folk music. As a British scholar observes: "A European coming fresh to the subject would expect to find amongst a race that had suffered a quarter of a thousand years of slavery a good many rude poems of revenge allied to vigorous music. But in Negro song, slavery is barely mentioned and vindictiveness is entirely absent. . . ." [2] In New Orleans jazz, feelings of vindictiveness would be incompatible with the prevailing good humor in the music and with the almost total absence of social protest. Freedom from vindictiveness is, of course, profoundly characteristic of genuine Christians, for they are required to love their fellow men and to turn the other cheek. It is, however, by no means characteristic of white men in general or of Africans, a fact vividly illustrated by recent history.

Mr. Blesh's belief that jazz is essentially African is consistent with the assumption, frequently indicated in the literature and table chatter on jazz, that the soul or essence of jazz is to be found in the innate, unique quality of the Negroes, manifested in its pure form in native African music. This interesting approach, with its exotic, escapist appeal, has had a seriously adverse effect on the study of jazz. Typical of its consequences is the casual observation by the jazz record reviewer of a widely read periodical that "African drumming . . . is at the very heart of jazz." This proposition, of course, is hardly supported by the facts, already noted, that fine traditional jazz is sometimes played with no drums at all and that leading musicians in this field insist on keeping the drums subordinate. African drumming has influenced jazz but it is obviously remote from "the very heart" of the music.

But the worst aspect of the jazz-comes-from-the-innate-African-ism-of-the-Negro approach is not the misunderstanding of jazz to which it leads. It is rather the curious Jim-Crowism that it implies, although the promulgators of the approach are, as a rule, sincere friends of the Negroes. New Orleans jazz becomes Afro-American music, created and played by Afro-Americans, i.e. Africans who happen to find themselves in America. Negroes, especially Negro jazzmen, are conceived as profoundly and innately different from the rest of us. They are the men of the jungle drumbeats, exotics with whom an elite among us (the promulgators of the approach and their followers) can attain a sort of rapport verging on mystical identification. Finally, the Negroes are endowed with superior musical ability (the inferior whites can show nothing much better than Bach or Beethoven) and even with a greater capacity for significant emotional experience. Here we have Jim Crow in reverse. Whether or not it goes so far in a given case, the approach under consideration leads, in both the study of jazz and the study of men, to the avoidance of every hypothesis that would require recognition of the profound and extensive common ground which American whites at their best share with American Negroes at theirs. It is on that common ground of Christian insight and abundant human vitality that one can find the "very heart" of New Orleans jazz.

In matters of form or mode of expression, New Orleans jazz includes elements apparently derived from African music. There is no need here to review these elements, virtually all of which (such as syncopation, polyphony, and polyrhythm) had also been utilized in European music. The important thing is that an ordinary listener who has no need to defend Afrophilism will find New Orleans jazz a special kind of Americo-European music rather than a kind of African music. One would expect, and the meager evidence on the subject appears to support the expectation, that African natives wholly unfamiliar with the European musical idiom would find jazz meaningless or at least unimpressive. In any case, the African contributions to the jazz mode of expression have a significance quite secondary to that of the expressed content of the music, which lies essentially within the European-American tradition. It is seen, then, that New Orleans jazz is not in any profound sense an Afro-American synthesis.

The proposition that jazz represents a synthesis of Negro and white elements comes a little closer to the significant truth. The creators of New Orleans jazz utilized both the music that American

Negroes had already created, especially the spirituals and blues, and music that whites had created, especially marches. Much of the Negro music was strongly religious in nature; the white music was chiefly secular and, in the marches, strongly characterized by a predominantly secular type of vitality. The synthesis, adequately expressed, of such vitality with Christian feeling or insight is the secret of the immense appeal of New Orleans jazz. It is only very roughly equivalent to the Negro-white synthesis, however, for there was earthy vitality in some of the American Negro music that influenced New Orleans jazz, and the white music included hymns. If one seeks to go beyond the prior music utilized by the creators of jazz to the basic human elements involved, one will note that Christianity came to the Negroes from the whites and that neither whites nor Negroes could claim a monopoly of secular vitality. It becomes, then, a little confusing to speak of a Negro-white synthesis in the content of jazz. All the elements were both Negro and white.

II   Alan Lomax, an authority on folk music, finds the life-giving synthesis in the coming together, through jazz, of blacks and mulattoes or Creoles. The two groups had been separated by the Creoles' social and racial prejudice against the blacks, which was not unlike the whites' prejudice. With acumen, Mr. Lomax observes that jazz fused "tan knowledge with black inspiration." [3] (In the early days of New Orleans jazz, a Creole musician was generally better educated in his art than a black musician.) He believes also that the "emotional power" of jazz derives from "the human triumph" represented by this "black and tan wedding." "Two neighborhoods," he writes, "disjoined by all the sordid fears of our time, were forced to make a common cause. This musical union demanded that there be not merely acceptance and understanding, but respect and love on both sides. In this moment of ecstasy an interracial marriage was consummated, and the child of this union still jumps for joy wherever jazz is hot." [4]

Although the Creoles were by no means without inspiration, Mr. Lomax is certainly on solid ground in finding significance in their contribution of knowledgeable musicianship. One may question, however, the truth of his proposition that the overcoming of racial prejudice between blacks and mulattoes created the emotional power of jazz. The extraordinarily strong and valid emotional substance that went into the content of jazz surely antedated the development of this music. Jazz was a satisfactory means of expressing certain strong feelings and emotional attitudes, but it hardly can be said to have created them. Much of the emotional substance can be felt in the spirituals and has, indeed, given them much the same power as New Orleans jazz to survive as living music. If the reader will listen to Mahalia Jackson singing spirituals and gospel songs, he will immediately perceive that this music and New Orleans jazz share a source of strength.

Jazz is often compared with the music of Bach. Indeed, traditional jazz has been compared with his music more often than with that of any other nonjazz composer. It has been pointed out, for example, that both traditional jazz and Bach's compositions are generally polyphonic and strongly rhythmic; Bach often used dance forms and dancelike rhythms. His melodic lines and embellishments have been found comparable with those in traditional jazz and, occasionally, with those in other types of jazz. In this connection it is maintained both that traditional jazz resembles the music of Bach because it consists of two-bar and four-bar phrases, and (by other persons) that modern jazz is comparable to Bach's music because of its long phrase lines. From all this, one gets the impression that a Bach–jazz resemblance on a deeper level has been felt but not fully expressed. This impression is reinforced by consideration of a statement made in a 1919 magazine article by the Swiss orchestral conductor Ernest Ansermet. He observed that the solos of the New Orleans clarinetist Sidney Bechet had a "brusque and pitiless ending like that of Bach's Second Brandenburg Concerto." [5] The fact that Ansermet brought Bach in—dragged him in, one is tempted to say—for so superficial and unenlightening a comparison, causes one to suspect that he felt the existence of a deeper common ground.

This deeper basis of resemblance is one of content rather than form. In spite of the interrelationship between form and content, comparisons primarily with respect to form do not reach the heart of the matter. But content varies significantly even within the field of traditional jazz. In narrowing this field for purposes of homogeneity, one turns naturally to New Orleans jazz because of its historical and normative importance. The very core of the substantive content of New Orleans jazz is a synthesis of the secular with the religious, of human vitality with Christian feeling or spirit. If a similar synthesis were found in Bach, the resemblance between the two bodies of music would be so profound that the obvious and striking differences between them would appear almost trivial by comparison.

The religiousness of Bach's music, including his nonchurch music, has already been adverted to and is widely recognized. Scarcely less recognized is its vitality. F. A. Waterhouse calls Bach "undeniably a masculine figure"; [6] Albert Schweitzer writes of his "immense strength"; [7] Hubert Parry, of his "vigorous" orchestral music, of the "warmth and vigour" and "extraordinary vitality of the details" of his organ works. [8] The pursuit of the musical idea in the *Brandenburg Concertos,* writes Dr. Schweitzer, "is not in the least formal, but alive from beginning to end"; in Bach's clavier works even the legato is vital—"much less pianistic and much more vital" than that of various other composers. [9] Several things written about Bach's strength or vitality could be said almost as appropriately about that of New Orleans jazz; for example, that it "functioned without self-consciousness, like the forces of nature." [10]

The combination of Christianity and abundant human vitality brings about much the same consequences in Bach's music as in New Orleans jazz: good humor, freedom from sentimentality, sometimes exuberance. In both bodies of music, the religious element is consciously experienced, at times, as a kind of sermon, for the combination of religion and human vitality suggests not a monk or religious philosopher but a preacher. It has been shown that jazzmen, especially trumpet composer-performers, in or close to the New Orleans tradition have often been thought of as preachers. The same is true of Bach, whom Widor calls "the greatest of preachers." [11] Leichtentritt finds Bach's religious music similar to "a profound sermon of a great preacher." [12] This is not a thing generally said of a composer just because he gives effective expression to a religious content. It would be inappropriate, for example, to Palestrina, whose greatest religious music has little vitality in the layman's sense of the term. Nor, very obviously, would it be appropriate to the great mass of ostensibly nonsacred music. The use by various persons of the preacher analogy for both jazzmen and Bach is therefore seen to be significant, especially in the light of the other evidence of the synthesis which, in both, it is thought to indicate.

III   Closely related to the synthesis of Christian insight and human vitality is the balance of expression and restraint. In New Orleans jazz, this balance is a fairly reasonable one, for it permits the music to be exuberant but discourages it from becoming frenzied or *ausgelassen*. Of the formal restraints, the most important in this connection is imposed not by the simple, prescribed harmonic progressions or by the variations structure, but by the polyphony. The clarinet and each of the brasses must co-operate with the other two to create a satisfactory whole; thus the exuberance of each is restrained and channeled.

At least as important as formal restrictions, however, is the restraint imposed by the traditional ways of thinking and feeling which comprise the content of New Orleans jazz, as previously described. If overstated, the content changes: vitality becomes wildness or brutality; exuberance becomes mania.

To what degree religious understanding and Creole education and temperament, respectively, have contributed to this restraint and wholesome balance need not be determined. For in any case the outcome is an art thoroughly acceptable on the basis of humanistic standards. These standards, although they require rejection of the naturalistic, do not require acceptance of the religious. They represent an intermediate level of human experience and judgment, in which emphasis, as has been noted, is on reason, reasonableness, and moderation, which in turn necessitate emotional restraint. The humanistic critic often speaks of "good taste," a term frequently used in recent criticism of traditional jazz. The aspects of New Orleans jazz that recommend much of this music to him are its happy balance between expression and restraint, and the exclusion from its expressed content of the consequences of emotional laxity and vulgarity. Conspicuous among these consequences, and therefore anathema to the humanist, are sentimentality and brutality.

Humanism is associated with classicism. Haydn, Mozart, and the early Beethoven produced music close to the humanist's ideal. The fact that there are strong religious elements in some of this music does not disturb him. He simply approves it for other reasons and, logically, does the same in the case of New Orleans jazz.

The history of European music from Bach to the present is, in its broad sweep, a story of the weakening of the religious point of view and of the humanistic point of view, with inevitable frustration leading ultimately to an effort to return to humanistic or classical ideals. Jazz, developing at a time when the old, civilized points of view were already weak, nevertheless represented at first those points of view. It was a sort of cultural ghost, doomed to repeat in its own way the cycle of European musical and, one might almost say, spiritual history.

94

9. *The apostasy of Louis Armstrong*

I   Jazz performances cannot be classified in clear-cut, mutually exclusive categories, but they can be studied in relation to certain norms or centers of reference. It is in this sense that the authors will refer to Dixieland, Chicago jazz, hot-solo jazz, sweet dance music, swing, symphonic jazz, and "modern" jazz.

Dixieland may be identified roughly with the music of the Original Dixieland Jazz Band, the New Orleans Rhythm Kings, and Tom Brown's Band from Dixieland, all of which are examined in Chapter 20. Most of what has been said in prior chapters about New Orleans jazz applies also to Dixieland. There are differences, however. For one thing, the Dixieland beat tends to be lighter. Also, the Dixieland brasses and clarinet generally play in more regular meter than their counterparts in New Orleans jazz, who often hit notes slightly behind the beat or irregularly lengthen or shorten notes and phrases. In Dixieland, syncopation of a regular nature replaces in some measure the more informal rhythmic variety of the Negro music. Thus the humor of New Orleans jazz at the expense of the solid beat and of that which the beat represents is a little less prominent in Dixieland. Dixieland has much of the general good humor of New Orleans jazz, but it is often a less relaxed good humor. Some of the Dixieland players tend to "push" in what might be considered a slightly aggressive fashion.

Religious feeling and, at times, a sadness profoundly colored by the religious feeling were seen to be among the elements characteristic of New Orleans jazz. They are somewhat weaker in Dixieland jazz. Dixieland's earthiness and vitality, however, are close to these elements in New Orleans jazz. Also, its nonimitative counterpoint has much the same effect as that of New Orleans jazz in creating an intellectual-emotional experience of integration of coexistent, dissimilar, largely independent elements, i.e. the feeling of unity-in-diversity.

The type of music sometimes called Chicago jazz was developed in that city, chiefly in the late 1920's, by young musicians who had admired the New Orleans and Dixieland bands playing there in the early 1920's. They used the same instrumentation except that they used a saxophone—very often in place of the trombone but sometimes as an added instrument. This music may be identified with that of McKenzie and Condon's Chicagoans. The synthesis and balance that gave New Orleans and Dixieland their classic aspect were substantially weakened in Chicago jazz. A sort of feverish excitement partly replaced the basic elements in the old content; this has been associated by some persons with the omission of the trombone in much of the music. In this connection, it is interesting that the feverish "modern" jazz groups that began to be heard in the middle 1940's generally used no trombone; like the Chicagoans, however, they found the saxophone almost indispensable. James Weldon Johnson's book *God's Trombones* was significantly named. One can hardly imagine anyone speaking of God's saxophones. In both the Chicagoans and the "moderns," the replacement of genuine vitality by other elements may reflect the inability of the human spirit to maintain its vitality at full strength without the spiritual antithesis of that vitality.

The element of restraint imposed by the polyphony, as well as the feeling of unity-in-diversity, were weakened by the tendency of the wind instruments to exaggerate their mutual independence. In the ensembles, the approach often seemed to be every-man-for-himself, with little attention paid to the distinct, separate roles of the several wind instruments.

Solos came to occupy a larger proportion of performance time in Chicago jazz than in most New Orleans or Dixieland jazz. The

Bunk Johnson and the Yerba Buena Jazz Band. *On platform, left to right:* Pat Patton, Bill Dart, Squire Girsback. *In foreground, left to right:* Turk Murphy, Bunk Johnson, Ellis Horne, Burt Bales.

Bunk Johnson at a Chicago session. *Left to right:* Don Ewell, John
Lindsey, "Snags" Jones, Bunk Johnson.

music felt the influence of what the present authors call, for want of an established name, "hot-solo jazz," which tended to dominate Chicago jazz and all other quasi-Dixieland jazz. By the early 1930's, "pure" Chicago jazz had virtually lost its identity.

II   Hot-solo jazz grew out of both New Orleans jazz and Dixieland, but it received its most powerful impetus from the apostasy of trumpeter Louis Armstrong, perhaps the most influential and certainly the most famous of all jazzmen. After an apprenticeship in New Orleans jazz, both in that city (of which he was a native) and in Chicago—he played under Oliver in both cities—Armstrong sought fuller expression than was apparently possible within the limitations of the New Orleans contrapuntal style. Solos in New Orleans had generally been subordinated to the ensembles in both frequency and importance; in some bands, indeed, virtually no solos were played. The performer, no matter how celebrated, was primarily part of the group. Armstrong, however, had achieved an almost unprecedented popularity, and the larger the audience the larger the proportion of persons to whom bold, vivid homophonic expression is more comprehensible and satisfying than the nice balance of three- or four-part polyphony.

Impelled by popular taste, as well as by his own drive for expression, Louis Armstrong changed the position of the highly talented individual (or, in some cases, individuals) to one of domination in the band. This did not mean the total abandonment of polyphony but rather a change in emphasis. There were more solos and sometimes greater domination by an individual in the ensembles. This new direction is clearly evident in the recordings in 1925 and 1927 by groups under Armstrong's leadership.[1] These records are rightly considered milestones in the history of jazz, but Armstrong's influence during the same period as a live performer was at least as great as the influence of his records. He was, and is still, imitated by both white and Negro musicians.

If a helpful analogy can be drawn between the position of Oliver and Morton in the history of jazz and that of Haydn and Mozart in the history of classical music, perhaps one may be suggested also between Armstrong and Beethoven. Steeped in the tradition of a classical norm and working within that norm during their earlier years, both men subsequently opened the floodgates—or perhaps the Pandora's box—of intense individual expression. Where Beethoven pushed in the direction of mysticism, inwardness, and super-

97

natural strength, however, Louis Armstrong produced an outspoken expression of emotional expansiveness on a naturalistic level—an expertly controlled barbaric yawp curiously intermingled with the religious underpinning of the New Orleans jazz tradition. Although this underpinning is clearly perceptible in Armstrong's music, his emphasis on naturalistic expansiveness and on the individual entailed a weakening of the religious and "integration" or unity-in-diversity elements in the content of the norm. In the music of many of the performers whom Armstrong has influenced but who lack his New Orleans roots, these elements of content are further weakened and diffused, but they never wholly disappear.

The more one studies the several types of jazz, the more evident it becomes that Louis Armstrong stands historically at the crossroads. The main tendencies in jazz lead to or away from him. That the world was ripe for the changed content which he so expertly expressed and still sometimes expresses, is evidenced by his immense popularity and by the critical adulation he has received in America and, even more, in Europe. Robert Goffin, a Belgian writer on jazz, calls him "the one who made jazz great." [2] Hugues Panassié, the well-known French jazz critic, maintains that "any other musician pales in contrast" to Armstrong, who is "of such extraordinary ability that he is above all possible praise." [3] A prominent "serious" European musician is reported to have shouted, at one of Armstrong's concerts, that Louis was "the greatest musician in the world." [4] George Avakian, veteran American writer on jazz, considers Armstrong "the greatest of them all." [5] Thus it is seen that Armstrong, again like Beethoven, has taken on the aspect of a Titan.*

This critical acclaim may be accounted for, in part, by what Virgil Thomson, an American composer and critic of "serious" music, describes as Armstrong's combination of "the highest reaches of instrumental virtuosity with the most tensely disciplined melodic

* The extent of the public interest in Armstrong is indicated not only by his professional success but also by the fact that four books about him have been published—a rare honor for so young a musician. (Born in 1900, he was only fifty-five when the last of the four was published.) One is a biography, *Horn of Plenty*, by Robert Goffin. Two—*Swing That Music* and *Satchmo*—are autobiographical. *Trumpeter's Tale: the Story of Young Louis Armstrong*, by Jeanette Eaton, is written expressly for young people. This book, by an author whose three prior works had been on Lee, Washington, and Gandhi, respectively, brings Louis Armstrong into the company of the indisputably immortal.

98

structure and the most spontaneous emotional expression." [6] One
suspects that the nature of the emotional content, which surely
affected the content of subsequent hot jazz, also affected the judgment of some critics. Undisciplined, sometimes savage emotional
expansiveness, made intelligible and artistically acceptable by disciplined presentation and mixed with an element of religious feeling, provides an almost irresistible cocktail for the listener whose
emotional responsiveness and aesthetic sensibility exceed his ability
to distinguish the wholesome from the destructive in the content
of an art product.

Moreover, Armstrong is accepted by many as the virtual embodi-
ment, or the first great performer, of jazz. For example, Jorge Guinle,
a Brazilian amateur who wrote a book on jazz, says that he is the
"very spirit of jazz." [7] Rex Harris, an English writer, says that
Armstrong's name "has become synonymous with jazz." [8] A "modern"
jazz composer began a work entitled *A History of Jazz* with music
in the style of Louis Armstrong. He omitted prior jazz because, as
he told one of the present writers, he considered Armstrong's music
the consummation of earlier developments and the beginning of
the main line of jazz history. Apparently thinking in much the same
way, Barry Ulanov maintains that "it is as a background for Louis
and his successors that early New Orleans jazz has its most lasting
interest." [9]

A listener who accepts Armstrong as the culminating representative of the best in early jazz is suspect of not understanding New
Orleans jazz. For Armstrong departed from the tradition of that
music in both content and form. In the matter of form, as has already been indicated, the departure was associated with his emphasis on the solo. This emphasis was at first merely symptomatic.
It did not, in itself, carry Armstrong's music far from the New
Orleans norm. In this connection, much may be learned from a
comparison of the records made by Louis Armstrong and His Hot
Five in 1925 with those made in 1927 by the same group and by
Louis Armstrong and His Hot Seven. In the 1925 records, Armstrong's style was still close to the norm, especially in the ensembles,
in which he played a basically New Orleans lead. This may be
noted particularly on the 1925 records of *Muskrat Ramble* and
Heebie Jeebies. Before long, however, Armstrong evolved a style
that lent itself less to a true ensemble approach. His remarkable
performance on the Hot Seven's *Potato Head Blues*, for example,
splendid tour de force though it may be, is no longer true New

99

Orleans jazz. In both style and mood, it is another music. The final ensemble, where the trumpet is soaring through grandiose, excited phrases, shows no thought for the role of the other voices in jazz polyphony. One of the 1927 recordings of the Hot Five, *Ory's Creole Trombone,* perhaps indicates the changes even more markedly than *Potato Head,* if only because this record obviously represents an effort specifically in the New Orleans idiom. The dramatic, Pagliacci manner of much of Armstrong's subsequent work is suggested here. There is also some good New Orleans humor, but the element of frenzy in the trumpet solo and the considerable use of relatively high-register horn are of another origin and clearly show Armstrong to be preoccupied with stylistic ideas foreign to his earlier manner of playing.

In later years, Armstrong moved still farther away from the New Orleans norm. Even during the traditional-jazz renaissance of recent years, his bands, although playing many pieces from the traditional repertoire, have been New Orleans only superficially. Some have been little more than vehicles for vaudeville-like "showman-ship." Others, such as a so-called Hot Seven with trombonist Jack Teagarden, have featured performers whose basically solo styles were incompatible with the requirements of classic jazz. The results have been sometimes shoddy, sometimes interesting or even sensational, but they have almost never been genuinely representative of New Orleans jazz.

III   Farther removed than hot-solo jazz from the norm, and in an important respect antithetical to the norm and to traditional jazz in general, is sweet dance music. The types of jazz discussed so far are vigorous and unsentimental; in this aspect of their character lies a substantial part of their integrity and claim to respect. Sweet dance music, as a rule, is mildly sexual, languid, and sentimental, with a sort of sweetness that tends to cloy because there is so little substantial food offered with it. As such a mood cannot be maintained forever, the sweet bands sometimes play, by way of contrast, "novelty" numbers with a "peppy" tempo. It need hardly be added that "pep" is a sorry substitute for genuine vigor.

In the late 1920's and early 1930's, the popularity of sweet dance music, in contrast to that of traditional jazz, greatly increased. This development has been recognized as an artistic come-down even by some of the purveyors of the sweet music. Rudy Vallee, for example, said frankly that he liked "hot" jazz but that it "was over the heads of the vast majority of people who, after all, are those who buy the records and the sheet music." [10]

Although it uses syncopation, sweet dance music is far from traditional jazz in form and method of composition. The band or orchestra is relatively large—typically about fifteen pieces—and generally includes, in addition to a rhythm section, several trumpets, trombones, and saxophones, possibly to the exclusion of the clarinet, although, as a rule, at least one of the saxophonists "doubles" occasionally on the clarinet. The leader may be a regular performer, or may perform from time to time, or may simply conduct the orchestra. As a rule the performances are completely arranged. Solos are not uncommon, and even most of the ensemble passages are essentially homophonic. The pieces played are generally popular songs.

Even a reader unfamiliar with other types of jazz is hardly likely to require examples of sweet dance music. If one among the many prominent and influential sweet dance orchestras were to be selected as the most outstanding representative of this music, it would be Guy Lombardo and His Royal Canadians. Not only has this orchestra remained popular for an extraordinarily long time (since 1930 or earlier) but, unlike some of the others, it has kept the vast majority of its performances almost entirely within the class of sweet dance music.

When dance music becomes most unlike traditional jazz, it is scarcely distinguishable from what has come to be called mood music. Here mild languor has turned to revery and to an exaggeratedly sentimental sexuality. A great deal of mood music has been heard in the past few years. It is a sort of *reductio ad absurdum* of the tendency represented by sweet dance music. By comparison, Guy Lombardo's music is vigorous.

IV   It has been maintained that the word "swing" in relation to jazz should be used only as a verb. A jazz performance is said to swing, in one of the most frequently encountered meanings of the word, if it moves with a smooth, buoyant, propulsive rhythm.* Nevertheless the term has been frequently used as a noun to designate a type of jazz which enjoyed immense popularity from 1935 to 1940 or 1941. Its most prominent figure was the clarinetist and

* In some "modern" jazz circles, the verb *to swing* appears to have taken on a more profound meaning. *Infra*, page 275.

band leader Benny Goodman, although William "Count" Basie's band was at least as representative of this music as Goodman's band.

"In the Dixieland era and just after the war [World War I]," says Frank Norris, "it was called jazz. . . . Now they call it swing, but it's the same kind of music." [11] This premise—i.e. that there is no significant difference between traditional jazz and swing—has been widely entertained and often repeated. It supports the contention that "swing" should be used only as a verb, for if Mr. Goodman's and Mr. Basie's music is virtually the same as earlier jazz it needs no special name. Also, it gives the music and the persons associated with it some of the prestige which the approbation of an elite has conferred upon traditional jazz. Unfortunately the premise is false.

The significant differences between swing and traditional jazz in form and in method of composition are readily discernible. Swing is usually large-band music and is therefore wholly or almost wholly arranged. As in the case of sweet dance-music orchestras, the saxophone is featured. Thus, as they recorded in 1936, both Mr. Basie's band and Mr. Goodman's included four saxophones; the other instruments were three trumpets, two trombones, piano, guitar, bass, drums, and, in the case of the Goodman band, clarinet (Mr. Goodman). By 1940, both bands had five saxophones and four trumpets, and the Basie band had also acquired a third trombone. With its personnel of approximately fifteen men, a typical swing band is two to three times as large as a typical traditional-jazz band.

In swing greater reliance is placed upon rhythm and propulsion and less upon melodic and contrapuntal invention than in the case of traditional jazz. Consequently swing makes far greater use of "riffs" (short repeated figures). One piece, *In the Mood,* which was played with immense success by Glenn Miller's swing band, consisted chiefly of repetitions of a two-bar riff whose principal appeal lay in a not very novel polyrhythmic twist. Riffs tend to emphasize rhythm at the expense of melodic interest and variety. It is significant that, despite the emphasis on rhythm, the size of swing bands deprives the music of the freedom and consequent interest of the rhythmic invention in the respective melodic lines of the traditional-jazz trumpet, clarinet, and trombone.

It will be recalled that hot-solo jazz, although sometimes within the broad tradition of New Orleans jazz, represents a significant departure from the norm. There are clear historical connections between hot-solo jazz and swing, but the direction of development is centrifugal. Swing's relative remoteness from the norm is evident even in the small-group swing conspicuously associated with Benny Goodman. This music, played by groups of three to seven men, is little more than a succession of solos with rhythmic accompaniment. In hot-solo quasi-Dixieland jazz, unlike swing, full three-part-counterpoint ensembles generally introduce and terminate a performance, even if (as sometimes occurs) every instrument in the band, including those in the rhythm section, plays a solo in the course of the performance.

In content, swing represented a reaction against the supersweetness of the dance music that had dominated in the early 1930's. It achieved a measure of freedom from the languor and cloying quality of that music. This was an important achievement, but a negative one. What, then, is the positive content of swing? One is tempted to reply that, whatever it is, there is very little of it. Most conspicuous is a simple appeal to the motor impulses enhanced by the propulsive trancelike effect of the riffs. Apart from this, a certain freshness without depth; a pale reflection, thrice removed, of the vitality and humor of Dixieland; especially in small-group swing an almost purposeful flight from profundity on the wings of glibness, fast tempo, and virtuosity—and the content has been told. The fact that such content satisfied some people indicates not the richness of the music but the spiritual and intellectual poverty of these people. In this sense, swing may be characterized as the poor man's hot jazz.

Swing may also be thought of as the tyro's hot jazz, not so remote in form from sweet dance music nor in substance from the "light classics" that it will be unmeaningful to him, yet offering enough suggestion of the possibilities in jazz to stimulate the taste and the curiosity of a competent listener. This stimulation, and swing's failure to satisfy the stimulated demand, helped to provide popular support for the renaissance of traditional jazz which began about 1939. To many of the musicians and *aficionados* who participated and are still participating in the renaissance, swing is nearly as inadequate as sweet dance music, and to some, because of its pretensions, it is even more distasteful.

10. "Modern" jazz

1   Symphonic jazz is music for large orchestras—at least too large for the music to be considered chamber music—in which an effort is made to combine the jazz idiom with the European art-music tradition. The composer may seek to fortify or dignify jazz by borrowing from that tradition, or to enliven "serious" music by borrowing from jazz, or to do both. The most popular examples of symphonic jazz are still George Gershwin's *Rhapsody in Blue* and *Concerto in F*, first performed in 1924 and 1925, respectively.

In form and content the relatively few pieces of symphonic jazz that have been performed show little uniformity. One would anticipate heterogeneity, for the music comes from individuals with diverse musical and spiritual backgrounds, and it has no tradition of its own.

It should be noted that jazz was never wholly free of the European tradition. General structure, harmonies, phrase and melody lengths, even some specific melodies—marches, quadrilles, and others—in New Orleans jazz were of ultimately European origin. All these became an inherent part of jazz. Subsequently, conscious efforts

Notes to this chapter begin on page 304.

were made to combine this music with European musical forms and methods.

In large-scale works, the two have never quite jelled, perhaps because jazz, in proportion to its proximity to its norm, is unpretentious. New Orleans jazz expresses great things in modest form; therein lies its hold on the heart of a competent listener, who, when he thinks of such music, is likely to look upon the use of a symphony orchestra by a composer of Gershwin's stature, expressing the comparatively insignificant content of which Gershwin was capable, as in itself an act of pretentiousness. The content of Gershwin's best-known symphonic jazz is, for the most part, a composite of the elements found in sweet dance music and swing (see Chapter 9), plus the callow, kinetic self-confidence which many foreigners consider characteristic of Americans—all blown up to turgid proportions.

Symphonic jazz, without the name, has often found its way into the orchestral arrangements played in musical comedies and revues. Duke Ellington underwent the influence of Debussy and Ravel not directly but by listening to orchestrations written for Ziegfeld shows.

The combination of jazz and "serious" music has become fairly commonplace in "modern" jazz, in both small and large bands. Thus symphonic jazz tends to merge into big-band "modern" jazz, sometimes called "progressive" jazz.

II   By the middle 1940's, "modern" jazz had evolved into a clearly distinguishable type. It was called bebop or bop. Played at first by small, intimate groups of musicians, it consisted chiefly of improvised solos. In rebellion against the formal limitations of swing and of traditional jazz, the musicians utilized novel (to jazz) harmonies and harmonic progressions as well as phrases of irregular length—i.e. lengths other than four measures or multiples thereof. In basic structure, however, the variations form was used. The underlying themes were generally those of popular songs, some of which became favorites for the purpose of bop variation. Even when the title of a performance was new, an old popular song could often be perceived beneath the variations. The classic traditional-jazz pieces were conspicuously absent, for most of them were unsuited to the mood of the new music. Original blues, however, were sometimes played.

The emotional attitude of bop is almost directly contrary to that of New Orleans jazz. As already indicated, the weakening of the

105

Christian element in traditional jazz during the 1920's led to an expression of wildness and of feverish excitement. In swing, the need to appeal to a mass audience tended to restrain this element, or rather to reduce it to mild propulsive jitters. The frenetic line of development had nevertheless not disappeared. Louis Armstrong in the 1930's sometimes played a succession of high notes in which he seemed to be seeking not heaven but a screaming release of excitement. In the vapidity of swing, trumpeter Roy Eldridge, influenced by Armstrong, injected solos representing the borderline between vitality and frenzy. In bop itself, vitality virtually disappeared. As one writer says, "The élan of jazz was weeded out of bop because [to the bop performers] all enthusiasm was naïve. . . ." [1]

Eldridge was one of the two swing jazzmen (both of them Negroes) who probably exercised the most immediate influence on bop. The other was Lester Young, whose nickname Pres is justified, according to some, by his eminent position among tenor saxophonists. Both men played passages that suggested the later melodic and harmonic freedom of bop. Young, however, was not inclined to frenzy. His importance as a precursor of bop derives in part from his willingness and ability to create a completely new melody as a solo variation, his development of a saxophone sound comparatively free from the big, lush, excessively vibrato tone that had been (and still is) popular, and the mood of superficial brightness and underlying malaise that characterizes much of his playing. In a sense, Eldridge and Young, or rather the tendencies that they represent, converge on bop. Frenzy and unhappiness join in the music whose content has been characterized by one of its devotees as "jangled sadness" and a "frantic, almost desperate emotion." [2]

Along with bop, certain musicians' colloquialisms gained popularity. Especially significant was (and is) the use of "cool" and "crazy" as terms of approbation. No semanticist or psychologist is needed to tell us that these are terms of escape. It is interesting to speculate on the significance of their general acceptance in relation to the whole trend of jazz from Louis Armstrong to bop. Deprived of its spiritual check, vitality in jazz turned to wildness (of spirit, not necessarily of form) and then to frenzy. Only under principles by which the crazy is good can music expressing such emotional attitudes be accepted.

The term "cool" in relation to jazz has two very different meanings, which appear to represent two different interpretations of

106

"modern" jazz or perhaps a divergence in interest between two tendencies in "modern" jazz. According to one meaning, cool is the opposite of hot, which means exuberant or passionate. Cool in this sense means dispassionate. By the other meaning, cool jazz is jazz in which the emotion or feeling, although it may be intense, is understated or given a restrained expression. When "modern" jazz is cool in the former sense, it is a logical consequence of the weakening of the source of valid experience. The cool jazzman in this sense is a discerning critic of the kind of emotion that is offered him: he rejects both the wildness of Armstrong and the sentimentality of sweet dance music. Unfortunately, this jazzman has no adequate emotional substitute for the rejected emotions and sometimes falls back upon them in disguised or altered form.

The bopster generally considered most immortal (jazz literature recognizes degrees of immortality) is, perhaps significantly, a musician not regarded as typical. He is the late alto saxophonist Charlie "Bird" Parker, a direct musical descendant of Lester Young, whose malaise he turned into wistfulness and sometimes despondence. Parker was a tortured soul and often played like one. There is in his music a certain nostalgia. Both jazz and the civilization of which it was a part had lost something, and Parker felt the loss. In some of his blues one gets the impression that he was trying to find his way home from a great distance. Perhaps he caught tantalizing glimpses of the lost homeland.

Clarinetist-saxophonist John LaPorta told one of the present writers that Parker sometimes sounded to him like an old-fashioned preacher delivering a sermon. Lester Young has been called "saintly." [3] Although these characterizations may seem far-fetched to some, the music of Young and of Parker very likely implies a religious quest.

Such a quest is suggested also by the fact that a number of Negro bop musicians became Mohammedans. (There has long been a Negro Mohammedan group in the United States.) Among these is Art Blakey, a drummer who helped to found bop and who now plays "modern" jazz, sometimes with consciously derived African rhythms (he has visited Africa). Mr. Blakey calls his combination The Jazz Messengers, apparently with religious intent. During a period of illness, Parker used to have the Koran read to him. Some "modern" jazzmen have turned to Buddhism or to yoga philosophy.

These searchings symbolize the dilemma of "modern" jazz and

of the generation whose attitudes it expresses. Running away from religion, the music and the generation have nowhere to go—unless they go back to a religious attitude, on the basis of which they, like Bach and the New Orleans jazzmen, can ultimately produce something "solid." It is a pity that the search for homeland is handicapped by practices and ways of thinking that have become hardened through years of misdirected effort. The choice of exotic religions instead of Christianity may represent a social rather than a spiritual protest. It suggests, however, a quest not yet fulfilled, an insistence upon something "different" instead of something basic. The emphasis on love is weakened by the choice, and it is in part to this emphasis that the music of the New Orleans jazzmen owes its profoundly valid emotional content.

The musician with whom the public most firmly associates bop is one in whose music the religious quest is very difficult to recognize. He is the trumpeter and arranger John "Dizzy" Gillespie. Deriving in part from Roy Eldridge, Mr. Gillespie may be considered a musical grandson of Louis Armstrong. Much of his bop is musically logical but almost all of it is characterized by a nonsensicality of content, an end result which Armstrong never intended but which came as an almost inevitable consequence of the departure, which Armstrong symbolized and led, from traditional values and meanings. It is interesting that, although Armstrong recognizes Gillespie's ability, he has little use for bop, which, he says, "doesn't come from the heart the way real music should." Mr. Armstrong speaks here as a New Orleans jazzman.

Bop has left its mark and is, indeed, still played. Out of it, various tendencies have developed: experimentation with polytonality and atonality, attempts to improvise in "modern" harmonic progressions or with no predetermined harmony, and an effort to develop structures other than that of variations. "Modern" jazz in the 1950's is generally played by a very small combination, typically a quartet of piano, drums, string bass, and either saxophone or vibraphone. In the Dave Brubeck Quartet, which is the most popular "modern"-jazz group, the fourth instrument is a saxophone. In the Modern Jazz Quartet, which is the critics' current favorite, it is the "vibes." The instrumentation and method of playing generally make for blending rather than contrast.

Although there is some experimentation with structure, the variations form is still much used. The New Orleans classic pieces are still eschewed. The selections are generally popular songs or "originals," some of which are popular songs under new names. As a rule, some parts are arranged and some are improvised. Very common is the use of a fully written arrangement at the beginning and at the end of a piece, with free improvisation in between. Although there is some two-part counterpoint, especially in groups having two or more wind instruments, most "modern" jazz consists chiefly of solos with accompaniments.

Generalizations concerning the content of "modern" jazz are likely to be less valid than in the case of New Orleans jazz or Dixieland, because in "modern" jazz the individual composer or composer-performer is comparatively unrestrained in the expression of his "uniquity." In New Orleans jazz and in Dixieland the expressed content is part of a tradition. A performer of this music may think he is expressing only his mood of the moment, and indeed that mood may get into the music, but it is subordinated to the dominant spirit prescribed by the implicit tradition. For example, Eddie Edwards, the trombonist of the Original Dixieland Jazz Band, told one of the present writers that when he played his stop-time solo on the recording of *Skeleton Jangle* he was thinking of, and putting into the music, his resentment at being required to take the solo, a resentment resulting from the fact that, because the piano recorded badly in those days, the trombonist had to work harder throughout a recording performance than he did in an ordinary performance. The feeling comes through in the solo to some extent, but its sting is subordinated to and transformed by the humor and good nature inherent in the type of music.

In "modern" jazz there is less force in tradition with respect to expressed content than in the case of New Orleans jazz. Nevertheless, certain attitudes or ways of thinking tend to come through repeatedly. One of these is a certain playfulness, sometimes intellectual, sometimes pixyish or whimsical, sometimes both; the music is often clever or ingenious. Sometimes the playfulness merges into an almost cavalier attitude, manifested not toward music (about which almost all "modern" jazzmen are very serious) but toward the content of music.

Another element of content sometimes conspicuous in "modern" jazz is a sort of revery, closely related to that of mood music; indeed, "modern" jazzmen sometimes play out-and-out mood music. The devitalized sentiment found in sweet dance music is not unknown, either, in "modern" jazz. It makes what at first sight may seem a strange, but is really a wholly logical, bedfellow for the

109

cute, almost smart-alecky tricks and little jokes that characterize some "modern" jazz. This pair of bedfellows is found notably in the music of Dave Brubeck's group, which even descends on occasion to the slightly tricked-up performance of a sentimental waltz. And the content of bop has not been altogether lost in some of the nominally antibop "moderns."

Now and then one finds, especially in "progressive" jazz—a term sometimes used to denote big-band "modern" jazz—a sort of fierceness or savagery. Examples may be found in some of Stan Kenton's music [4] and in parts of Leonard Bernstein's *Prelude, Fugue, and Riffs*. Where, as in these examples and in so much other "modern" jazz, the old synthesis of New Orleans jazz has almost wholly disappeared, it is filled by the random eclecticism of many individuals; the substituted elements seem so much alike at times because, in the last analysis, their significance lies in the unity of that which they deny.

III   Moving away from swing and dance music, and from traditional jazz at the same time, "modern" jazz moved toward nothing positive in content. Frustration or a change in direction was inevitable. At the present writing, some "modern" jazzmen are turning back toward something regarded as the mainstream or "jazz tradition." But their concept of this tradition suggests a curious ignorance of jazz. Many "modern" jazzmen know almost nothing about New Orleans jazz. Only very recently, long after his rise to eminence, a "modern" jazzman highly respected as both pianist and teacher heard his first King Oliver record. Gerry Mulligan, "modern" saxophonist, band leader, and composer, is looked upon as old-fashioned by some. He considers himself a respecter of tradition and has written a magazine article entitled "The Importance of Jazz Tradition," [5] in which one would expect to find references to New Orleans jazz, Dixieland, or at least the Chicago style. There are no such references. Tradition to Mr. Mulligan means Dizzy Gillespie, Parker, Lester Young, Duke Ellington, and Woody Herman's 1945 big band. It is as if the American political tradition were thought to have its roots in Grover Cleveland.

But other musicians moved away from swing and big dance band music in a wholly different direction from that taken by the bopsters. Beginning about 1939, as already indicated, they created a renaissance of traditional jazz. This renaissance is still in full flower. When played by first-rate musicians who played it in the 1920's or earlier, the music usually contains much the same emotional attitudes as then. When played by young men, it sometimes does and sometimes does not. But the fact that they prefer it to the "modern" tendency suggests that they (and their listeners) are on the track of the old values. The chief danger appears to lie in an imitation of late models, especially Chicago-style models and later Armstrong, in which the element of wildness or frenzy was already conspicuous.

It has often been remarked that crises tend to polarize men, to push them off the fence, to drive them toward God or toward the frustration of denial. World War II and the events leading to it had this effect, which was felt even in the field of jazz. New Orleans jazz, with its profound religiousness, became newly attractive. "Modern" jazz, in general, took the opposite direction. But even in "modern" jazz the quest for spirituality has not been abandoned; it cannot be. The musicians and their applauders are simply looking in the wrong places.

11. Progress, novelty, and Dave Brubeck

1   Essential to an understanding and sound evaluation of jazz, or of specific types and performances of jazz, is an acceptance of the fact that New Orleans jazz represented a throwback to an outmoded way of looking at life. The long period of progressive secularization of European and American thought and feeling, beginning at least as long ago as the rise of rationalism in the seventeenth and eighteenth centuries, made and makes it virtually impossible for vast numbers of persons to receive or even to recognize the fresh faith and religious feeling which New Orleans jazz inherited from the spirituals and from the sort of men who created the spirituals. Even robust vitality, conspicuous in the content of New Orleans jazz, had become aesthetically out of date, replaced by Wagnerian mystical heroics, Debussyish revery, and the various other primitivistic or decadent substitutes for healthful vigor of spirit.

In a sense, Bach himself represented an outmoded point of view. The tides of rationalism and of incipient romanticism began to drown his spiritual voice almost before his natural death. By the time of New Orleans jazz, a thoroughly secular attitude, dominated

Notes to this chapter begin on page 305.

by romanticism and other forms of naturalism, had become orthodox. People were born into it as, many generations earlier, people
had been born into Christian belief and attitudes. Consequently,
both Bach and New Orleans jazz became rapidly incomprehensible
to persons who moved, spiritually, in the full current of contemporary attitudes. Such persons included, in both cases, the majority
of respectable music critics.

The general rejection of Bach by writers on music in the second
half of the eighteenth century has a close parallel in the rejection
of New Orleans jazz by the stylish jazz critics and musicians of
the mid-twentieth century. In both cases, it is in part a corollary
of a naïve faith in the inevitable coincidence of genuine progress
and the mere passage of time. The late eighteenth-century critics,
in Dr. Schweitzer's words, "were too simple to rank the art of the
previous generation as highly as that of their own. They were con-
vinced that music was always advancing, and as their own art
was later than the old art, it must necessarily come nearer to the
ideal." [1] Some of them even persuaded themselves that Bach's music
was crude. The advocates of the latest thing in jazz have taken
precisely the same attitude and, one suspects, it is quite as fatuous
in their case as it has proved to be in the case of Bach's early
critics. They assume that jazz is climbing ever upward on what
Leonard Feather calls "the endless ladder of jazz achievement."
New jazz is progressive jazz. The latest is the best. Early classic
jazz is referred to as the "kindergarten" phase, interesting chiefly
"as a background for Louis and his successors." [2]

Dave Brubeck, the most popular of "modern" jazzmen, says that
it makes him sick to see a young jazz musician confining himself
to Dixieland (which, in the context, appears to mean traditional
jazz). It is, he says, "like a concert pianist studying Bach all his
life, ignoring Bartok, Schoenberg, Hindemith, Stravinsky, Milhaud." [3] In point of fact, Mr. Brubeck confines himself to the playing of his own "modern" style of composition, with its limited content, just as much as any traditional jazzman is confined to his personal modification of the traditional jazz style and content. Mr.
Brubeck is therefore suspect of seeking—what, indeed, he achieves
in his own music—not a balance between Bach (traditional jazz)
and the "moderns," but the virtual repudiation of the former in
favor of the latter. Indeed, he intimates that lovers of Dixieland
are "squares" [4]—a dreadful colloquial condemnation of the uninitiate.
It may be noted that the occasional use by Mr. Brubeck and other

113

"moderns" of musical devices or techniques associated with baroque music or traditional jazz is wholly consistent with the substantive repudiation of the values and emotional attitudes in such music.

The analogy between a traditional jazzman and a concert pianist studying Bach all his life and ignoring the modern innovators is significant also from another point of view. Unlike the "classical" concert pianist, who is generally expected to serve his audience a dinner of many and varied courses, the jazzman is expected to play in the style or tradition that he has adopted. This expectation is reasonable because the jazzman, in small groups, is in part a composer. One would not ask a "classical" composer to write music in the styles, and with the content, of Bach, Bartok, Hindemith, etc. As a composer, he may find that the content of, say, Bartok's compositions is repugnant to him. Critics call Bartok's music lonely and fiercely proud.[5] A composer or, for that matter, a listener may consider fierce pride offensive and, if effectively communicated as the pervasive attitude of the music, positively harmful. The mere fact that a feeling is skillfully and eloquently expressed in music does not make the feeling desirable or healthful. Fierce pride is especially likely to be unacceptable to a composer or listener whose spiritual tradition is Judeo-Christian. It is not the fiercely proud, he is told on the highest authority, who will inherit the earth.

Concerning a series of works by Hindemith, the famous musicologist Alfred Einstein writes that "in each work his own spirit appears, savage and passionate, with renewed and almost terrifying vigor. . . ."[6] Here again the listener or performer who is interested in content, not merely in polytonality and form, may find reason to reject the music. He may not care for the savage and the terrifying. He may, indeed, care for fierceness and savageness just as little in "modern" jazz (where they are sometimes found—see Chapter 10) as in Bartok or Hindemith. Some of Hindemith's music and a good deal of "modern" jazz, including much of Mr. Brubeck's, are predominantly playful in character. A composer or listener may find playfulness without depth uninteresting and emotionally inadequate.

One of the present writers asked a number of traditional-jazz musicians for their opinions of recent types of jazz. Their answers suggest that they find them inadequate rather than repugnant. Asked what they thought of "bebop and music like that," the respective replies of three of the members of Paul Barbarin's band, all New Orleans jazzmen, are instructive. Mr. Barbarin himself said it was just a series of chords and a lot of notes without melody or meaning. Trombonist Bob Thomas replied, "I don't think anything of it. They don't give you any music at all, just chord progressions," but added that he enjoyed the technique of the performers. Clarinetist Willie Humphrey said that the music was short on "spirit"; that, although some bop performers played very difficult passages, a feat which any musician admires, the music lacked "this," pointing to his heart; and, finally, that the music had a lot "on top" but not much "at the bottom"—in short, that it was emotionally superficial.

These opinions are very close, in substance, to the reply of Jim Heanue, trumpeter of the Red Onion Jazz Band, to a request for his opinion of "modern" jazz. He said that this music appealed only to his intellect and that he wanted music that would address itself to his whole being. It is surely not for want of intellectual acumen that Mr. Heanue, who holds a graduate degree in philosophy, rejects "modern" jazz; perhaps, rather, his intellectual attainments make it unnecessary for him to overrate the importance of cleverness in music. In his own restrained but emotionally effective playing within the tradition, Mr. Heanue's intellectuality takes the form of an effort, not to be ingenious or clever, but to oppose each musical idea with a counter-idea in an effort to achieve a well-balanced synthesis on a higher level. Just as some "modern" jazzmen play their frustrations into their music, Mr. Heanue blows his confirmed Hegelianism. It is, so to speak, a different story.

Along the same line, Tony Parenti, a traditional-jazz clarinetist from New Orleans, replied that "progressive" jazz consists largely of "extemporaneous tricks," that it is intended to and does lack "feeling and expression," and that it arouses a "cold reaction" in him. Frank Gillis, a traditional-jazz pianist who holds a graduate degree in music, replied that he liked "earthiness" in jazz and found little or none of it in Dave Brubeck's music. In some modern jazz, however, Mr. Gillis finds that an element of earthiness comes through.

There are, then, reasons, possibly sound reasons, why a musician or a listener may choose to devote his attention to the jazz equivalent of Bach, to the virtual or total exclusion of the jazz equivalents of Bartok, Milhaud, et al. There is no need to seek "psychological" causes for the choice, as Mr. Brubeck does when he suggests that "a lot of kids like to do what their fathers did, and their fathers listened to Dixie." [7] This sort of thinking is a two-edged sword, and

115

the other edge is sharper; for young people tend to rebel and to reject the values that they associate with their parents. This may account, at least in part, for music that turns away not merely from the traditional manner but also from the traditional values.

II   The music and opinions of Dave Brubeck bring to mind a curious assertion of progress in jazz, made by a clergyman acting as "narrator" in a 1955 telecast on which Mr. Brubeck and his group were the only guests. The program, in WCBS-TV's excellent series "Look Up and Live," merits careful study because it indicates the hopelessness of the task undertaken by the clergyman-narrator and the script-writer in seeking to find religious significance in the music of the Brubeck group. So much is at stake in the accurate ascertainment of the existence or nonexistence of a strong element of Christianity in this enormously popular music that even the undoubtedly sincere and well-meaning narrator must not be spared.

The narrator sought to draw religious analogies from this new music. Wasn't the concept of an underlying theme beneath Brubeck's and others' variations much like the idea of an underlying truth beneath all the different creeds? "The truth is everywhere," said the narrator, "with each and every individual possessing an equal share, a theme upon which all of us may play our individual variations, held accountable only to God." But Brubeck had pointed out, earlier in the program, that his improvisations not only departed from the melody but created "a completely different feeling." Paul Desmond, the saxophonist of the group, had put the matter more graphically on another occasion: "The melody is just a vehicle. It's like an old Ford with a new Cadillac motor put in." [8] This figure would not have helped the narrator to make his point, but it undoubtedly represents the attitude of the group and of many other "modern" jazzmen toward the underlying melody (Ford) and their own very superior contribution (Cadillac motor). To find a kind of music in which the melody was respected although varied, the narrator might have looked to any of various New Orleans jazz bands, rather than to what the magazine *Time*, following Mr. Desmond's figure, calls "the strange, souped-up vehicle" [9] of the Brubeck group.

The narrator said that the music "flows along completely unrestrained and yet is held together by a firm foundation, a core called an arrangement." This is intended, one assumes, as an analogy to the reconciliation of free will and God's "arrangement." But Bru-

116

beck had stated that the arranged parts come only at the beginning and end of a piece, with improvisations in the middle, and that "when we're playing well, the out parts are ridiculous usually, because the inner parts have come up to the level where you're truly composing." Thus another religious analogy is vitiated by Brubeck himself. One cannot help sympathizing with the narrator, confronted with the task of making a silk purse out of a sow's ear when the owner of the sow's ear is embarrassingly candid about the nature of his possession.

The narrator found an analogy also in the concept of improvised interplay among the performers. "A good way of running the world," he said, "would be freedom of individual interpretation accompanied by universal co-operation." We need "freedom to explore, create, originate and improvise. . . . This is why we've coupled religion and jazz, two of the mediums of communication which speak a universal language and need no interpreters to touch the soul of man." The improvised music of Brubeck's group consists chiefly of solos with accompaniments and is therefore an especially unhappy illustration of free interplay and co-operation. Traditional jazz, with its three-part polyphony, would have served much better. But more significant is the narrator's failure to indicate a criterion by which his listeners might know what ought to be created, originated, etc.—in short, what sort of thing the co-operators ought to produce by their co-operation. Surely co-operation may have undesirable purposes and results. One wonders whether a consensus of authoritative religious opinion would not place the emphasis here, rather than on the mere fact of improvised co-operation. But such an emphasis would have required a determination and evaluation of the content of Brubeck's music and possibly its consequent rejection.

The narrator introduced the final piece as "a hymn, not the conventional familiar paean of praise, but the spontaneous, unrestrained atonal conversation of jazz, which too can be truly an act of worship." It is hard to see why atonality should be associated with worship. It is equally difficult to understand how lack of restraint—restraint, on which survival of our civilization depends—should be eulogized, especially on a religious program. If lack of restraint is a sign of progress, then the madman is superman; then New Orleans jazz is a poor and backward thing indeed, and the Reverend Alvin Kershaw (who spoke on other programs in the same series) made a great mistake in inviting a New Orleans jazz band—

George Lewis'—to play at church services. In truth, of course, Mr. Kershaw made no mistake but manifested great understanding.

The narrator was consistent enough to reject New Orleans jazz, at least by implication, as virtually obsolete. "Hearing you play," he said to Brubeck, "is really to demonstrate how far jazz has progressed since its early days in New Orleans." But progress, to a man of God, can mean only advancement toward godliness or grace. The narrator made no effort at all to show that Brubeck's music represented progress over traditional jazz in this sense, and indeed any such effort would have proved vain. Brubeck's final selection on the program was *When the Saints Go Marching In*, a piece suitable to the occasion but not usually played by him—he has never recorded an ostensibly religious number. The performance lacked all the aspiration and depth of feeling of the old spiritual. The narrator must have perceived this; any man with both a religious and musical background could not help perceiving it.

Brubeck had already stated in broad terms the content of his music, as he understood it. "Today's jazz," he said, "reflects the American scene, the hopes, dreams and frustrations of our generation." Here is the provincialism that one has learned to expect in centrifugal art, i.e. art moving away from the source of unity that is found in genuine religious feeling. It is a corollary of the cultural and musical tradition to which Brubeck has attached himself, manifested notably in the nationalistic content of much of Stravinsky's music and of Bartok's. Predominant emphasis on local color and local attitudes is characteristic of romantic art products and wholly uncharacteristic of the universality of Christianity. But Brubeck has gone the other nationalists one better. He is provincial in time as well as space. He seeks to express the frustrations and dreams of one generation of Americans, a generation which, although turning to religion more than its predecessor generation did, is certainly not marked by the devoutness out of which New Orleans jazz, with its more universal values, was created. Yet the narrator finds that jazz has progressed.

Brubeck is not the only one to remark the time-provinciality of much "modern" jazz. Charles M. Fair, writing about bop, states: "In its combination of technical wizardry and frantic, almost desperate emotion—in its occasional sterility, even—it too perfectly represents the era which produced it." [10] Of course there are other elements in the era, elements closer to the wisdom of the ages and therefore necessarily less *peculiar* to the era. One wonders whether it is not the creative artist's obligation to seek them out, to take them to his heart, to express them in his art product if he can, and thus to make both himself and his product something more than flotsam on the tide of time. If the Judeo-Christian tradition is thought to be at the core of the wisdom of the ages, "modern" jazzmen will have much more to learn from the clergy than the clergy from the jazzmen.

To the great credit of the narrator in the program discussed, he did not specifically attribute religious content or insight to Brubeck's music. In an earlier jazz program of "Look Up and Live," the Reverend Mr. Kershaw, in a context that suggests primary, if not exclusive, application to traditional jazz, spoke of "religious insight in music" and pointed out that it "doesn't necessarily have to do with what we traditionally think of as religious subjects." With a profundity that would have been altogether inappropriate on the Brubeck program, he stated that

true jazz played with feeling and inspiration seems to me more truly an act of worship than singing some of the religious songs I learned back in Sunday School. There's nothing wrong with those songs but a lot of them only touch our surface feelings. Our deep feelings about our loves, our agony, trust, at least as far as I am concerned, are left untouched. When Jesus taught the people about God, He created new stories about a father being rejected by his sons, about a salesman being attacked by robbers on a lonely road, about working men on a plantation, about seed and crops and rocks. About, in short, how God's love and punishment stream through the ordinary places and events where people struggle, find happiness, are born and die. Now, I want to say just one thing. When men speak to each other, in their own way and their own style, about all the complexities of life, in jazz the conversation usually ends in a chorus of praise. Life, for all its sadness and separation, is still good. Life forever gives us the chance to live joyously. Life is so big and wide and deep that you just have to go beyond what's superficial, and banal, and beyond what's phony. Faith rises above the streets, the slime and the suffering men, to the source of goodness Himself. In this sense, jazz becomes a glorious anthem of praise.[11]

As Mr. Kershaw observed on a later program in the series, a program dealing specifically with New Orleans jazz, this music "supports whatever it says upon . . . a faith in God who in His power and wisdom can restore health and brotherhood to the human family."

119

The growing interest in jazz manifested publicly by clergymen of various sects * can have a wholesome effect on the criticism and development of the music. It will have such an effect, however, only if the clergymen examine the subject, as Mr. Kershaw appears to have done, from a spiritual point of view, with standards derived from the study of Christ's word. So long as they try to be good fellows and to avoid, in their work with respect to jazz, the shocking radicalism of their Lord in the criticism of all human activity, they are likely to be as ineffectual as most of the lay writers on jazz. Such avoidance of Christian criticism could not be exemplified more strikingly than by the denotation of Christianity (in a passage previously quoted) as a medium of communication rather than as a body of beliefs and spirtiual attitudes. The clergyman's problem here runs deep, for, as everyone knows who cares to know, secularization of thought has not been confined to secular institutions. It would be worse than unfortunate if, as a consequence, the opportunity to apply Christian standards to the content of jazz were lost.

III   The void left in European thought by the weakening of Christian faith could not be filled by rationalism, for faith in mere reason lacked sustaining emotional power. Romanticism, with a strong impetus from Rousseau, rushed in to fill the vacuum. Its force was felt in virtually every type of creative art in the nineteenth century and on into the twentieth.

Close to the core of romanticism is a "thirst for novelty." The romanticist is "adventurous rather than purposeful." [12] In this connection, one is reminded of the jazz classicist Bunk Johnson's puzzlement upon hearing some "modern" jazz played by a band led by the trumpeter Dizzy Gillespie. Johnson, it is reported, turned to Gillespie and asked, "What is this music for?" The question is apposite, and one may be forgiven for wondering whether the literature on "modern" jazz has produced an answer. It is doubtful whether the writers and other listeners who adore the latest thing even recognize the need for an answer. Off on today's new musical adventure, they would, in any case, have little time to formulate one.

In its thirst for novelty, "modern" jazz has followed the course of

* Mr. Kershaw is an Episcopalian. The narrator in the program with Brubeck is a Presbyterian. The Reverend Joseph M. Miller, author of "I Like Jazz," *America*, October 1, 1955, p. 17, is a Catholic. Father Norman O'Connor participated in one of the panels in the 1955 Newport Jazz Festival.

120

European music and, more broadly, of European-American popular thought, the thought that culminated in the use of "different" and "new" as terms of approbation. In its most naïve form, the quest for novelty becomes a quest for the exotic. This is essentially an aspect of the romanticist's insistence on the local and the peculiar; in requiring that they be exotic rather than familiar, he is merely indulging in a "dicty" sort of provincialism. But romanticism is allied to naturalism (as is seen in the case of Rousseau), and the quest of the exotic therefore tends to merge into the quest of the primitive. "Let's get away from it all" and "Let's get back to nature" go hand in hand. The noble Indian of early romantic literature and Stravinsky's savage *Sacre du Printemps* alike reflect the romantic-naturalistic quest.

Stravinsky, it may be noted, has indicated an interest in jazz—he has even composed what he considers jazz—and many "modern" jazzmen find in him a kindred spirit. His use of polytonality, his diminished fifths, his manner of writing for small, irregular groups of instruments, and his way of using rhythm to make palatable what might otherwise be a dull and forbidding melody line, hold an obvious interest for them. One of his styles, the one that they presumably admire, has been called, like their own music, "cool." [13] But Stravinsky has also had his intensely romantic phase, in which the colorful, the exotic, and the primitive were sought and expressed. This romanticism is closer to the cool music than some of his admirers probably suspect; by the same token, the sentimental romanticism of sweet dance music or mood music is close to cool jazz. Sainte-Beuve's observation that nothing resembles a swelling so much as a hollow has here its perfect application. For both the cool and the romantic are denials or rejections of the genuine vitality and spirituality which, in synthesis, provide a central, universal point of reference for valid human emotion. This point of reference shows the exotic to be merely peripheral and the cool to be merely negative. Stravinsky's coolness and that of some "modern" jazzmen are alleged to be baroque or classical in spirit; but the most celebrated works of the baroque and classical composers were far from cool.

In "modern" jazz, the quest for the exotic and the primitive have led chiefly to Africa and Latin America—often to both at once, as in Afro-Cuban rhythms. In at least one of his compositions, Charlie Mingus derives rhythmic and other elements from Belgian Congo music; the result is intensely exotic music. Stan Kenton, pianist and orchestra leader, with whom the term "progressive jazz" is most closely associated, went through a Cuban phase, which left a mark on his music. Duke Ellington's band has played with Latin-American rhythmic appliances and, although Mr. Ellington rightly objects to the idea that Negroes are primitive people, his band has exploited the use of "jungle" sounds. Its "jungle-istic" (Mr. Ellington's expression) numbers have included *Echoes of the Jungle, Jungle Blues,* and *Jungle Nights in Harlem.* Bop musicians and other "modern" jazzmen sometimes use bongo drums and tom-toms, not merely for incidental effect but to give the primary quality and orientation to the music. "Latino" passages are common.

Incidentally, the very fact that the use of African rhythms and "atmosphere" has an exotic effect in jazz indicates the absurdity of attributing an essentially African character to jazz. It would be curious indeed if a familiar type of music that derives its "very heart" from African drumbeats could provide the thrill of strangeness by employing such beats.

Although the effort to achieve Africanism in content or in rhythm is comparatively new, traditional-jazz musicians have sometimes employed Spanish or Latin-American rhythms. Examples of a habanera-like rhythm may be found in several of Jelly Roll Morton's compositions, notably *The Crave,* and in some of W. C. Handy's blues, including the *St. Louis Blues.* The occasional use of Spanish rhythms in traditional jazz is somewhat analogous to Beethoven's use of Russian tunes in two of his so-called Rasoumovsky quartets. The exotic is assimilated to a basically classic approach. Although the Spanish or Latin-American rhythm is prominently featured in some of Morton's music, he appropriately called it merely the "Spanish tinge."

In "modern" jazz, however, the exotic element, when used, often tends to dominate the spirit of the music. Its dominance introduces a content alien to that of the old jazz tradition but apparently welcome to the "modern" jazzmen. If one listens, for example, to Dizzy Gillespie's rendition of *Swing Low, Sweet Chariot,* he will find an utterly un-Christian content in the shell of the fine old spiritual. The famous bop trumpeter has played and sung the piece with Afro-Latin-American rhythms and a degrading irrationality of content, beating the bongo drums and singing "Swing Low, Sweet Cadillac." (Mr. Gillespie's is not the only example of the perversion of the title of a spiritual in "modern" jazz: a "modern" clarinetist features *Let My Fingers Go.*)

122

The irreverent bad taste in the use of a spiritual as the vehicle of this nonsense goes beyond the iconoclastic joshing of Louis Armstrong's Reverend Satchelmouth, but Armstrong nevertheless pointed the way that Gillespie followed. Gillespie plays with great virtuosity, but at times with an emotional irresponsibility which is the logical consequence of Armstrong's vehement assertion of the right to express the outpouring of undisciplined emotional expansiveness. The lack of restraint in content, aided or not by the quest for the strange, has produced in some of Gillespie's music and that of other bop-minded "modernists" a sort of emotional gibberish. Persistent rejection of the source of meaning can end in no other way.

IV   The quest for novelty in "modern" jazz is by no means confined to discursions into the exotic. It is part of the "modern" jazzman's day-to-day, feverish, brain-tormenting burden. Creative concepts, sometimes hard come by, are quickly outdated and the jazzman tries to move on to something new. Commenting on the fact that certain recordings made in 1949 still sounded "fresh" in 1953, the discographer and writer Frederic Ramsey, Jr., observes, perhaps a bit wryly, that "four years is a millennium in 'modern' and 'progressive' jazz circles." [14]

The quick rejection of successive styles suggests a foreknowledge that what is produced will have no permanent value. One gets the impression that many of the "modern" jazzmen really want, not to turn out meaningful music, but rather to hide from the necessity of doing so. In the late 1940's the post-bop "modern" coterie was something close to a secret society. Popularity was considered a sign of failure—really, one suspects, of failure to fail. The music was apparently intended as a rejection of society and of the vestiges of traditional thinking that society represented. This attitude is, in 1955, not nearly so strong as it was, but it has left its mark on much of the music and, even more, on some of the critics, who seem eager to reject a "modern" jazzman as soon as he achieves popularity.

The irregular two-part historical canon of "classical" music and post-traditional jazz, in which jazz repeats what has happened earlier in "classical" music, is illustrated by the parallel between this coterie, formed after World War II, and the coteries in "serious" music after World War I. The following account by Sidney Harrison of the latter could be accurately applied, almost word by word, to the former: "New music became more and more an affair of coteries and studio-gatherings. Musicians, writing more and more for one another and less and less for the dwindling lay audiences, began to speak an almost secret language, until plain diction came to be derided, unquestionably, as platitude and cliché." [15]

It is tautologous to point out that the quick death of so much "modern" jazz, composed and performed by competent musicians, is a consequence of lack of vitality in the music. No extended reference need be made to the inadequacy, as a source of vitality, of the cleverness and ingenuity in which "modern" jazzmen have sometimes sought newness. More inclusive and more interesting is the effort of "modern" jazzmen to create new syntheses by introducing in their music elements already well established, or in some cases already outmoded, in European art music. Those jazzmen who are also arrangers and composers generally do this with knowledge of the sources. Debussy, Ravel, and (as already noted) Stravinsky are especially favored, but Bartok, Hindemith, and others are also looked to.

One must distinguish here between a synthesis of content and a synthesis of form or musical devices. With respect to the former, it should be noted that, where jazz, even if not strictly traditional, is still predominantly jazzy in content, as in some of the playing of trumpeter Ruby Braff, it is inimical to certain other types of content. It tends especially to repel the "coolness" and ultraromanticism of much of the European music in question. Combining as it does vitality and Christian feeling, the jazz tradition has little to do with Debussy's revery or with Ravel's wistfulness and pixyish playfulness. The opposites here do not blend into a higher or more meaningful synthesis. Vitality and spirituality blend, because the latter creates the former and because vitality cannot survive as such without spirituality. These are old truths and may be accepted as axiomatic. But revery and wistfulness are alien to the spiritual vigor of the traditional music. Successful blending requires a pre-existent inner affinity.

So far as the new jazz has broken free of the traditional content—and most of it has broken free very conspicuously—synthesis of content with "classical" music is unnecessary, for wistfulness, revery, pixyish or cerebral playfulness, etc., became prominent in both jazz and European art music when the more solid elements of content had been weakened or eliminated. They are the effete remnants of a tired and disoriented civilization, turned away from valid, wholesouled experience. In both jazz and "classical" music they represent the dregs of a dying romanticism and the shadow of the rejected content of a preromantic world view. Sometimes, with an almost romantic yearning for what has become exotic by the passage of time, the new music (whether "serious" or jazz) turns to the eighteenth or an even earlier century. Jazzmen write fugues and choral preludes; European composers as well as jazzmen write "cool" music, formal and precise. But they are unwilling to adopt (one wonders if they even perceive) the depth of feeling without which Bach's music would be dry and Mozart's merely polite and delicate. Paul Desmond's lacy saxophone playing in the Dave Brubeck Quartet reminds some of Mozart, but it is only the lacy side of Mozart, without the profundity. "Modern" jazzman David van Kriedt writes in baroque forms, and the music is clever and interesting, but where is the deep appeal to the God-loving soul of man? And so, with a played-out romanticism and a rejected or unassimilated classicism, the "modern" jazzman gives us wistfulness in place of the rich sorrow of the religious man or the *Weltschmerz* of the passionately romantic; he gives us the revery of "mood" music as the final devitalization of romantic love; and he gives us whimsicality in place of hearty classic good humor.

The parallel of European art music and post-traditional jazz therefore does not depend on intentional imitation of content. The intentional imitation is formal rather than substantive. The parallel in content simply reflects a parallel in extramusical attitude and thought.

The "modern" content in both jazz and "serious" music tends to represent one or another of certain conventional interrelated responses. So far as both European and American creators have turned their backs to the synthesis of Christian feeling and healthy human vitality underlying the classics in both traditions, they can travel in only one direction, just as persons moving away from the north pole can travel only southward. The meridians diverge, and the voyagers think they are traveling in different directions—such as romanticism and cool "classicism"—but if they persist in keeping their backs to the north they will meet again, for the meridians also converge at the opposite pole.

Far from that traditional synthesis, the composers are disoriented. Improvisation governed by such a tradition is not nearly so nerve-racking as improvisation in which the performer must produce meaning out of man-made sources. Searching within himself for inspiration, he is almost foredoomed to frustration, unless he is too

125

shallow to recognize the poverty of what he is producing. Bach was a great improviser and, so far as history shows, a well-integrated individual. New Orleans jazzmen improvise within their tradition without, as a rule, suffering great frustration. But some of the best "modern" jazzmen have been driven to narcotics and to other manifestations of abnormality. The reason usually given is the mental strain of improvisation. Undeniably, their improvisations are sometimes more demanding "musically" than those of traditional jazzmen. But more important is the fact that they improvise without the help of an adequate tradition of human thought and feeling. The disorientation of "modern" jazz is not musical but spiritual.

12. Mass-man's taste in jazz

1   As part of the creative art of the Western world in the nine-teenth and twentieth centuries, jazz has undergone the influence not only of romanticism and progressive secularization but also of the domination of effective taste and judgment by what Ortega y Gasset calls mass-man. The late Spanish philosopher emphasizes two fundamental traits in mass-man. One is his indulgence in "the free expansion of his vital desires." [1] The other is his "radical in-gratitude" [2] toward the efforts and principles that have created the civilization he enjoys. At least the former trait shows mass-man to be, in an important respect, a naturalistic romanticist.

Here again it is important for one to remember that New Orleans jazz represents a throwback to an earlier world view and emotional attitude, in which the principles of Christianity and of individual and group vitality on which Western civilization is built were humbly and joyfully honored. The development of very different types of jazz, like the development of types of European music remote from the baroque-classical norm, represented a departure from that attitude in the direction of mass-man's emotionally expan-sive but provincial point of view.

Notes to this chapter begin on page 305.

The effects of mass-man's questionable but pervasive taste are very much the same in both areas of musical development. For one thing, expansive mass-man likes bigness, which he associates with strength. Accordingly, he prefers a large orchestra to a chamber music ensemble. The orchestra's quantitative aspect, whether reflected in volume of sound or simply in a mass hush, gives him a sense of power and hides any lack of validity in the music's (or in his own) substance. "The fanciful notion that virility is synonymous with immensity," says F. A. Waterhouse, "is a favorite popular fallacy." [3] Like most popular fallacies, however, it is strongly motivated and has roots deeper than logic. For a listener can lose himself in the music of a large orchestra.

The fact that a conventional "big band" in jazz consists of only about fifteen musicians does not bring it into the chamber music category. It is dominated by wind instruments—brasses and saxophones—one of which, as the composition of the conventional symphony orchestra shows, is the equivalent of several string instruments. Mass-man made big bands popular, whether they played sweet dance music or swing.

One often hears or reads complaints that meretricious entrepreneurs foisted big bands on the public and thus led the public away from the better music played by small groups. The facts do not support this proposition. The entrepreneurs merely exploited the public's bad taste. If the public had paid as much and as consistently to hear a small group, the businessman would have been pleased, for expenses would have been lower and profits higher.

Unfortunately, an increase in the number of musicians playing at once does not signify a musical advance; if any generalization in this area were justified, it would be the contrary. So far as validity of content is concerned, we tread the same downhill path from Haydn's small and simple orchestra to Tschaikowsky's big and more complicated one that we tread from the small New Orleans or other traditional-jazz combination to Paul Whiteman's or even Count Basie's big band. But mass-man in both cases thinks he is climbing. He has little sense of altitude or of true orientation because, as Ortega y Gasset points out, he is ignorant of the history that created the values underlying the civilization whose fruits he enjoys. He does not inquire into the state of soul to which Bach's music gave expression, although that is the state of soul that created much of the greatness in Western civilization and without which the civilization may well perish. In the jazz field, he is utterly uninterested

Bob Scobey.

Kid Ory.

in, and probably incapable of understanding, the state of soul that produced the content of New Orleans jazz, although it, too, reflects the vital spirituality behind the civilization that he inherited. His taste and interest run in other directions.

They run, for example, toward the sort of content that can be best expressed in a single melody line with harmonic accompaniment. Mass-man has little use for the polyphony of Bach or for that of traditional jazz. The attention that it requires interferes with the emotional or conative expansion that he wishes to experience in listening to music. When he is in a "romantic" mood, therefore, he likes the homophony of sweet dance music or mood music. When he is in the lively mood that appeared to predominate in the middle and late 1930's, he turns to the general homophony of swing. The feeling of unity-in-diversity, with its religious connotations, has little significance for him. It implies a cosmic quest that is meaningless to him, for his orientation is egocentric and, therefore, although utterly fallacious, is simple and, so to speak, homophonic.

Related to his preference for homophony is mass-man's desire to worship a Great Man, generally conceived in romantic terms. This desire is reflected in music and other forms of art as well as in philosophy. The sort of feeling that led to the philosophical conception of the superman led Nietzsche's acquaintance Wagner to conceive his Siegfried and causes mass-man to worship Beethoven or Louis Armstrong as a Titan. The whole mass-man-romantic atmosphere is one of hero worship which, together with mass-man's ignorance of the true sources of that which he enjoys, leads to idolization of the virtuoso performer. The concept of polyphony is hostile to that of virtuoso worship, for polyphonic solo playing, except on a keyboard instrument, is seriously handicapped. Somewhat less obviously, the interplay of musical voices may be thought to discourage the state of mind in which the greatness of the individual man is sung, except where a specific program shows the voices to be the chatter of the hero's detractors or some other subject matter not identified with the hero himself.

In jazz, the demand for the Great Man may be associated with Louis Armstrong's declaration of independence from the limitations of New Orleans jazz. Mr. Armstrong, it will be noted, carried jazz in mass-man's favorite direction—toward free emotional expansion. He carried it also in the direction of solos and exhibitions of virtuosity. Although hot jazz had had outstanding musicians before Armstrong, the group concept had dominated. A band organized by Armstrong in 1925 was, according to George Avakian, "the first band built quite frankly around a musical personality—the prototype of hundreds of bands since which have been fronted by a Benny Goodman, Count Basie, or Harry James."

"But for recordings," Mr. Avakian continues, "Louis returned to his first love—the New Orleans style. The Hot Fives are among the classic examples of Crescent City jazz, although they did not rely as heavily on traditional ensemble work as did (for example) the Oliver band. The new emphasis on solos was perhaps inevitable, for in Armstrong and clarinetist Dodds the greatest one-two punch of all time was in operation. In addition, Kid Ory was unquestionably the best trombonist of his time. . . ."[4] Mr. Avakian is right about the inevitability of the emphasis on solos, but his reason—the presence of musicians of outstanding ability—perhaps does not tell the whole story. Dodds, Armstrong, and Ory all had performed in bands with Oliver, bands which nevertheless played chiefly polyphonic music with few solos. But mass-man's impatience with polyphony, his love of the virtuoso, and his demand for emotionally expansive music—together with, but not primarily because of, virtuoso soloist Armstrong's eminent qualifications as a purveyor of such music—led very naturally to the emphasis on solos. The emphasis on solos continued, even in bands lacking such outstanding musicians as those in the Hot Five, because hot solos responded to a need of the men (whether listeners or performers) whose tastes dominated. Indeed, by combining homophony, virtuosity, and in some cases naturalistic emotional expansiveness, hot solos tended to satisfy two or three interrelated needs of dominant mass-man.

II   Expansive, and ignorant of or uninterested in the part played by emotional restraint in the development of art, mass-man tends to like overstatement. Unfortunately, overstatement and loss of validity in content generally go together. The sort of overstatement of vitality that one finds in Louis Armstrong and in some of the jazzmen of the Chicago school (for example, Wild Bill Davison) sometimes results in an expression not of vitality at all but of something close to barbarism and moral irresponsibility. Overstatement of sweetness in dance music and of sentiment in mood music results in an expression not of sweetness and sentiment but of saccharine insipidity and sentimentality. Mass-man, the receptive audience in all these cases of overstatement, does not seem to know the difference in any of them.

130

Perhaps "overstatement" fails to indicate precisely what has happened in these cases. As in "modern" jazz's replacement of rich sadness by wistfulness or despondence, the significant thing is a weakening or omission of something essential, which leaves the transmuted remainder at once exaggerated in relative importance and weak or vapid in itself. There is, in a sense, a diminution of substance. This is especially obvious in the case of swing, which, by its stress on rhythmic propulsion, overemphasizes the rudimentary mechanical vitality in the music but, by weakening or omitting the emotional attitude that gives that element its validity and significance, it actually diminishes the importance of the element that it overemphasizes. As a consequence, swing represents a great deal of motion with almost no matter.

Jazz, including jazz of the types referred to, that lacks the selective emotional restraint or, still worse, the basic synthesis that characterizes the jazz norm, is a poor thing and cannot long satisfy a discerning listener, although it may momentarily interest him. Accordingly, such music requires every external, artificial aid that it can command, including large bands (already referred to), highbrow or arty pretentiousness, and flashy theatricality. Some of the purveyors of this sort of music, notably Paul Whiteman and Benny Goodman, have been touted as prophets of a great and thrilling new popular art, worthy of performance in the concert hall and of approbation by those critics of classical music whose erudition has not dulled their capacity to respond emotionally to fresh, vital stimuli. Paul Whiteman has long since been deflated. Mr. Goodman's Carnegie Hall debut in 1938 suffered deservedly at the hands of the "serious" critics.

Because of his transitional position, Louis Armstrong cannot be disposed of in this way. Armstrong has deep roots in traditional jazz, and therefore his music has much greater validity than that of Mr. Whiteman or Mr. Goodman. Nevertheless, the value of his music has been immensely, and harmfully, exaggerated. Unpretentious himself, Armstrong has had pretentiousness thrust upon him.

Although Armstrong's musical ability speaks for itself, his showmanship has doubtless augmented his popularity. He has shown himself quite willing to assume the professional role of the grinning darkie. Such a role would have been wholly alien to Bunk Johnson, Jelly Roll Morton, and the other New Orleans jazzmen who continued to respect the tradition. It would be out of the question for any of the genuine New Orleans jazzmen of today, such

131

as Paul Barbarin. The fact that it is accepted and even appropriate in Armstrong provides some indication of the nature of the jazz revolution that he symbolizes. It was a revolution against a sort of dignity, the genuine dignity that is consistent with liveliness and humor because it flows from the greatest source of human strength. Accordingly, the revolution could lead, as it has led, only to effeteness.

An interesting example of the power of pretentiousness and flashy theatricality in jazz may be found in the career of Duke Ellington. He engaged his highly competent, longtime drummer, Sonny Greer, because Greer, in Mr. Ellington's words, "used a lot of tricks" and was "flashy." [5] Even his admirer Barry Ulanov considers Ellington's piano style "florid" [6] and refers to one of his compositions as "very flashy, very sophisticatedly aware of all the tricks of the time." [7] Ellington himself is referred to as "flashy." [8] His bass player went in for "tricky syncopation." [9] As a young performer, Mr. Ellington developed "flashy handwork" and learned "the trick of throwing his hands away from the piano," [10] a trick which he still uses. Everywhere flash and trickiness. To borrow a phrase used by Abram Chasins in another connection, most of Mr. Ellington's music may be expected to go the way of all flash. But his employment of expert soloists, his genuine musical talent, his willingness at times to use the strength of the jazz tradition, and his quick recognition of changes in public taste have earned him great popularity. Nevertheless, his music has been called pretentious and, with respect to a great deal of it, the charge is justified. One piece that the American critic John Hammond found pretentious was the subject of the following comment by an English critic: "I believe that Duke has allowed us to 'tune-in' on his mind at work." [11] These two judgments are not necessarily inconsistent, for Mr. Ellington's expressed thoughts have sometimes been pretentious.[12]

Duke Ellington has, on occasion, played something fairly close to traditional jazz. He is said to be a man of deep religious conviction. He is also a man of talent and imagination. If he set his heart and mind to it, he might help find a way to perpetuate the eternal values in New Orleans jazz while expanding the idiom. But his musical imagination turns to the theatrical. He is, indeed, a sort of jazz Wagner. He has the same sort of dramatic feeling about Negroes that Wagner had about Germans. He wants to get back to the soul of his people, which he associates with their African past, much as Wagner turned to Teutonic mythology. He has even

132

criticized Gershwin's opera *Porgy and Bess* by the use of standards fairly close to those that led Wagner to establish a new kind of music drama.[13] But, in spite of his talent, his musical training and equipment appear inadequate for ambitious dramatic works. His *Black, Brown and Beige*, which he calls "a tone parallel to the history of the American Negro," contains some moving passages, but seems musically unsure of itself. More important, it lacks the vitality and optimism that characterize the best New Orleans jazz and which Ellington might accept as essential elements in the spirit of both Negroes and whites at their best.

One suspects that if Duke Ellington were to search religiously (so to speak) in the emotional content of New Orleans jazz, he might find, even now, a solid path to a new music of his own which no one could call arty or pretentious. Other extratraditional jazzmen with better technical equipment might find such a search even more rewarding, provided of course that the jazzman's spiritual acumen has not been so dulled that he can no longer understand that content.

Symphonic jazz, by its very nature, makes pretentiousness almost inevitable. Reference has already been made, in this connection, to George Gershwin. In the 1940's and on into the 1950's, the most downright pretentious music in the field of jazz has been that of Stan Kenton, pianist and band leader. With suggestions of symphonic jazz and all sorts of arty effects, this music, even apart from its ballyhoo—a longplay record is preposterously called "The Kenton Era"—is, in the words of a reviewer of that record, "uniformly pretentious, although a great deal of technical skill is lavished on it." [14] Mass-man, for all his ignorance, or perhaps because of it, likes to think that he appreciates high-class art. Even mediocre symphonic jazz, if properly publicized, therefore has a special appeal for him. Part of Dave Brubeck's success is doubtless due to his use of canonic or fugal snatches and the like—just enough to show that the music is high-class and thus to flatter the listener without boring him.

III Among the twentieth-century European composers to whom "modern" jazzmen turn and from whom they expressly derive ideas and methods, one great composer is conspicuously absent. He is Jean Sibelius. Why did they omit him? Because he is more a purveyor of moral and spiritual values than a technical innovator. The significance of the omission may be grasped in the light of Hugo Leichtentritt's observation on the contrast between Sibelius and the other recent composers who have influenced Dave Brubeck and the "modern" jazzmen in general: "The craving of the more mature and serious minds of our time for something of intrinsic worth, something durable and substantially sound in contemporary music has been too often disappointed. If one surveys recent music with the aim of discovering not merely interesting experiments and fashionable isms but an accomplished art of monumental aspect, weighty contents, and ethical values, with a philosophy of life as background . . . one finds it not in the work of Schoenberg, Stravinsky, Ravel, or Hindemith, but perhaps in Jean Sibelius, whose symphonic output within the last fifteen years has shown its creator capable of a unique spiritual elevation." [15]

Sibelius' greatest works, although they have romantic elements, indicate that the strength of the classical tradition in musical content and the values for which it stands have not become inaccessible to all composers. It shows also that an eloquent musical expression of spiritual elevation can still be achieved by fairly conventional means and, when achieved, has far greater value and significance than all the new music produced through polytonality, atonality, the new dissonance, and the rest of the paraphernalia.

All of this is as true in jazz as in "serious" music. In jazz, too, classical values are still purveyed. Bands of Negro and of white musicians, some of whom played New Orleans or other traditional jazz in the 1920's, others of whom have just begun their musical careers, are giving original expression to universal values through the traditional-jazz idiom. When played by fine musicians, this is not old music. As Schoenberg said, "All music, in so far as it is the product of a truly creative mind, is new. Bach is just as new today as he ever was—a continual revelation." [16] So it is also with New Orleans jazz.

As in "serious" music for some time, so now in jazz there appears to be a reaction from novelty and experimentation, even among some of the "moderns" themselves. There are signs in "modern" jazz of a search for something worth expressing, not just for new modes of expressing frustration. The search leads almost inevitably in the direction of traditional jazz. In his notes for a phonograph record in which this direction is very evidently taken, S. W. Bennett observes: "Because these two musicians have so much to say, they make no effort to hide the roots of their music in tradition."

One must hope that the searchers will be impelled to follow their noses all the way back to New Orleans jazz, not necessarily so that they may play it but so that they may understand how the jazz idiom can be used in the original expression of traditional, universal values. The important aspect of the search is in the values themselves. Once a competent musician catches their scent, he will be on his way to the creation of important music, whatever its formal resemblance to or difference from the highly civilized music which has been scorned as the kindergarten phase of jazz.

13. Cornets and trumpets

I   In the foregoing chapters, New Orleans jazz or, more broadly, traditional jazz is seen to be at once the nucleus or norm by which jazz may be defined and the most important type of jazz yet developed. It merits, therefore, a more intimate study. In the present chapter and the three succeeding ones, the roles of the usual instruments in traditional jazz bands will be examined. Subsequent chapters will be concerned with the specific concepts of traditional jazz expressed by significant individual musicians, bands, and schools.

In traditional-jazz ensemble choruses, the cornet or trumpet generally plays an approximation of the underlying melody, referred to by jazzmen as the lead part. It is therefore frequently called the lead horn. ("Horn" in the following discussion will mean the trumpet or cornet.) Because of this basic role, it receives more attention than other instruments in the band. Some remarkable individuals have played the horn, and many of the most stirring moments in jazz have been created by its sound. Its range of notes and widely varied tonal possibilities create an instrument which, in the hands of a superior musician, can express an endless variety of musical thoughts.

136

The great flexibility of the horn, while it is a blessing in wise hands, is a source of considerable damage when used improperly. Too often a brass man feels that, because his is usually the melodic line, the other instruments are merely there to accompany him. Such a performer tends to play too many notes and fails to create opportunities for the other musicians to share in the true counterpoint that is at the root of all good jazz. No matter how stirring such performances may be, they remain something apart from the uniquely fascinating sound pattern that constitutes a traditional-jazz ensemble. Generally, early master horn men used very economical phrasing, in marked contrast to the fashion now all too prevalent in many areas. While their phrases formed a logical theme, they were so constructed that they blended into the ensemble, instead of riding stridently over the other instruments. The latter technique is never a satisfactory approach in a traditional-jazz performance.

The right tone for jazz cornet is something for which a specification cannot be drawn. There have been many widely varied tonal approaches that have proved effective. On the other hand, it is not difficult to cite a few tonal characteristics that are most unsuitable. Playing "hot" and making shrill noises are not one and the same thing. The thin, "cool" tone often found among "modern" trumpet men bears a relationship to jazz similar to that of dishwater to gin. Jazz does not suffer from an overpowering need for the saccharine tonal qualities often delivered by Harry James or his followers, either. Lastly, the ability to play loudly is in no sense a measure of tonal value. This latter fallacy is one that badly needs clearing up among jazz lovers.

In keeping with the unique relationship between jazz instrumental music and vocal music, voice qualities are important in judging tone on a cornet. Where there is a conflict between classical instrumental standards and vocal standards, it will pretty generally be the vocal standards that may best be applied to jazz horn. While "serious" horn teaching decries the use of vibrato, the proper application of it can be most beneficial in this field. Important, too, is a degree of resonance, much as it is important to the male voice. "Modern" tone leans to a close, compact effect, but this sort of playing results in a most anemic sound for a jazz band. Such a tone may be suitable when six or seven trumpets are playing through an arrangement loaded with obtuse chords, but it does not suffice when a lone cornet is freewheeling alongside a clarinet and trombone on *Sister*

137

Kate. Whatever else may be requisite, a certain mature virility is always essential for a good jazz horn tone.

Jazz mythology is full of tales concerning the tremendous power of various cornetists. While many good cornet men have played with great power, they haven't all made a practice of playing fortissimo 100 per cent of the time. Power on the horn ensures a strong tone at lower volume as well as the ability to blow loudly. As a result, some of the most powerful of horn men could and did play rather quietly much of the time. One of the basic secrets of good jazz is an implication that far more is present than is apparent —few things can create this impression better than a powerful horn played softly.

There is, of course, a great difference between playing with power and playing loudly. One can get some utterly horrible, loud noises out of horn and still have a thin tone. In addition, there are those horn men who play a nervous, frantic style of horn that gives an impression of loudness when in fact it is merely irritating. On a visit of an Eddie Condon group to San Francisco, a well-known New York trumpeter "sat in" on a concert stage with Lu Watters and gave a most convincing demonstration of this. The Condon representative is known for a loud, frenzied style, yet throughout the selection played with Watters, only the Watters horn was clearly to be heard. The New Yorker did manage at one or two points virtually to throw himself into his horn and make one or two sounds that were discernible, but the calm, controlled horn of Watters remained in full command and was not to be gainsaid.

II   While tone is vital, it is in the art of phrasing that the musicianship of a horn player is tested most severely. One can overlook many tonal defects if phrasing is inspired and interesting. Syncopation, sustained full tones, staccato passages, terse notes divided by moments of silence fraught with as much meaning as the notes or more, these are the stock in trade of the jazz horn man. Melody is his rule and guide, and his ability to enhance it by recasting the original phrases without destroying them is the real test of his ability as a jazz instrumentalist. Any skilled technician can run up and down the scales within the chord structure of a given tune. It is quite something else again to recast the tune in a manner that leaves it fully recognizable, yet makes of it something new, fresh, and different through intelligent use of the art of phrasing or rephrasing. It sounds deceptively simple when done

138

by a master, but when one realizes that the lead horn has to re-member what to expect of the other four to six instruments around him and the idiosyncrasies of the musicians as well, the simplicity is suddenly gone. Small wonder that many horn men end up blow-ing whatever comes into their heads and thus force the rest of the players to settle for the provision of his background. The real reason not too many present-day horn men are willing to attempt true New Orleans jazz is that it just is not easy music to play. The lead horn man clearly has his work cut out for him.

There are many arguments concerning rhythmic versus melodic horn styles, but all jazz horn work is pronouncedly rhythmic in character. Although some horn men are considerably more em-phatic in their rhythmic accents than others, rhythmic patterns are never less significant than the notes themselves in jazz playing. Among those horn men using a very legato style, this is less appar-ent. Horn work that is extremely legato, however, ceases to be good jazz.

It is at this point that the element of "swing" enters the picture. As the word implies, this is the ability of the instrumentalist to impart a sense of smooth, free motion or buoyancy in his playing. This element is considered the one basic essential by some people, but it is only a single plane of the many-faceted jewel that is tra-ditional jazz. A capable player can swing mightily while playing fast cascades of short, interconnected notes in ascending or de-scending phrases, but this is not an adequate interpretation of a melody. Phrases may swing, yes, but good phrases are the primary requirement rather than swing for its own sake.

A marked tendency to hit their notes behind the beat is charac-teristic of many New Orleans horn men. Properly used, it is a tre-mendously effective device. Playing around the beat rather than on it does much to make horn style interesting. The unexpected in rhythmic devices is desirable, although the grotesque is always to be avoided.

Concrete rules for cornet players are easy enough to create, but circumstances invariably force the player to modify them occa-sionally. In some instances when a horn seems overdominant, it is because the other instruments are not properly performing their functions. In such a position, a horn player is forced to replace the missing function as best he can. Great taste and discretion must be used in these cases, and while a remarkable virtuoso performance may result, it is still not desirable to have one horn trying to fulfill

139

all the functions of a full band. In a trio or quartet, where a cornet is the only wind instrument, the situation is different, but where a clarinet and trombone are wallowing around while the cornet carries the structural burden in its entirety, a muddied sound is the inevitable result.

III One factor given most insufficient consideration by the jazz student is the nature of the instrument itself. Many a performance has been ruined by a bad horn. Conversely, some otherwise mediocre musicians have been made to sound better through judicious selection of horn and mouthpiece. The most obvious choice lies between cornet and trumpet, but there are variants here as well, including "compromise" instruments with various characteristics of both.

The two horns are mechanically similar. They are played in the same fashion, and a musician can usually switch from one to the other without any great difficulty. While the parts are essentially similar, the proportions are different. The bore of a true cornet is conical, starting at the mouthpiece with a small diameter which gradually increases until the bell is reached. In addition, the piping is so coiled that the horn is short and looks like a very complicated piece of plumbing. The conical bore and the curvature of the pipe give the cornet its characteristically mellow, smoky tone.

Trumpets have a circular bore whose diameter is constant from the mouthpiece to the beginning of the flare for the bell. They are long horns with fewer bends in the piping. The typical trumpet tone is brilliant and piercing.

While these differences are sufficient to be notable, the trumpet and cornet are not too widely separated in character. In the case of some musicians who use both horns, it even takes careful listening to discern which they are using. As to choosing between them for jazz playing, careful consideration must be given to the nature of the specific band and the tonal effects desired. The cornet would seem better suited to the purpose generally, as its broader tone can give a sound of greater richness to the three to four wind instruments of the typical group, particularly in the middle and lower registers. On the other hand, many jazz players feel the trumpet is a little freer blowing in the upper registers. Another factor given considerable weight is the smoother appearance of the trumpet, although modern cornets are now fairly "streamlined" as well. Many musicians who seek the larger tone found in the cornet stay with the trumpet because they fear that they would not look "sharp" with the short horn. No person is more violently conventional in these respects than the typical "popular" musician.

Concurrent with the gradual revival of jazz interest has been the slow return of the cornet to the scene. The appearance of cornets with a cylindrical trumpet-type bore, but with the other characteristics of cornet construction, has added impetus to their reacceptance, as this makes a horn with several favorable characteristics of both instruments. Some relatively long cornets have also appeared, but this sort of thing eventually reaches a point where one of the shorter trumpets is virtually the same thing.

One of the most important parts of any horn is the mouthpiece. The musician must consider his comfort while playing and the sound that he wants to achieve in making a selection. A large measure of musicians with "phenomenal" high ranges can thank a shallow mouthpiece rather than any unique ability. The real trick of the trade lies in the achievement of range using a mouthpiece of sufficient depth and proper diameter to give a good, full tone as well. It might also be noted that in the playing of traditional jazz, it is perhaps most important to execute properly in the middle and lower ranges of the instrument. Cornetists who play a great part of the time in the upper register are rarely effective ensemble musicians. In the case of New Orleans cornetist Freddie Keppard, for example, although he was famous for a remarkable and consistent high range in a time when neither horns nor musicians' embouchures were developed for the purpose as they are today, he was equally famous for the beauty of his playing in the lower register. It is in this latter area that many of the younger jazz horn players have shown their greatest weakness.

While the traditional manner of playing has been changed and corrupted by many influences in the course of years, a great reappraisal of all things in jazz has been proceeding since World War II. More and more young musicians are coming to realize the significance and beauty of the basic principles expounded and practiced by earlier New Orleans and Dixieland cornetists. The influence of Bunk Johnson and Mutt Carey in this regard has been of the utmost significance, the former through his work with his own bands and the latter in his performances with the post-World War II Kid Ory band. Other younger men who have also exercised a considerable refining influence over the wild, swing-Chicago-hot-solo stylists have included San Francisco's Lu Watters and Bob Scobey, Johnny

141

Wiggs in New Orleans, and Chicago's Muggsy Spanier. All these cornetists or trumpeters have steadfastly upheld the principles enunciated by the fine instrumentalists of preceding generations. The continuance of this attitude of mature restraint cannot but have a salutary effect upon the continuing evolution of traditional jazz as an art form.

14. The role of the trombone

1   The trombone fills one of the most important and least understood roles in the traditional-jazz band. It has on occasion been
a solemn, noble, dignified voice in a music not frequently accused
of these qualities, yet half of the real humor in "pure" jazz seems
to emanate from this same source. The right musician can work
wonders with it, but it has too frequently been mistreated or forgotten by bandsmen who should know better.

While both valve and slide trombone have been used in jazz
bands, it is the latter that most concerns us. Valve trombones are
pretty much a jazz oddity today, although they were somewhat
more common in the very earliest jazz bands. Old pictures of the
almost legendary Buddy Bolden band show trombonist Willie
Cornish using a fierce, complicated piece of plumbing that must
have been the caveman ancestor of the mild-looking valve trombone
of today. Constant improvements in slide construction, however,
have eliminated the interest of most musicians in valve trombones.

Newer trombones are made with somewhat smaller bells than
in the past, and the earlier conical bore has given way to the circular, trumpet-style bore in the tubing. Some claim that the older,
conical bore is preferable, but the lower cost of manufacturing an

143

instrument of this size with a constant-diameter bore has undoubtedly affected horn production and design.

Some downright peculiar things have happened to jazz trombone as time has passed. In the earlier periods it was an essential and important part of virtually every band, yet certain critics have slandered its use in New Orleans as "crude" or "trite." Its propulsive capabilities did much to put life into what was going on, with such musicians as Zue Robertson, Roy Palmer, Honoré Dutrey, Eddie Edwards, Kid Ory, and a few of the Brunies brothers by no means considered "inferior" to their contemporaries on other instruments. Contrary to the allegations of a few "critics," the New Orleans musicians knew what they were doing in selecting and using the instruments they did in their ensembles. In the case of the trombone perhaps even more than other instruments, some writers have failed utterly to note any but the most obvious of playing characteristics when evaluating the structure of traditional jazz.

During the 1920's, various musicians in other localities, notably New York and Chicago, who were attempting to play New Orleans jazz decided to "improve" the trombone's part. They thought New Orleans trombone style was achieved merely by hitting spasmodic notes in tuba fashion to fill out chords, with an occasional slur added for punctuation. The role of the instrument in the construction of contrapuntal patterns was totally overlooked. This is painfully clear in many early recordings where various would-be Dixieland bands include trombone parts representing a sad travesty on the New Orleans manner of playing. As a result, when Miff Mole started playing a more complicated and legato melodic line than had ever before been heard on a trombone in jazz, many others rapidly jumped on the band wagon, turning the trombone almost into a sort of second trumpet. Following this, Jack Teagarden introduced a style that might easily be transposed to trumpet with no real difference in effect, placing great emphasis on solos, the ensemble role of the trombone being all but forgotten. Once again virtually a generation of young trombonists hurriedly adopted the style and moved yet another step from the traditional role.

It would be a mistake to deny that some very interesting music came from Messrs. Mole and Teagarden as well as several of their followers. It would be a worse mistake to deny that their work was inferior to that of their New Orleans predecessors in the creation of traditional-jazz ensembles.

The dilution of the trombone style in New York and elsewhere was exceeded by its virtual elimination by the Chicagoans, who substituted a saxophone in many of their excited, hell-for-leather jazz battles. In this manner of playing, tailgate trombone, as the more common phase of the traditional style is frequently called, would be utterly out of place. However, because the Chicago musicians of the late 1920's played pretty much the same sort of thing on one instrument as on another, the trombone's occasional appearance remained in keeping with the idiom, bearing little or no resemblance in playing to its function in New Orleans jazz.

II   In the late 1930's, with the traditional-jazz revival, the old-style trombone received belated attention. George Brunis (he has dropped the "e" from "Brunies"), who had recorded with the New Orleans Rhythm Kings in 1923, left Ted Lewis's big band in 1939. In the company of Muggsy Spanier's Ragtime Band, he proceeded to demonstrate that the Dixieland ensemble art was still something very much alive. He also made records with various remnants of the old Chicago groups who were gathered with guitarist Eddie Condon. Here, in his usual brash fashion, Brunis virtually bullied some of the happy-go-lucky Chicagoans into something nearer a traditional ensemble than many had ever previously played. About the same time, one Melvin Alton Edward "Turk" Murphy was playing a trombone with the newly formed Lu Watters band in San Francisco that was equally far removed from New York and Chicago "improvements."

It is very largely due to the work of these two men that real ensemble trombone has been slowly returning to the fore. Paradoxically, despite this gradual ensemble improvement, many trombonists feel called upon to be Teagardenesque in their solos. Excellent musician though Teagarden is in his unique fashion, his solo style simply does not fit, as a rule, the pattern of traditional ensemble playing. One may be rather startled when, after a high-register, trumpet-style solo, the trombone suddenly shoots down a full octave and proceeds into the ensemble sounding very much like a grandfather to its own voice in the preceding solo.

Among the earlier players, two fairly distinct trombone styles were apparent. Most common was a brusque, clipped style, replete with sudden upward thrusts and tricky rhythmic patterns of an economical nature. The other, marked by long glisses and sustained notes coupled with short runs, provided at once a harmonic bass and a simple countertheme to the cornet. Many New Orleans men

145

played both styles, although usually favoring one somewhat more than the other. Kid Ory, for example, although known in the past for the former style, frequently has used the second of the two approaches, particularly in the revival period, switching readily between the two manners of playing in the same performance.

The brusque style is what is usually thought of as the New Orleans "tailgate" style, although it would seem certain that both styles were heard over the tailgates of New Orleans band wagons in the "golden age." It has also been said that this was the marching band style, yet there are examples extant of the other type of horn in marching band recordings as well. Many ardent jazz enthusiasts have argued heatedly as to which style is the "true" style, but it seems evident that both are valid from a traditional viewpoint. Paradoxically, the simpler sounding style is the more difficult in the opinion of many trombonists.

To a certain extent, choice of trombone style is affected by instrumentation, with the simpler preferred where there are two cornets as in the case of the King Oliver Creole Jazz Band. Oliver's trombonist, Honoré Dutrey, exemplifies this style almost perfectly. Choice is also affected in some measure by the presence or absence of tuba or string bass. The brusque, highly rhythmic trombone approach affords additional support in this area when needed.

Although individual players varied considerably as to intonation, the older New Orleans trombonists generally played a very full-throated, powerful horn of a vibrant, markedly masculine tone. The characteristic use of vibrato was as evident here as on the other horns, with "blue" notes very much a part of the equipment as well. Even when the trombone was playing softly, a resonance not characteristic of "legitimate" concert playing was always apparent. It is in this respect that many younger trombonists have been most remiss, although the growing movement of young bands who play for the sheer love of the traditional music is producing new performers who are more markedly aware of the trombone's jazz potentialities.

Because of its size and the manipulation required in its playing, the trombone lends itself to clowning. As a result, it has sometimes been considered an inferior instrument in jazz. Conversely, some have become unduly self-conscious because of the prevalence of clowning and try to appear as if paralyzed when playing. Either pose is bad, for the best efforts can come only from relaxed musicians who are fully free to concentrate on the music.

In the 1930's, many jazz groups were not using a trombone, and

146

even today it is regarded by some as "less important" in ensemble playing than the other horns. Careful attention to the better recordings of New Orleans and Dixieland bands will prove the fallaciousness of such thinking. A few groups using trombone and clarinet have suffered very little for want of a cornet. On occasion a cornet and trombone have also produced respectable performances without a clarinet. No one instrument is "superior" in traditional jazz— it is rather the musicians that make the difference. A band without cornet sounds far better than it would with the wrong cornetist. The trombone is neither more nor less "useful" in a jazz group than the clarinet or cornet.

15. The clarinet—complement and contrast to jazz brasses

1   The clarinet has received more varied application in jazz than any other instrument. It is the perfect counterfoil of the brasses in a traditional-jazz band and often serves as a catalyst, igniting fuel provided by the lead horn and trombone. The instrument's full range is of value in jazz. The variety of styles in which it can be utilized within the traditional idiom gives the instrumentalist a wide area in which to develop his talents and ideas.

Comparisons between performers are made somewhat difficult by the vast differences among instruments in this category and by the variety in techniques possible on the individual instruments. A wide basic difference exists, for example, between the Boehm and Albert system clarinets, on which the fingering is quite different. The Albert system was and still is favored by many of the old-line New Orleans players. The Boehm, which is the more modern system, has many adherents who insist that jazz can be played in the New Orleans style just as readily on their newer instruments. Although some tonal superiority may exist in the Albert due to the smaller number of holes in the body of the instrument, it seems that any person technically competent to play the full range of the clarinet would not be likely to phrase very differently in the different systems. A case in point is some of the "revival" clarinetists who have approaches clearly related to early New Orleans styles despite their use of the more modern Boehm-system instruments.

A wide variety of reeds, differing in hardness, size, shape, and texture are available for the clarinet. Each of these characteristics bears a distinct relationship to tonal possibilities. A harder reed, for instance, will generally give a larger, more brilliant tone, but makes execution of complex passages more difficult. The soft reed yields a softer sound and facilitates rapid flights around the scales. Recognizing this, it becomes apparent that Johnny Dodds, for one, was a pretty powerful man with his horn, blowing some very smart passages through a reed from which a few modern "virtuosos" would be incapable of obtaining the tricky phrases characteristic of their styles but achieved on softer reeds.

Clarinets are available in several keys, although the jazz instrumentalist generally favors the B-flat instrument. Even in this category there are variations, as witness the difference between the tiny instrument of French origin used by veteran Alphonse Picou and the instruments used by most other jazz players.

Embouchure holds an important place among the jazzman's facilities. Although several jazz musicians have used a classical embouchure, there are others who maintain that to play jazz necessitates a somewhat different position of the lips and jaw structure in relationship to the mouthpiece. They state that a jazz tone must be obtained in a different manner from the thinner, purer classic tone. In the case of Bob Helm, former clarinet player with the Turk Murphy band, this would seem to be clearly indicated. He uses an entirely different embouchure when playing jazz from occasions when he is playing Bach. His hard, Dodds-like tone in jazz work is in marked contrast to the tone he achieves in playing European art music.

Although objective comparisons among stylists seem to be made more difficult by the varied technical facilities available, it might also be noted that this leaves the musician less grounds for claiming that he is limited by his instrument. The area for development of his tastes is vast, and the man must therefore stand or fall on his willingness to develop the necessary skills for proper performance.

II   The fusion of brass band and blues influences is nowhere more apparent in jazz than in the styles of traditional clarinet players. Phrasing of a distinctly vocal nature is clearly evident in really blue

149

clarinet work, while march characteristics are found in various facets of counterpoint and in the use of obbligato and trills of types commonly used by flutes and piccolos in marching bands, as well as in typical clarinet phrasing from the same source. Another very considerable influence has been the classical vein stemming directly from the French Opera era of New Orleans Creole music.

Because of the wide variety of influences, even the earliest clarinetists played in sharply different styles. The Creole clarinet style of Alphonse Picou is no less valid than the bluer style exemplified by Dodds or the more legato style of Jimmy Noone. It was Noone's style that later became the foundation for the "swing" clarinetists, although, from the traditional standpoint, their work would be considered a degeneration of the parent style.

In large measure, clarinet ensemble parts have been played in upper register above the lead, although this is by no means essential, some of the players having a tendency to use low register much of the time. While a considerably more legato phrasing than that used on cornet or trombone is acceptable, the traditional instrumentalist must none the less make certain that his playing does not clash with that of the other horns and, equally important, must create phrases more meaningful to the formation of a melodic line than mere rapid exercises up and down the scales. It is in this latter respect that the Goodman-Shaw imitators seem to be most remiss in their traditional-jazz efforts.

Tonally, there are great variations among clarinetists, far more so than the variations of tone found among brass players. The classic tone of the Creole as exemplified by Albert Nicholas is a sound far different from the big, hard tone of Dodds and his followers, or the somewhat thinner, sourer, more metallic qualities utilized by Ed Hall and certain others. The soft, limpid nature of the Goodman tone is not well suited to traditional jazz, although many "compromise" musicians attempt its use in the field. Some of their work is of value, but generally this is in spite of, rather than because of, the tone they affect.

The Creole style is characterized by a clear, individual attack on each note, with little or no slurring and a clean albeit warm tone. The phrasing is light, buoyant, and lacy, with limited or no use of the vibrato. On occasion, the use of piccololike phrasing is apparent in the work of various Creole clarinetists.

The "blue" style is of a more markedly vocal quality, utilizing considerable variation in tone and vibrato. The phrasing is more economical than that of the Creoles and not quite so fluid. It is generally more powerful, with tonal qualities of a somewhat "brassy" nature as compared to the distinctly reed quality of the Creole intonation.

Obviously it is an oversimplification to describe the basic New Orleans clarinet styles in this brief manner. Obviously, too, most of the pioneer players overlapped stylistically to some extent. However, a comparison of the Creole approach of George Baquet and Alphonse Picou with the blue style of Johnny Dodds clearly illustrates a basic difference in approach.

The extremely legato, "pure"-toned style of the Goodman school is something else again. Although no pretense is made at evaluation of this style in its own "swing" idiom, there is little doubt of its impropriety in the traditional ensemble. At the time he was playing music closer to the tradition than in his subsequent swing efforts, Mr. Goodman himself used a considerably more virile tone. The tone for which he is commonly known, however, lacks the necessary stamina to create a proper balance with cornet and trombone in traditional ensembles. This ceases to hold true only when the other horns are of a similar tonal nature, in which case one wonders why any attempt is being made at all to play this essentially robust type of music.

The great flexibility of this instrument makes it something to be utilized cautiously. Various tonal aberrations that are possible may, on occasion, be highly dramatic or convincingly humorous. Too often the temptation to use them leads the player across the line separating good taste from foolishness, especially among those whose understanding of their function is rather vague. The cute and "jivey" are a little out of place in most areas of traditional jazz. Where humor is concerned, traditional jazz tends toward geniality or hearty laughter rather than smirks or sneers.

In the right hands, the clarinet is perhaps the most soulful and expressive of the wind instruments in jazz, but its soulfulness does not suggest a lack of vitality.

Although the two brass horns are volumetrically more potent, the contrasting tone of the reed permits the clarinet part to stand out clearly. Properly, the part should be formed in a strong counterpoint, usually above the melodic lead, phrased in a relatively fluid manner to impart a sense of motion to the ensemble pattern. In this way the voice of the clarinet becomes the very spark of life in the traditional-jazz ensemble.

151

16. Rhythm instruments in traditional jazz

1   Although there has always been general agreement in orthodox traditional-jazz circles that the wind instruments in a band should be a trumpet or cornet, a clarinet, and a trombone, with possibly a second cornet or trumpet, there is nothing close to unanimity of opinion as to the instruments that constitute a proper rhythm section. Many have felt that four rhythm instruments should be used, while others prefer two or three. On occasion more than four have been used, but this is a most unusual occurrence, in all probability dictated by circumstances other than purely musical desirability. Disagreement on the number of instruments in a rhythm section is but one indication of a wide area of disagreement throughout the subject.

The basic instruments utilized in rhythm sections include sets of drums and accessories (referred to simply as drums), banjo, guitar, tuba, double bass (usually referred to as string bass or simply bass), and piano. Where the banjo is used, guitar normally is not, and where tuba is used, the string bass is not generally employed. It is readily apparent, then, that there exist two major areas where opinions may differ in the selection of instruments. Directly related to such selection is the fact that bands using guitar generally use string bass, while bands with banjos frequently use tuba as the bass instrument. However, there are many examples of bands using banjos and string bass, and in a few instances guitar and tuba have been employed. In general, a "full" rhythm section consists of four units, probably the two most common being (*a*) banjo, tuba, piano, and drums, and (*b*) guitar, string bass, piano, and drums. Some groups have used men who "doubled" on instruments, a string bass player also playing tuba, or a guitarist playing banjo, with various shifts occurring from selection to selection in their work. On the famous recordings made in 1926–27 by Jelly Roll Morton and His Red Hot Peppers, virtually every conceivable combination of instruments in the rhythm section was utilized, with only drums and piano remaining fixed, to wit: banjo, string bass, piano, drums; banjo, tuba, piano, drums; guitar, string bass, piano, drums; guitar, tuba, piano, drums. A similar situation exists in a group of recordings made during the "revival" period by Graeme Bell's Australian Jazz Band for the Czechoslovakian Supraphone label. While such wide variation within the same band at the same time is not common practice, there have been other groups than these in which it has occurred. More commonly, a schism is found dividing the banjo-tuba advocates and the loyal guitar-string bass users, with one or the other of these pairs being used exclusively in conjunction with piano and drums.

Where fewer than four instruments are used, several possible combinations of two and three may occur. A relatively common rhythm trio in Dixieland bands is piano, string bass, and drums. The combination of piano, banjo or guitar, and drums is also not uncommon. Three-piece groups using bass, however, are more usual than the latter. In the early New Orleans period there were often groups using no piano, the unit consisting of banjo, tuba, and drums; guitar, string bass, and drums; banjo, string bass, and drums. A two-piece rhythm section consists most frequently of piano and drums, sometimes of piano and banjo, and, in some instances, of banjo or guitar with tuba or string bass.

As if the combinations described provided insufficient diversity, there is wide divergence both in the techniques applied to the instruments and in their construction. In the case of the banjo, the four-string tenor banjo is commonly found in jazz bands, but some players tune it in the same manner as a ukulele while others prefer normal tenor banjo tuning, the strings ascending in fifths, C-G-D-A. Yet another method of tuning this instrument follows the tuning of the upper four strings of a guitar. The banjo situation becomes still more complex when one considers the five-string plectrum banjo and the six-string instrument, which is tuned like the six-string guitar and is, indeed, used chiefly by musicians who usually play such a guitar.

As for the guitar, the six-string instrument is commonly used, but certain players utilize the four-string instrument, notably banjoists who wish to "double." The Chicago guitarist Eddie Condon, for example, although he speaks with scorn today of the banjo, utilizes the four-string guitar because his basic instrument was the banjo and he has not essentially changed his method of playing.

There is little conflict within the field of the string bass over any really major phase of design, but tubas are to be found in several sizes and shapes. The lap model seems to be most favored, but the Sousaphone, which surrounds the player's trunk and was originally designed to facilitate the carrying of it in marching bands, is also used in jazz groups. The basic method of playing the tuba remains the same, but different models have different tone qualities and certain instruments in the tuba class are in keys different from the usual B-flat tuba.

The jazz band is indeed rare that can specify the type of piano it will use. As a rule, the piano used is the piano that happens to be on the premises. Jazz pianists are of necessity a hardy lot. They are divided into two camps—those who are apparently content with any instrument on which the strings are not actually broken and those who are never content with any instrument that comes under their hands.

Drums vary from a simple set comprising bass drum, snare, perhaps a couple of cymbals, and a block, to huge, complicated assemblages including not only the devices mentioned but also top-hat cymbals, tom-toms, kettledrums and countless other appurtenances on which varied noises may be obtained. In the playing of traditional jazz, it is too frequently true that the quality of the drummer's work varies in inverse ratio to the amount of equipment with which he surrounds himself.

Whatever may be the area of discord in discussions concerning traditional-jazz rhythm units, one particular question of taste finds at least a substantial level of agreement: specifically, recognition of the rhythm section as subordinate to the wind instruments. It is recognized that the rhythm instruments function primarily in support of the horns in the ensembles and as accompaniment to solos.

Rhythm instruments may themselves be featured to some extent in solos, but the basic character of New Orleans and Dixieland bands has always been determined by the ensemble playing of the groups. Rhythm instruments are used primarily in support of the horns in ensemble playing.

The beat used in traditional jazz varies in over-all nature between an unaccented four-four and a beat in which the offbeats of the measure are accented to a degree virtually constituting duple time. A group whose beat approaches the latter is referred to as a "two-beat" band. Although both New Orleans and Dixieland bands have used various beats, the colored New Orleans style tends somewhat more to the unaccented four-four, while the white Dixieland groups are usually two-beat. In the Chicago style and in the subsequent swing era, the unaccented four-four was the most common, although it was by no means invariable.

II   The history of drums in the traditional jazz band has been a spotty one. Where a drummer is possessed of a keen sense of rhythm and accompanying good taste, his support is doubly beneficial, giving greater unity to the sound of the group while at the same time lightening the effort required of the horns. A good drummer's ability to free other players from rhythmic preoccupation is of particular value where the other musicians have the mental ability to utilize creatively the added instrumental capacities his playing affords. Conversely, a poor drummer, one who overplays, races, or drags the beat, is far worse than no drummer at all. Not only does he detract from the group sound, but he forces the other musicians to work harder to less purpose. Brass players note particularly that their lips tire more rapidly when playing with a bad drummer. Similar or related effects are common among players of other instruments as well. Several bands that have not used drums have avoided them as much because of this phenomenon as for any other reason. A number of phenomenal drummers have existed in jazz, however, men such as Jimmy Bertrand, who combined great power and skill with great taste. Bertrand showed similar capabilities in use of the washboard, which is occasionally used in place of drums, possessing qualities in this use as yet unappreciated except in traditional jazz and a few categories of folk music. He was one of the few who could use virtually all the myriad tools available to a drummer without disrupting the playing of the other musicians. Minor Hall, considered by many to be the best of today's drummers and recognized for his superiority in the past as well, uses one of the simplest sets of equipment extant, consisting of little more than bass drum, snare, top-hat cymbal, plain cymbal, and wood block. His accurate beat, sensitive dynamics, and tasteful rhythmic punctuation add considerable zest to the Kid Ory band, in which his beat, described by some as a tight four-four, is ideally suited to the group requirements. It is interesting to note in passing that the afore-mentioned top-hat cymbal is frowned upon by many traditional drummers, evidently because it brings within a performer's command various possibilities that are not suited to traditional jazz. However, in a drummer of Hall's impeccable taste the danger of such misuse is virtually nil.

Taste in drumming, as in all things, is not readily measurable in concrete terms. Certain major faults, however, can at least provide an implication of the area in which the limits of good taste may be found. The drummer who plays so loudly that ensembles seem but accompaniments to drum solos certainly is in bad taste. Anyone familiar with the efforts of the Chicago expatriates sometimes referred to as the Condon clique is painfully familiar with final ensemble contests wherein all horns blow their loudest while the drummer bends every effort to be louder than all by considerable use of cymbals, leading almost invariably to an eight-bar drum solo before an eight-bar ensemble closing. Similarly in bad taste are the players who "accompany" piano solos with a gusto that drowns out all but a few straggling notes from the piano.

Harder to define are faults in the quality of the beat itself. Two of the major ones found in many drummers are obvious, one of these being a tendency toward acceleration ("racing"), the other being the opposite tendency ("dragging"). However, a drummer may have a consistent beat and still be unsatisfactory because of his failure to impart a feeling of motion and/or buoyancy to the rhythm consistent with the needs of the specific group. Various types and degrees of these qualities are desirable under different circumstances. At one time, the basic demand was for a drummer who performed with a high degree of "swing" or buoyancy. However, this quality is now assuming a role of somewhat lesser significance, as in the classic period of traditional jazz, when it was considered more as a desirable effect than as a solitary goal. If a further reference may be made to the metaphoric jargon of jazz musicians, the ability to "rock" or to "strut" is considered of at least equal significance to "swing" at the present time.

In "four-beat" drumming, where beat accents are even, the basic meter is usually established through hitting the bass drum on each beat, while a fairly common type of "two-beat" drumming utilizes bass drum and cymbal on alternate beats to establish the underlying meter. Over and above the rudimentary beat, the various accessories are used to procure syncopation or create texture. Use of these rhythmic elements plus certain purposeful disruptions of the normal beat and various "tricks" such as the rim shot (striking both rim and surface of drum coincidentally with a drumstick) provide punctuation. Further variety is achieved by the use of wire brushes as alternates to drumsticks.

In listening to the drums on various older recordings, it is unfortunately true that only a most distorted picture can be gained. The bass drum created such serious problems for recording technicians upon the old acoustical records that its use was either minimized or eliminated. As a result, the full dynamics normally utilized by Warren "Baby" Dodds are not found on the King Oliver Creole Jazz Band records, and Tony Sbarbaro suffers similarly on the various recorded performances by the Original Dixieland Jazz Band. Only a distorted impression of what their natural styles included can be found on these early recordings. An incidental effect of this was the creation of a school of drummers who learned their craft from phonograph records, with the result that their styles were based largely on the limited drumming techniques necessitated by nonelectric recording exigencies.

The various Dixieland groups developed a school of drummers who used certain "stylized" effects with no little success, but the tidal wave of swing, which converted most drumming to a monotonous series of dull thuds overridden by loud cymbal crashes, all but wiped out this style. However, its brash and bouncy exuberance, even if a little noisier than needed at times, did much to add to the general feeling of well-being created by the better Dixieland bands. Several exponents or partial exponents of the style are still providing us with happy reminders of the joyous rhythmic possibilities lurking in large cowbells and wood blocks. Bob Thompson, leader-drummer-washboard player of the Red Onions Jazz Band and Homer Welch of the Castle Jazz Band have done much to maintain the respectability of both, with veteran New Orleans drummer Ray Bauduc, a master technician who was featured with the quasi-Dixieland band of Bob Crosby during the "swing era," clearly demonstrating that flashy technique may still be a handmaiden to good

157

taste. The same may be said for George Defebaugh, a drummer in Los Angeles whose rapid technique with rim shots borders upon the incredible.

Among the New Orleans style drummers, Paul Barbarin, Zutty Singleton, and Minor Hall are good examples—men who have been playing excellently behind fine musicians for many years. Baby Dodds also falls in this category, but shares with Mr. Singleton an occasional tendency to overexuberance that is sometimes damaging in ensembles. In all fairness, it should be noted that these men have played from time to time in groups where this attribute is considered a virtue, but when playing under proper control with New Orleans groups, they are without a present-day superior.

III   Banjo players are roughly divided into two-beat and four-beat categories, the two-beat men quite often playing in a rhythm section including tuba, which accents the alternate beat, while the four-beat players are more generally found in bands utilizing string bass. Laurence Marrero, banjoist with the George Lewis band, is an excellent example of a four-beat banjoist. His playing creates a rhythm of remarkable strength coupled with harmonic simplicity. Johnny St. Cyr, who was featured in Louis Armstrong's Hot Five and is heard also on the famous Jelly Roll Morton Red Hot Pepper recordings of 1926–27, plays in both styles, varied to suit the occasion. Pointing up the versatility of the strange and peculiarly American instrument are the "trombone" style accompaniments sometimes effected by St. Cyr, in which he uses single-finger phrases in the lower portion of the instrument's range, creating an effect remarkably like that of "tailgate" trombone played softly. His work on the Armstrong record of *Muskrat Ramble* points up his four-beat approach, while much of his work on the Morton recordings is primarily two-beat. On these latter he may also be heard playing excellent guitar.

Although the basically two-beat approach has been used by several capable players, Lou Black of the New Orleans Rhythm Kings was particularly outstanding. Unfortunately, the old recordings do not show him to best advantage, but if one can remove the focus of one's concentration for a moment from, say, Rappolo's clarinet solos on *Tiger Rag* and *Panama*, it may be found that no little portion of the vitality in these passages may be attributed to the syncopated, flowing banjo support.

The guitar is most often utilized in playing of a four-four beat

158

even when the band is itself basically oriented to a two-beat style. Numerous fine musicians, including the afore-mentioned Johnny St. Cyr and the late Bud Scott of Kid Ory's band, who also played banjo in earlier years, have provided excellent support to various groups on this instrument. The less assertive, legato qualities of the guitar, in contrast to the banjo, lead to its use in a more closely blended style of playing, wherein the individuality of the perform-ance is "sacrificed" to the creation of an over-all group tone. Although one may listen purposefully for the guitar, casual atten-tion to a traditional group utilizing it will rarely bring the instru-ment forcibly to the ear's attention. Such a contrast exists between it and banjo that many bands have utilized both alternately for dif-ferent selections because of the greater over-all variety afforded to the group sound.

IV   The hot-and-heavy battle of tuba versus string bass is at fever pitch once again at the time of this book's publication. For many years, all but a very hardy little band of the faithful would have no part of the tuba. Today, a large group of musicians and enthusiasts are again favoring the huge brass instrument. It went virtually into oblivion for some time save in a few sweet bands where its harmonic possibilities and a lack of extreme tempos made it quite suitable. The fast four-four tempos characteristic of much of swing found it lacking in requisite mobility and its clearly defined notes provided a sharp punctuation not in keeping with a highly legato style. However, the traditional-jazz renaissance found new groups and new musicians relearning some of its virtues. The string bass, of course, is considerably more flexible. An adept string-bassist can play single-string passages bordering upon guitar technique, if he wishes, over a very considerable range. Fast tempos hold no terrors and sustained passages utilizing the bow are also possible. It is well suited to a four-beat attack and unquestionably gives a considerable rhythmic lift to the other members of groups in which it is used. Moreover, even though not always clearly audible, the deep tones it exudes enrich the total group sound heard by the audience.

While the tuba does not have quite the mobility of the string bass, it offers other compensating virtues of considerable impor-tance, explaining its reappearance on the jazz scene in recent time despite the considerable economic disadvantage of a very high pur-chase cost of the instrument itself. An adequate tuba may cost its owner more than six to seven times what would be paid for an adequate string bass, thus explaining in no small part the reason for the instrument's having more listening enthusiasts concerned about its use than playing musicians. Unlike the string bass, the tuba is a highly assertive instrument that is distinctly audible even when blown softly. Harmonic mistakes that can be casually ignored by a string-bassist are not easily overlooked on the tuba, as any error stands out with brutal clarity. Herein lies a strength rather than a weakness, for the tuba can and does add greatly to the harmonic content of the music without obstructing the clarity of the melodic counterpoint played by the three principal horns. In a sense, a good tuba player can fulfill a harmonic function that is too often filled by the addition of a saxophone which almost invariably detracts from the clarity of ensembles. This is frequently accomplished by the addition of a sustained note to complete a chord where necessary. A most important advantage of the tuba lies in the freeing of the trombone to fall into its natural line rather than causing it to assume a constant bass part in an effort to achieve a balance that a string bass often does not provide. Turk Murphy, leader and trombonist of one of the best-known renaissance groups, is strongly in favor of the tuba, the reasons cited above representing basically his thinking with respect to the instrument.

v   The function of a piano in the jazz band is extremely varied. In many groups it becomes the most important instrument in the rhythm section, while others have found that it was either unnecessary or a downright hindrance. Traditional bands, particularly New Orleans-style groups, have been almost indifferent to it, finding it of some use in enhancing the work of others, but not feeling particularly discommoded if the pianist were sent on an errand, leaving the band to play on without the benefit of his presence. The early New Orleans attitude seemed to give greater consideration to the piano as a strictly solo instrument. Indeed, Jelly Roll Morton has stated that the pianist should be imitating a band or orchestra in creating his solo style, an attitude clearly illustrated in his own playing. As such, the piano might very well be considered largely a duplication of the group effort. One result of this attitude makes itself apparent in the number of traditional pianists who were limited to playing simple "one-two" style, this being a musicians' term for a piano style restricted to playing the chords of the harmony on the beats without further embellishment. While this can be an effective device, many excellent band pianists have developed abili-

George Lewis.

Laurence Marrero of George Lewis' band.

ties to play more complex accompaniments without impeding the flow of ideas from other instruments and without detracting from the sound of the ensemble. Morton himself played a pronouncedly rhythmic style, yet at the same time executed many interesting little variations behind the horns that only tended to point up the work of the horns themselves. Others such as Joe Sullivan, Hank Ross, and the uniquely talented ragtime pianist Walter Rose, have developed ensemble styles of similar balance albeit stamped with the distinct flavor of their own personalities.

The passage of years brought a diminution in the vitality of piano stylings, with emphasis on rhythmic capabilities shifting steadily to a lighter approach. The robust left hand, with its interesting bass figurations, became passé in the swing era, with only a few hold-outs such as the late Thomas "Fats" Waller still championing this hearty approach. In its place, a group of followers of Earl Hines and others of his type rose to the fore. The approach became one of a single-finger trumpet line in the right hand over light harmonies in the left. Mobility of a high level and legato phrases of great length were the order of the day. Teddy Wilson, pianist with early Benny Goodman groups that spearheaded the swing movement, was viewed as a major step away from the traditional approach into a new era for the piano. In retrospect, this becomes rather amusing, for the clearer sense of proportion that time brings to us all indicates that the Wilson style was little more than a rather weak variety of Dixieland piano. It was something that would have been quite at home, perhaps, with the Memphis Five of Brooklyn fame or a Red Nichols group.

Ragtime piano is, of course, a subject in itself. It was basically a music utilized by solo pianists rather than bands, principally because the highly complex melodies were in large measure extremely difficult for effective orchestral treatment. The famous old *Red Backed Book of Rags*, utilized by many early traditional bands, contained several excellent orchestrations of these pieces. Some of these are included on an LP by Bunk Johnson discussed in Chapter 27 of this volume. A number of these pieces required the use of an E-flat clarinet in order to cover the range necessary for proper execution, and all of them required no little practice. For the pianist, however, they were somewhat less of a problem because of the range of the instrument. Many of them were avoided by all but the finest pianists, but the problems of one man are proportionately far smaller than those encountered in properly orienting an instru-

161

mental group to such fare. It may be fairly stated, nonetheless, that in no segment of jazz does an excellent technique stand a musician in better stead than in the performance of piano rags, particularly when played "as written." As jazz developed alongside ragtime, a very large measure of this music seeped into what is believed the younger form, being particularly noticeable in the piano stylings of many band players. All the work of the Original Dixieland Jazz Band shows a marked ragtime influence, while many older musicians state that the typical jazz trombonists played in styles differing in no substantial degree from the trombone styles found in the early relatively "pure" ragtime groups.

Although the piano has been found in all but a very small portion of the recorded jazz bands, there have been several groups that did not use piano, both among the earlier players and among the renaissance groups. Much of Bunk Johnson's recorded work included none, while a young white band, the Dixieland Rhythm Kings of Dayton, Ohio, discarded piano for a considerable period, resuming its use only after the addition of a ragtime scholar to their personnel. There is a feeling on the part of some traditional musicians that piano only muddies the work of either a banjo-tuba or guitar-bass team, or perhaps a banjo-string bass team. In those groups not using piano, there is a rather unusual flexible flavor to the rhythm that is perhaps refreshing as much for its contrast as it is for any inherent virtue in the instrumentation. It is true that the piano is too frequently used as a crutch for bad or lazy musicianship in other sections of a group, but a tasteful pianist has certainly been an asset in his own right in many other cases. It is a very difficult point to resolve. The writers find justification for thinking on both sides of this question both from listening and from personal playing experience.

Piano jazz as a solo art cannot, of course, be treated even remotely with the respect that is its due in the short confines of a chapter or a few pages. It is, rather, a subject about which many books could be written. For this reason, little more than an indication of the piano's role in a jazz band is given here. Its study, like the study of the jazz band, can be a most rewarding experience.

Qualitative comparisons of various rhythm sections are not easily made. While one may readily compare the instrumental capabilities of individual musicians, comparison of groups varying from two to four in number must take other matters into consideration beyond individual techniques. They must further take into consideration the ends in view of the particular group. The rhythm section of the New Orleans Rhythm Kings, for example, a consistently interesting unit despite various personnel changes from time to time, would create only consternation behind the horns of Lu Watters' Yerba Buena Jazz Band, while the strong two-beat style favored by such groups as Turk Murphy's would cause only unhappiness in Kid Ory's Creole Jazz Band. The real measure of quality in the rhythm unit, then, must be the degree to which it fulfills the needs peculiar to the organization of which it is a part. Moreover, it is perhaps one of the primary reasons why few jazz bands ever succeed in any degree at an effort to copy other groups. No two rhythm sections ever seem to sound alike. The rhythm section is a portion of the band performance that is most highly subjective, a portion that stamps its nature indelibly not only on every performance, but upon the style of all who are accompanied by it. It is the introverted aspect of each band's personality, its role solely to support it, but its support a primary governor upon the actions of the horns. Reconsider for a moment the exchanges of rhythm sections considered above. Assuming for a moment that the Yerba Buena Jazz Band and the New Orleans Rhythm Kings could have exchanged rhythm sections for an occasion, can there be any doubt whatever that the horns would have been forced to change their styles of playing considerably? Any musician will agree that this is indeed a situation in which the tail wags the dog. Out of such exchange, of course, an element of compromise would result, but whatever the compromise might prove to be, both bands would sound radically different from their former selves. Even in large commercial bands where written arrangements, strictly adhered to, are the order of the day, the rhythm sections develop characters of their own, and any personnel changes result in alteration of their character.

17. *King Oliver and his Creole Jazz Band*

1   Joseph "King" Oliver, New Orleans cornetist and band leader, was deeply respected by virtually all jazzmen of his day. The performances of his Creole Jazz Band recorded in 1923 are now considered classics. Beyond all doubt, his music has been and still is one of the most powerful forces in the jazz tradition.

The individual styles of the musicians must always be important in a music where so much of the creative responsibility rests upon the shoulders of the performers. The Oliver band is especially significant for the lesson it offers in group concept and discipline as applied to the traditional-jazz idiom. It is readily apparent that Oliver knew the goals toward which he was working. He possessed an ability, rare among highly creative individuals, to transmit his thoughts to his fellow musicians with such clarity that his personal concept and the band concept were almost synonymous. This is made clearly evident when the styles of various members of the group in their recorded performances with Oliver are compared with their styles in recorded efforts elsewhere.

In the case of the second cornetist, Louis Armstrong, the point is demonstrated most forcibly. In any other group with which Armstrong has recorded, whether or not he was nominally the "leader,"

164

he has always dominated the performance with his assertive style. Even in arrangements where his work was restricted to a short solo passage, the manner and approach are invariably wholly his own. In contrast, there is a subdued, almost introspective quality in much of his second-horn work. It is particularly evident in passages on record where the cornet parts are spaced widely in the ensemble and Armstrong can be followed easily through a chorus. There is some beauty in his later work, but it is beauty of a radically different kind. It is ironical that the first records in which he ever participated are undoubtedly performances of far greater maturity than any of those that have followed.

No less a contrast is evident in the case of Johnny Dodds. In fairness to this clarinetist whom some venerate as perhaps the most inspired jazz artist ever to record, it must be noted that in both his recorded and live performances he exhibited a remarkable ability to vary his approach without departing from the idiom. Nonetheless, his manner in all recorded performances with Oliver shows a basic restraint and a lyrical approach bordering upon the Creole manner. This clearly indicates the application of personal disciplines in an effort to achieve the Oliver concept. It has often been stated that the Dodds style changed radically through the influence of Armstrong and the Chicago environment during his period with Oliver and immediately thereafter. In reality, it would seem that he merely resumed a manner of playing that he had always used prior to association with Oliver.

Honoré Dutrey, Oliver's trombonist, evidences perhaps the least contrast in manner. Dutrey played in a style that was rarely recorded elsewhere, although New Orleans musicians state that it was not uncommon. Even Kid Ory, the famous exponent of so-called "tailgate" trombone, on occasion shows distinctly the influence of this style. Dutrey played a smooth melody line which, although not merely a harmonic bass part (he left that to the piano or, when available, tuba), enhanced the harmonic richness of the performance. His style, characterized by extreme simplicity, sounds deceptively easy. In reality, it is considerably more difficult of satisfactory execution than the better-known "tailgate" style of New Orleans. Dutrey's manner of playing certainly was well suited to Oliver's requirements. If he shared equally in the quasi-anonymity of the other musicians, he did so with but little change from what recordings elsewhere indicate to be his usual approach.

It is this quasi-anonymity of the individual performers that seems

165

to be the hallmark of the Oliver band. Unless the old recordings are listened to with a conscious effort to abstract the work of one particular artist, the normal tendency is to regard the work of the band as a whole with little or no particular consciousness of individual personalities as "standouts" at any point. Indeed, the paucity of solos and the stable dynamics of the horns * in ensemble is such as to preclude the gymnastics associated with "stars" in jazz music. The rhythm section remains uniformly subordinate to the horns, limiting itself to a strong supporting role, the usual function of such a group in traditional jazz.

II   Although Oliver's Creole Jazz Band is a classic example of the New Orleans jazz band, it was atypical in certain respects. The second cornet, common in the instrumentation of marching brass bands in New Orleans, is unusual in the traditional jazz dance band. The addition of second cornet very sharply changes both the over-all tone quality and the structure of the counterpoint, particularly when the second cornetist is a person of Louis Armstrong's capability. The brass band quality that is always implicit in these bands becomes particularly dominant in Oliver's group. The choice of material as well as its treatment emphasizes this quality still further. Most of the pieces recorded by the group are multi-theme original or traditional compositions. Many of them are of common march structure and therefore have two or more strains with strong overtones of ragtime. Typical of these are *Chattanooga Stomp* and *High Society*. Each of the blues selections for which this band is justly famed, such as *Working Man Blues, Room Rent Blues* and *Chimes Blues*, contains two or more related themes. In the performance of "pop" tunes, as exemplified by the recording of *Sweet Lovin' Man*, both verse and chorus are played. The consistent use of multiple themes and the heavy emphasis on ensemble playing clearly indicate the brass-band ancestry of Oliver's concept. Indeed, only very minor changes in instrumentation would have been necessary to convert the group into a marching band, for all the horns had considerable experience in the street marching bands of New Orleans as well as in dance jobs.

The very limited use of the solo comes as a great surprise to

---

* In jazz parlance, a horn is any wind instrument or performer of such an instrument. The tuba is generally excepted when one speaks of the horns collectively because it is considered a part of the rhythm section, while "horns" are "melody" instruments in jazz usage.

listeners accustomed to the so-called Dixieland bands of recent years. When a solo is played in the recordings of the Creole Jazz Band, it always performs a definite function. In doing so, it constitutes an integral part of the composition as rendered, never a sort of postscript adding one instrumentalist's impression of something that might be done with or to the chord structure. A particularly noteworthy example of this is the Armstrong cornet solo on the band's recording of *Chimes Blues*. Instead of using the solo merely as a vehicle for the presentation of a chorus of raw emotion or technical virtuosity, Armstrong fulfills the function of presenting the fourth strain of the melody. He plays it twice in a straightforward manner, presenting only slight variations in the phrasing rather than a devious improvisation. Too often in the intervening years, jazz musicians have used solos as mere unrelated extensions of themes, or a group of solos as a virtual medley of various musicians' impressions, without regard to the unity of the whole. In Oliver's recordings, the few solos are functional units of the formal structure, and in this respect are similar to solos in large brass-band music. The full expression of individualism in the group's work seems to have been restricted to the use of breaks. A short, unaccompanied two-bar statement by one instrument often was utilized to spice the composition with an effect considerably more dramatic than could be normally attained through the use of a solo chorus.

The beat achieved by the Oliver band rhythm section is truly remarkable when one remembers the limitations under which the old recordings were made. The tuba of Bill Johnson was used on some of the later ones, but the first records were made with no bass or tuba. The unit consisted of banjoist Johnny St. Cyr, drummer Warren "Baby" Dodds, and pianist Lillian Hardin, one of the few women musicians to grace the personnel of a major traditional jazz group. Despite the lack of a bass instrument, even to the elimination of bass drum, these musicians created a steady, powerful rhythm on their initial recordings that is still the envy of jazz musicians. The achievement is doubly significant when it is realized that it was necessary to establish a rapport with four horns instead of the usual three. Moreover, the horns often played with a fluency that required great independent strength in the rhythm unit, instead of playing constant processions of rhythmic figures tending to bolster the rhythm, as is frequently done in various other groups. Here we have an especially clear indication of the superiority of the Oliver band. Each musician had full confidence in the others. Thus he was able to follow the natural functional line of his own instrument instead of impinging upon the functions of others. Rare indeed would be a jazz band without tuba or string bass in which the trombonist did not almost automatically drop his playing into the role of a more mobile tuba. Instead, trombonist Dutrey plays a highly contrapuntal line more nearly approximating the harmonic role of a baritone voice, greatly enriching the over-all sound texture. Clarinetist Dodds indulges in solos of a most lyrical quality, obviously unfettered by any necessity to enhance the rhythmic punctuation. It is implied, not that the horns were not rhythmic in their playing, but rather that they were not preoccupied with the necessity of maintaining the rhythm. Thus it may be seen that, while the rhythm instruments in New Orleans jazz are limited primarily to a supporting role, they may strongly affect the manner in which the horns are played. Lack of satisfactory rhythmic support in many instances has been the downfall of other bands in which horn players were forced, in a sense, to play their own accompaniments. Thus they were led into complicated stylicisms that beclouded rather than enriched their work.

Listening to the Oliver recordings has never been easy. All the Creole Jazz Band sides were recorded by the acoustical method, and later Oliver bands that were recorded electrically were markedly inferior musically. Oliver himself was known to be unhappy with the latter groups, but he knew that the addition of saxophones and adoption of a more or less ordinary dance-band approach had become necessary if he were to obtain employment. To hear the important music of Oliver, then, one must study the earlier recordings. Fortunately, the recent great strides in production of high fidelity record playing equipment have made possible a far greater control of listening conditions than in the past. It may truthfully be stated that now, more than ever before, one can manage to hear clearly on record what this band had to offer. Close listening and relistening to this group can be a most rewarding experience for a jazz *aficionado*. The writers have never played these recordings without finding some new element, either in the basic concept of a selection or in the approach of one or another of the individual musicians to his part. It is not surprising that many highly critical listeners consider Oliver's Creole Jazz Band the best jazz band of them all.

18. Jelly Roll Morton—the Cellini of jazz

1   One of the most complex, colorful personalities yet produced in a field noted for such individuals was Ferdinand J. "Jelly Roll Morton" La Menthe. He was a bragging, ill-tempered, loose-loving, gambling charlatan of a most vicious kind, but he was also one of the most vital and talented composer-musicians in traditional jazz.

In certain respects Morton may be considered a peculiarly American phenomenon. A horrible example of virtually all the faults Europeans accuse Americans of possessing, he possessed in equally large measure a uniquely American capacity for the effective achievement of goals through unorthodox yet rational methods unknown and unappreciated in the Old World. He also possessed a bellicose, outspoken nature which made him his own best advertising representative. He made preposterous claims to one distinction in jazz after another. Most of these ultimately proved surprisingly true. However, despite his sharp practices in many other matters, in his music he was a person of the most rigorous discipline and firmest principle. In his later years he fought desperately to bring not only to his own personal music but to all New Orleans jazz the recognition, as an art form, that he believed it deserved.

169

His efforts were viewed as ludicrous and even pathetic at the time of their making, yet it is generally conceded today that Morton's work was one of the most potent forces in the creation of the jazz renaissance. In his later years, in addition to cajoling the Library of Congress into recording the now famous Morton documentary recording series and writing the fabulous letter to "Believe It or Not" columnist Robert L. Ripley (with carbon copy to *Down Beat* Magazine) in which he stated "I invented Jazz in 1902," he did numerous other things that were less spectacular but no less amazing in his crusading efforts. At a time when jazz was not quite fashionable intellectually, and college appearances of jazz musicians as lecturers or performers were utterly unheard of, none other than Jelly Roll Morton appeared as a guest lecturer-performer at New York University on at least one occasion. Time has proved that this semiliterate intellectual was one of the most important creative artists in American music.

With the exception of Louis Armstrong, Jelly Roll Morton is perhaps the best-known name in New Orleans jazz. However, there are vast differences between these two men musically. Indeed, the differences may go considerably deeper than that. Despite their presence in Chicago during the same period, and despite the impossibility of their being unacquainted or unaware of each other, they never recorded together. To the best of the writers' knowledge, they never played together save perhaps at an occasional informal gathering of musicians. Morton has stated that Armstrong was only the fourth best jazz cornetist, following Freddy Keppard, who Morton and others have stated possessed a phenomenal range, Buddy Petit, and King Oliver, an order of excellence with which Morton felt certain Keppard would agree.

Morton certainly possessed one of the most immense egos ever to appear on the jazz scene, but his music was characterized by a restraint and control clearly indicative of his mastery of both the idiom and the instrument. Armstrong, on the other hand, while no shrinking violet, is not and never was an egotist of the sort that Morton was. In his playing, conversely, there is an uncontrolled passion and an overexuberance representing a far different concept or capacity from that expressed by Morton. In Armstrong it is apparent that the form and the composition are only vehicles for extemporization. Morton obviously has high regard for a composition as such, even when he is "transforming" it with his own interpretation. Where Louis is "hot" by virtue of his wild, loose, highly emotional flow of ideas, with a tension bordering on the nervous, Morton is "hot" by virtue of his ability to express exactly the thought he wants to express, with a technique sufficient to his every purpose. If Armstrong is famous for his great drive, he is also famous for the number of missed notes and unresolved phrases checkering much of his recorded work. Great though his gifts, it is not unlikely that, in the years ahead, the stature of Morton will maintain a higher level than that of Armstrong. As jazz thinking matures, this conclusion seems almost unavoidable.

There have been other New Orleans pianists worthy of note, but almost none of them has been captured on record. The names of some have survived only through Morton's mention of them and his descriptions of their playing. There is reason to believe, however, that much of the music recorded on Morton's piano is stylistically similar to the playing of many another anonymous New Orleans pianist. Some of the early recordings of the Kid Ory band, circa 1944–45, indicate that the late Buster Wilson, for one, had a style markedly similar to that of Morton.

As a highly gifted jazz composer and pianist, Morton displayed a thorough knowledge of music theory. Although many reviewers and most of the "progressive jazz" coterie have tended to dismiss him as technically limited, there can be little doubt that their low evaluation of him is based on a difference in taste rather than on an objective judgment of capacity. The "heaviness" that they have found in his style was, in reality, a purposeful use of force of a highly functional nature. There are ample recorded evidences of Morton's ability to produce a light touch when and where desired, but much of the time he is found playing things in which his unique power style was preferable. His "archaic" left hand, so described by his detractors, was in every sense the antithesis of the weak, shallow, rhythmically unimportant bass of many more modern musicians, all of whom met with the scorn of Morton. On the 1939 Library of Congress recordings Morton stated that the only then current pianist who "has a tendency to go in the right direction" was the late Bob Zurke of the old Bob Crosby band. Zurke's left hand showed much of the strength characteristic of Morton.

The writing and arranging done by Morton are clear evidence of his knowledge of theory and his musical inventiveness. His occasional later forays into the recording of larger bands resulted in arrangements possessing adventurous qualities radically different from those of contemporary "swing" arrangements. A few

171

touches of sentiment appear in his work, but the over-all quality is muscular, never cute or quaint. When there is laughter, it is robust laughter, even to the use of vocal introductions consisting of snatches of strangely disjointed conversation roughly pertinent to the selection to be rendered, and conversation guaranteed to please any connoisseur of the type of humor known as "shaggy dog."

Morton believed very strongly in an orchestral concept of the piano's role. He felt that the only proper approach was for the pianist to realize that his resources were analogous to those of a band and to use them accordingly. It is certain that Morton's bass figures were created largely with trombone parts in mind. Many of his upper-register passages tend to emulate the liquid flow of the clarinet or the hard-hitting lead of a New Orleans cornet. The early Gennett piano solo recordings, and subsequent versions of the same pieces by bands under his leadership, make it readily apparent that he thought in terms of a band at the time the solos were made. The Gennett piano solo of *Kansas City Stomps* recorded about 1923 and the 1928 Victor band recording of the same number show a marked resemblance. Solos and breaks by the band instruments are closely reminiscent of the manner in which Morton had played them in solo.

A further indication of Morton's preoccupation with band music may be found in his trio recordings. Here it becomes clearly apparent, notably in a trio record of *Shreveport Stomp* with clarinetist Omer Simeon and drummer Tommy Benford, that his purpose in utilizing the trio form was to give himself an opportunity to become more nearly a major function in the traditional ensemble, the piano assuming various of the horn parts in counterpoint with the clarinet. There are some very beautiful and unusual choruses in this performance where the lead is actually in the right hand of the piano, with the clarinet playing its normal ensemble function and the left hand of the piano filling in, not only rhythm, but a structure closely related to the trombone part in a full ensemble. In passages where the clarinet carries the lead, Morton plays in an entirely different manner.

However Morton may have phrased his opinion in the matter, there can be no doubt that he regarded his music as an art, not merely a profession. It seems significant that perhaps his best recordings with bands were made at a time when there is reason to believe that music was very much a secondary source of income to him. In Alan Lomax' book, *Mister Jelly Roll,* information may be found concerning Morton's strangely varied and not always respectable sources of income, as well as many other fascinating facets of this (in Mr. Lomax' phrase) Creole Benvenuto Cellini.

II   Earlier in this volume, reference is made to a group of performances recorded by Morton in 1926 in which may be found music considered by some to be perhaps the best-recorded examples of New Orleans jazz. Although there are a few touches on certain of the numbers that are of other origin, or are stylicisms uniquely Jelly Roll Morton's, the general effect is most authentic. Fortunately, the quality of recording is far superior to that of the average records then being produced. With the exception of four selections, *Someday Sweetheart, The Chant, Smokehouse Blues,* and the Oliver tune, *Doctor Jazz,* they are all Morton originals. All eleven selections were recorded by the same personnel, augmented by violin on *Someday Sweetheart* and by two added clarinets for certain choruses of *Sidewalk Blues* and *Deadman Blues.* George Mitchell, a cornetist from Louisville, is the lead horn on these recordings. Here, as in other performances, Mitchell plays in the genuine New Orleans style, indicating that it can sometimes be acquired elsewhere than in New Orleans by a capable sympathetic musician. Omer Simeon's clarinet is recorded here at its best, while Kid Ory's trombone performance is emphatically classical in nature. As to the rhythm, the tasteful but powerful drumming of Andrew Hilaire gives excellent propulsion yet never obtrudes. Morton's own solos are totally unaccompanied and thus have greater clarity than would have been possible if the rhythm instruments had continued support through them. John Lindsey switches with impunity from tuba to string bass, playing both with taste and dexterity of such an order that it is difficult to identify the instrument used in a particular selection. Johnny St. Cyr, whether playing banjo or guitar, produces a highly effective rhythmic chording utterly in keeping with the music interpreted. Morton himself rounds out a superb rhythm section at the piano. Here were indeed seven of the best men who could have been assembled to illustrate the nature of this music. The opportunity was not wasted. All the numbers were well rehearsed with a minimum of repetition or waste motion. Morton had clear-cut ideas of what he wanted to achieve, and many of the solos as well as much of the ensemble playing reveal the presence of his master hand. There is a sufficient difference between the first and second masters of some of these selections to indicate

173

at least a reasonable degree of improvisation, but improvisation is not present to the extent that many have long believed.

Later recordings made in New York in 1928 are also of considerable interest, among them the afore-mentioned trio performance of *Shreveport Stomp*. The band selections are particularly notable for the beautiful playing of Simeon and the extremely lively banjo of Lee Blair. Using the orthodox tenor tuning, his style is one of the most completely "banjoistic" ever recorded. He is largely responsible in particular for the exuberant tone of *Kansas City Stomps*, where he takes a solo of the quality described by jazz enthusiasts as "hot." Also present on this record are trumpeter Ward Pinkett, who plays a very warm-toned lead horn, and trombonist Geechy Fields. In addition to Morton and Blair, the rhythm section includes the Benford brothers, Tommy playing drums and Bill the tuba. Bill Benford's remarkable performance greatly enhances the beautiful integration of the group. Some of these records, including *Shreveport Stomp*, utilize what appear to be clarinet solos, but are, in reality, polyphonic choruses in which the rhythm instruments participate on an equal footing with the clarinet.

Morton's earliest recordings were a group of piano solos for the Gennett label, made at the same time the New Orleans Rhythm Kings were producing their first records. Morton appeared as pianist on some of these, marking the first recording in history of a "mixed" band of Negroes and whites. These were followed by a few sessions consisting of Morton piano solos or using small bands under his leadership. Subsequently the classic Victor items previously described were issued. After the 1928 session with Simeon and a slightly later one with Albert Nicholas replacing Simeon in substantially the same group, Morton made a number of record dates with larger groups. The New Orleans influence was always strong in these, although certain qualities that were purely Morton's own were more apparent here than previously. A late group of records for Victor in 1939, although using nine pieces instead of the usual New Orleans maximum of seven, found him returning strongly to the tradition. The personnel was somewhat mixed, but was clearly the best that could be assembled in New York at the time. It is a particularly interesting recording session because of a performance of *High Society* in which Alphonse Picou's traditional chorus is played as a solo by both Sidney Bechet and Albert Nicholas in the order indicated. Although Mr. Bechet is the more famous, it is clearly Mr. Nicholas who proves the more adept at interpreting this most difficult and beautiful selection.

Morton's stature as a jazz composer is, without question, of the greatest magnitude. The jazz repertoire has been greatly enriched by numerous and varied Morton compositions. Most of the selections he recorded were originals. Many interpretations of the works of others, including various compositions in the Library of Congress documentary recordings made under the supervision of Alan Lomax, lend further emphasis to his unusual capabilities. This is particularly noticeable in his playing of certain ragtime selections, where he would take strains with very simple left-hand configurations and build up whole new bass harmonies without in any respect altering or destroying the melodic line in his right hand.

As to his scholarship, the documentary recordings reveal a mind with a prodigious memory for names, places, and styles of playing, and with a deep-seated understanding of all the many facets of traditional jazz. It is particularly interesting to note that the accuracy of his imitations of various early cornetists was authenticated after the making of these recordings. His whistled imitation of Bunk Johnson's style was recorded for a generation that had never heard Bunk play. Johnson, after his subsequent "rejuvenation," played in a manner markedly similar to the whistled passages of Morton's imitation. Furthermore, Johnson himself made a documentary recording giving his own whistled imitation of the almost legendary style of the early New Orleans cornetist, Buddy Bolden. The manner tallies perfectly with a whistled Bolden imitation of Morton's. The ability of these men to whistle imitations of cornetists heard thirty-five to forty years earlier indicates their great devotion to the musical tradition from which they derived their strength and which they, in turn, so magnificently strengthened.

19. New Orleans jazz at home

1   Of all the music that has been created through the years that jazz has existed, probably no portion has been so completely neglected, and most improperly so, as the music in New Orleans itself following World War I. Everyone seems to assume that after Oliver, the Original Dixieland Jazz Band, and the New Orleans Rhythm Kings arrived in Chicago, New Orleans promptly ceased to hold any interest for the jazz enthusiast or student. The unfortunate truth of the matter is that the world is too prone to consider jazz solely in relation to the existence of phonograph records. Because the New Orleans recordings were few and little publicized, the continued existence of the purest of this music has been greatly neglected, both in the New Orleans style and in the Dixieland phase of the tradition. Worse yet, when the few records that were made in New Orleans in the 1920's were cut, the recording directors, with the foresight and understanding apparently typical of the breed, proceeded to cut numerous discs that were devoid of jazz interest, or nearly devoid of it, despite the presence of numerous excellent jazz musicians on many of them. It is fortunate, indeed, that a scant few sessions of some merit did manage to get issued or perhaps we should be without any indication whatever of the

really worth-while music of New Orleans in the post-World War I period.

The music of the colored New Orleans musicians has continued to the present day as a vital force. There has been no period when some of these men have not managed to keep bands of some sort going, particularly marching bands. Groups such as the Eureka Brass Band and the George Williams Band are still active in the city, playing for parades and funerals as they have always done. Another good brass band is led by clarinetist John Casimir, whose soulful playing is considered by many one of the very finest examples of New Orleans clarinet style, but has never been adequately recorded. Casimir and others in these bands have played in various jazz bands and dance bands, and are still doing so when such work is offered to them. Similarly, members of the George Lewis Band, which has been working in many different cities as a jazz group, take part in the activities of the street brass bands when they are in New Orleans and can do so. During Mardi Gras, not only are the "regular" brass bands found in action, but many other groups are formed just for this period. These usually include a number of veteran jazzmen and marching men who play in large measure for the sheer love of it. Even the venerable Alphonse Picou (originator of the famous *High Society* clarinet solo, standard test piece for New Orleans clarinetists) can be found in the line of march on occasion, still most active in a musical career that spans virtually the entire history of jazz as we have known it. Thus it may be noted that, while little attention has been given to the colored New Orleans bands representing the period from approximately 1920 until recently, the music was at no time really dormant. The Negro musicians have continued the tradition in the home city during a period when it received little notice from the world beyond.

Fortunately we do have a few examples of New Orleans bands as actually recorded "on the scene" with portable equipment during the 1920's. Two notable sessions in this category were those made by Louis Dumaine's Jazzola Eight and Sam Morgan's Jazz Band. Both groups consisted largely of musicians little known or unknown so far as jazz listeners outside New Orleans are concerned. Both offered ensemble playing of typically New Orleans style somewhat marred by the presence of the saxophone. The Dumaine band used a tenor sax, while the Morgan group used a tenor sax and an alto sax, with one of these played by a musician who "doubled" on clarinet part of the time. The Dumaine group is of significance because of the excellent trumpet work of Dumaine himself, recalled by many as one of the better players in the style. The Morgan band is historically important for the earliest recorded work of trombonist Jim Robinson, who was suggested for Bunk Johnson's recording band years later by collectors recalling these records.

The Louis Dumaine recordings include four selections, *Red Onion Drag, Franklin Street Blues, Pretty Audrey,* and *To-Wa-Ba-Ca-Wa.* The last is one of a number of variant titles applied to a traditional selection perhaps more frequently entitled *The Bucket's Got a Hole in It.* The traditional trombone solo for which the number is known is played by trombonist Earl Humphrey on this recording. Four selections are but scanty fare on which to judge any musician or group, but viewed rather as evidence in support of a reputation enjoyed among other musicians, they serve admirably as an indication of Dumaine's excellence. His style is very much in the tradition, possessing a melodic quality that is genuinely "pretty" without in any sense becoming cloying or maudlin. There is classic economy in his phrasing and ample evidence of fine technique for his purposes, marked particularly by a close, well-controlled vibrato, a most desirable attribute in any jazz cornetist. Work of this quality from players virtually unknown, save to their brother musicians, is a clear indication of how much of this music has been lost, and how much justification there must be to claims of ability for other cornetists such as Buddy Petit and Chris Kelly. These are two among many who are still remembered with great admiration by musicians who recall their playing from a period more than forty years in the past.

The Sam Morgan records are of particular interest as an illustration of instrumentation somewhat akin to that of King Oliver's Jazz Band, albeit not on quite the same level of musicianship. Recorded electrically in 1928, they offer the distinct advantage of a clarity not found on any of the Olivers of a half decade earlier. While the brass team, consisting of Sam and Isaiah Morgan, trumpets, and Jim Robinson, trombone, is perhaps not on the Olympian level of Oliver, Armstrong, and Dutrey, respectively, it is a team nonetheless to be reckoned with. The vibrato and somewhat sour intonation, combined with a certain strange quality of dignity, stamp their work as the purest of New Orleans efforts. More than most, this group seems to typify the efforts of well-practiced but unschooled musicians of the kind found in many of the "street bands." Perhaps the best recording of the group made by them is *Bogalusa Strut,* an excellent example of the type of selection referred to as a "stomp," possessing a melody that lends itself to forceful rhythmic treatment in a medium tempo. All the Morgan records are largely ensemble in nature with occasional "solo" passages more frequently utilized by several instruments from the ensemble. The afore-mentioned selection, for example, features passages which at first appear to be alto saxophone solos but are found to be saxophone duets in which a close harmonic polyphony is provided by the tenor sax.

Perhaps one of the most important of these little-known sessions recorded by New Orleans-style bands at home in the 1920's was a small group of selections by the Original Tuxedo Jazz Orchestra, once again a group featuring two cornets. In this instance Oscar "Papa" Celestin (who became leader of one of two groups which subsequently emerged from this organization) is first cornetist, while "Kid Shots" Madison plays second horn, and William Ridgely (nominal leader of this group and leader of the second faction when the split occurred) is the trombonist. Later records by the group under "Papa" Celestin are of some interest, but the few sides recorded with Ridgely and Madison are classics of their kind. Madison was always noted as an exponent of the difficult and uncommon "second-cornet" style, no better example of which is to be found on record than here. His playing, notably on *Careless Love*, reveals a part in which the harmony of the second horn is carried in a variation behind the melodic lead of Celestin's horn that adds immeasurably to the beauty of the performance. "Shots" Madison was not to be heard again on records until the jazz renaissance of the 1930's and 1940's, when he was recorded as lead horn on records with the band that normally was playing with Bunk Johnson at the time. His death shortly thereafter precludes any further additions to the evidence of a work universally admired by those familiar with his playing.

From the later 1920's until the summer of 1940, virtually nothing was done to preserve the continuing music of the colored players. In 1940, however, Heywood Broun, Jr., made arrangements to record a group of New Orleans veterans in an effort to capture the music of individuals known and respected by fellow jazz musicians but never recorded, with the additional motive of recording the music as played by the most archaic instrumentation possible. As a result there now exists a group of selections featuring Henry "Kid" Rena, a trumpeter of considerable repute, clarinetists Alphonse Picou and Louis Nelson, two of the most respected clarinetists in

179

New Orleans, Jim Robinson, found previously on the Sam Morgan records and subsequently to achieve his greatest fame with Bunk Johnson and George Lewis, guitarist Willie Santiago, Albert Gleny on string bass, and Joe Rena, drums. No piano is present and the rhythm is simple and uncluttered throughout. Kid Rena was the victim of a stroke sometime prior to the making of these discs, with the result that his face was partially paralyzed. His pleasing middle-register performance is, therefore, truly a remarkable accomplishment. Rena's approach is very straightforward, showing considerable respect for the melody "as written." His variations tend more toward simple embellishment than alteration, the original notation clearly implicit within each phrase enunciated by his horn. The use of two clarinets is rather unusual and interesting, although a certain degree of out-of-tuneness is present, marring the efforts. Both of these men were subsequently recorded during the present renaissance, Nelson having been captured on wax shortly prior to his death, playing selections showing clearly the full, warm tone and simple yet liquid styling that was a tremendous influence on many other New Orleans clarinetists. Picou plays his *High Society* solo on that selection and repeats it as a duet with Nelson in the final chorus, creating a magnificent ensemble with the brasses in a superb example of uncluttered yet complex New Orleans counterpoint. Robinson's playing throughout is in the rather personal style of tailgate trombone for which he has subsequently become famous. These records were made in the fear that they might represent the only examples extant of the playing of several pioneer jazzmen. Fortunately, renewed interest and a growing understanding of this music has led to a number of other recording ventures utilizing available talent in New Orleans. The work of William Russell and his associates has been particularly noteworthy and commendable in this field. Through recordings of many previously unrecognized musicians, a whole new concept of the scope of this music has been established, leading to a reassessment of values among the listeners and critics that has brought a stature to traditional jazz previously accorded it by a scant few devoted followers.

II   One of the by-products of the recent recording activity has been a growing realization that many, including perhaps some of the finest, New Orleans musicians are not recognized even today outside their immediate circle. Two 1955 LPs by the Paul Barbarin Band (Atlantic 1215 and Concert Hall Society CHJ-1006) indicate this most clearly. Most non-New Orleans audiences would be familiar only with leader-drummer Paul Barbarin and his popular nephew, banjoist Danny Barker. Perhaps Milton Hinton, bass, would be a familiar name as well, but he is not a regular member of this band, substituting for Richard MacLean, who is admired in New Orleans but is little known in the "outside" jazz world. The names of others present are familiar in part to more serious students of music. A little healthy consideration of these men and their backgrounds cannot but arouse some sober reflections on the part of those who feel that all the significant New Orleans instrumentalists have been recorded or are well known in the field through references made to them in various studies, articles, etc. It is all too true that many fine past and present New Orleans jazz instrumentalists have remained unsung and undiscovered while others not always worthy of attention have been lionized.

Paul Barbarin is a veteran of many years in music. In addition to New Orleans jazz, he has played in larger dance bands led by Armstrong, Luis Russell, Red Allen, and numerous others. Always a strong rhythm man, he consistently holds the drums in the musical background, an admirable display of a good taste that few other band leader drummers have shown.

Barbarin knew Oliver well and played with him for some time in Chicago prior to the formation of the group with the Dodds brothers and Louis Armstrong, known as King Oliver's Creole Jazz Band. Barbarin feels that this group was the best jazz band of all time. His admiration of Oliver is clearly reflected in his present band, which plays a number of Oliver's tunes, including a featured arrangement, similar to Oliver's, of *Someday, Sweetheart*. The dynamics of Barbarin's group also reflect this influence—in Barbarin's words, "I try to keep my band from blasting. Oliver is my model."

While the Oliver influence is present in the substance of Paul Barbarin's band concept, the form of the group differs somewhat from that of the Creole Jazz Band. Barbarin uses only one trumpet and solos are utilized more frequently. The band's repertoire, which is most varied, also includes a few Barbarin originals, such as *The Second Line* and *Bourbon Street Parade*, the latter being a very beautiful New Orleans march and perhaps the first new jazz tune of note to be produced in New Orleans since the jazz renaissance began. Even such unexpected fare as Ray Noble's *The Very Thought*

181

of You receives interesting traditional treatment from this organization.

Willie Humphrey, clarinetist in the group, is an outstanding musician whose father and grandfather were similarly notable performers. He has studied violin and plays saxophone, but prefers clarinet. In addition to his excellent jazz work, he has played in groups utilizing European classical material (overtures, etc.) and played in a Navy band during World War II. He has also played in swing groups, including a period on sax and clarinet with Red Allen's Band. When the famous test piece, *High Society*, is called for, Humphrey not only provides a flawless rendition of the difficult traditional solo, but plays, as well, a melodic original second-solo chorus that adds greatly to the interest of this beautiful old march. It might also be noted that Willie Humphrey is that rare individual, a capable instrumentalist who possesses tasteful showmanship. His effective stage presence is possessed of an intimate good humor, yet never at the cost of dignity or self-respect. Perhaps the most unusual attribute of this many-sided personality is his ability as a teacher of music. Humphrey is very well known in New Orleans for his fine work in this respect. Although his particular specialty is reed instruments, he has proved capable in other areas.

One of Willie Humphrey's students, John Brunious, first acquired a horn in 1938 and became a hit within a few weeks. The book *Jazzmen*, which was being written at that time, makes mention of his playing. Brunious is the trumpeter on the Barbarin LPs mentioned earlier and has been with this group for some time. He is a graduate of Piney Woods College, where he studied music. He pursued his musical studies in New York at the Juilliard School. Brunious has done arrangements for the popular dance bands of Del Courtney and Johnny Long, has played with the modern Negro vocalist Billy Eckstine and, surprisingly, with the "be-bop" trumpeter Dizzy Gillespie. It is most refreshing to find an instrumentalist possessing so varied a background, but maintaining both skill and taste within the jazz tradition.

Pianist Lester Santiago, who has been with Barbarin for several years, comes from a family known for the musical activities of several generations. His facile technique and dependable rhythm would be assets in any jazz group. The piano certainly was a natural instrument when one realizes that his eleven brothers and one sister have all been fine pianists. Burnell Santiago, a brother who has since

182

died, was discussed in *Jazzmen* as an example of an outstanding New Orleans pianist of the time (1939).

Stylistically, Lester Santiago and Alton Purnell of the George Lewis Band are of particular note for considerable differences in approach from that of Jelly Roll Morton. While Purnell and Santiago are quite unlike each other, both differ particularly from Morton in their use of the treble. A fine example of Santiago's piano is to be found on the afore-mentioned Atlantic LP, his solo at the start of *I Wish I Could Shimmy Like My Sister Kate* being an excellent example of his facility and taste.

Banjoist Danny Barker is, of course, a familiar figure on the jazz scene. He is well known for his guitar and banjo work with various groups, particularly in New York. He is also familiar as a vocalist in certain Creole tunes and blues.

The most surprising personality in this band, however, is a gentleman unknown outside New Orleans prior to traveling with this group. Trombonist Bob Thomas, who was born in 1898, has been playing trombone since the age of fifteen. He is one of those modest, soft-spoken persons who rarely receive the attention they deserve, even though possessed of creative abilities. Clarinetist Willie Humphrey's grandfather, another Humphrey who played many instruments, gave Thomas lessons on the trombone around 1913. In 1915 he played with Louis Armstrong in the Young Olympia Brass Band, most of whose members were in short pants, playing jazz in parades and at dances. He recalls Louis as "kind of a bad boy" who came from a tough neighborhood. Thomas used to dance to Kid Ory's band in 1916; at the time it included Mutt Carey, cornet, bassist Ed Garland, and a violinist named Bigard (Carey and Garland were to be found with an Ory band again thirty years later), and remembers first hearing Ory at a school function in 1906 or 1907. Thomas himself played with many of the famous jazz musicians, including Kid Rena, whom he considered a wonderful trumpeter. A schooled musician, he has played in many large dance bands and a thirty-four-piece symphonic group in addition to numerous jazz bands. Stylistically, he appears to have a strong resemblance to Honoré Dutrey, for whom Thomas professes considerable respect. Upon hearing himself recently on records for the first time, he is said to have been astonished at his resemblance to Jack Carey. Carey, never recorded, was the famous trombone-playing brother of Mutt Carey, and it is said that, in early days, *Tiger Rag* was known as *Play Jack Carey*. Thomas, although capable of "rough"

183

playing, prefers a soft style and states that the others in the Barbarin group share this feeling. While his phrasing is simple, it is possessed of subtleties that are very rewarding to the closely attentive listener.

As a musician Thomas is important in jazz. As a symbol of the little known and unknown jazz musicians who clearly are superior to many jazz "greats" he is equally important. Too many persons listen to shoddy imitations or second-rate players only because they were available at the door of a New York or Chicago recording studio. Trombonists such as Bob Thomas or, for that matter, Ed Pierson or Bill Matthews remain almost completely unknown. In New Orleans, and in many other places, good musicians and good music are being neglected because they are not sufficiently convenient to the entertainment industry's assembly lines. This is a principal reason why the interested listener never takes too seriously the popular acclaim of a musician, preferring always to judge by listening for himself or on the basis of opinion expressed by truly qualified observers whose standards of judgment can withstand the listener's scrutiny.

III Similarly active at the present time is the hard-driving, rough-and-ready band of George Lewis. Perhaps only two of its members could qualify as reading musicians, but the group's creativity in jazz is nonetheless very considerable. The leader's clarinet is played in a very liquid style with much of the Creole influence in evidence, but the blues manner also is present. Lewis himself acknowledges the very considerable influence of "Big Eye" Louis Nelson upon his playing. Although untrained and unschooled in the usual musical sense, George Lewis plays many passages that require great dexterity in execution. His style contains a level of emotion that is obviously inspired, particularly on a piece such as his own *Burgundy Street Blues,* where the instrument sounds very much like the voice of a contralto singer.

With Lewis, since the time when both played with Bunk Johnson, is Jim Robinson, a colorful trombonist whose shouting style of trombone is possessed of an incredible rhythmic force. His hard-hitting attack is the perfect foil for Lewis' clarinet. Where Lewis plays introspectively or at least expresses the serious side of life, Robinson is overflowing with the joy of living, expressing it lustily in a most determined trombone style. He has said that it is his desire in music to make people happy, and when those listening or dancing are enjoying a "good time," he feels his music is accomplishing its purpose. Hearing Robinson in good spirits before a contented audience is, indeed, quite an exhilarating experience. The counterpoint established between Robinson and Lewis is frequently of real beauty. On occasions when no trumpet is present they will take turns playing lead, creating very great contrasts in their treatment of individual selections.

A comparatively recent arrival in this group is Avery "Kid" Howard, a trumpeter whose playing and singing have proved him to be most worthy and well qualified. Although he is an interesting performer, a degree of wildness was present in his work as recorded on one date with Lewis in 1943. Today, however, a greater degree of restraint is in evidence, and his typically New Orleans lead style, at times very powerful, is well suited to this band. He is a more schooled musician than most members of the group, but fortunately is at least equally a "natural" musician, an essential quality in any trumpet playing with this band. His sincere approach on spirituals is very moving, while his rollicking lead on an old-timer such as *The Bucket's Got a Hole in It,* recorded on Blue Note LP 7027, is utterly delightful.

The unobtrusive drumming of Joe Watkins, always in good taste, is the keystone of the rhythm structure in this happy combination. Rarely playing solo, he contents himself with an occasional pleasant vocal and then disappears behind the drums once more, caring only about maintaining his unfailing support of the others.

Alton Purnell, pianist, also sings some of the group's selections. Very much the band pianist, his occasional solo forays are similarly interesting, often possessing a strange, almost oriental charm in the treble phrasing.

Banjoist Lawrence Marrero and string bassist Alcide "Slow Drag" Pavageau are old and good friends of George Lewis. For many years it was the practice of all three to gather at the Lewis home and play for their own amusement. These men and Jim Robinson were the nucleus of the Bunk Johnson band which recorded in 1943, and they have worked and played together ever since save for a period when Marrero was in ill health and the very adept "Creole George" Guesnon occupied his chair. Marrero and Pavageau create a very powerful four-four beat that has always been a trademark of this group.

Like the Barbarin band, this group has brought to light several musicians who would have remained unknown and unsung elsewhere. The only records of Elmer Talbert, an excellent New Orleans trumpet player who died in 1950, were made with George Lewis, while "Kid" Howard is not found elsewhere on record either. Lewis himself had never been recorded in all his years of playing and remained unheard of outside the home city until Bunk Johnson's first records were released. When Johnson was asked to use trombonist Jim Robinson at the time, Johnson himself suggested Lewis as the proper clarinetist to play in a group with Robinson.

The effect of this group in the jazz renaissance has been most significant and unusual. Because of the absence of contrived polish, harmonic and other, in its performances, one would expect the public to reject it. People trying to "merchandise" jazz to a new audience always feel that a sweeter-toned band with a docile ensemble approach is the best introduction. The Lewis group, however, can probably boast of more overnight converts to jazz than any of the compromise groups. In recent years it has developed a large following, including many listeners with no previous acquaintance with jazz.

The Lewis and Barbarin bands represent only a small portion of the Negro jazz players in New Orleans. Such men as Albert Burbank, the Creole clarinetist, and trumpeters Al Alcorn and Ernie Cagnoletti are always ready to play the music. Every Mardi Gras produces innumerable bands, many of which play good jazz using musicians who are unknown save to their immediate audience. Today, as in the past, there is more music in New Orleans than the casual observer can ever hope to hear. The more diligent of traditional jazz recorder-scholars, including Frederic Ramsey, Boris Rose, and William Russell, have created impressive recorded evidence of the jazz tradition's continuing fecundity.

20. White New Orleans: the Dixieland school

1   Of all the factions constituting traditional jazz, none has been
the subject of more acrimonious dispute than the white musicians
and groups from New Orleans. During and immediately after World
War I, they were important beyond New Orleans on the jazz scene.
Many of the musicians who went north were rapidly swallowed up
in very non-New Orleans type bands, while a large proportion of
them chose to return to the comforts of their home town. Had New
Orleans been a major center of the phonograph record industry,
their influence would have been far greater, but only a small number of records made in New Orleans have been issued. Records
made there have been just sufficient in number to imply how much
of the very best of this music was not being heard in Chicago or
New York or Los Angeles. Stars were made of others fortunate
enough to be near the means of "communication."

   Because the white records were few and little known at the time
of issue, they were largely overlooked. When the jazz revival got
under way in the late 1930's, the more obvious frenetic style of the
Chicago school became the dominant influence so far as "white"
jazz was concerned, while the reverse-Jim Crowism that has too
frequently been found in jazz criticism focused all attention given

187

New Orleans music on the work of the Negro. Moreover, the comic effects in the records of the Original Dixieland Jazz Band and others were pointed out as examples of "corn," a term of opprobrium that any young pseudo sophisticate of the middle 1930's considered the ultimate in artistic condemnation.

Luckily, this particular brand of jazz managed to hold a small but dedicated group of admirers through the years, plus a number of musicians within the fold who took the music very seriously and have fought doggedly to preserve and develop it. It is probably true that the real Dixieland groups are only now beginning to get the long overdue recognition among jazz students and enthusiasts that they have always deserved.

A great deal of heat, and very little light, have been shed on the relationship between Negro and white musicians in New Orleans. Much emphasis has been placed upon the differences between the musicians in their ways of playing, their personalities, and just about every other category of reference applicable to human beings. That there have been some differences in approach and manner is certainly an established fact. It is an established fact that the Negro popular musician and the white popular musician have shown similar differences in concept elsewhere. What is too often totally overlooked, even by some of the musicians themselves, is the existence of strong similarities between the styles of the Negro and the white jazzmen of New Orleans.

Although racial tensions and the limitations of Jim Crowism and custom imposed barriers between musicians of the two races, these barriers were perhaps far less significant in the early part of this century than many have assumed. Musicians of both races fraternized to a considerable extent before or after working hours, and much of the so-called "lifting" of each other's styles that supporters of either school frequently accused the other of practicing might better be described as gifts from these sessions rather than thefts. On the one hand there can be little doubt that the basic origins of the music were largely Negro; it cannot be denied on the other that white musicians very early took to the music and were largely instrumental in its development. The multiplicity of bands and of occasions on which bands could be heard in early twentieth-century New Orleans was such that a very considerable amount of give-and-take between groups, separated more by mere custom than by racial feeling, was inevitable.

Today, discussion of the early days with the white New Orleans

188

veterans shows that many of them took a keen interest in the music of both groups and certainly were not lacking in knowledge of the Negro musicians and their efforts. It was a startling experience for one of the present writers to discuss this matter with clarinetist Gus Muller and cornetist Raymond Lopez in the spring of 1955. They enumerated more than sixty Negro musicians by name, from circa 1910–11, naming their instruments and in most instances commenting on their individual manners of playing. Such familiar names as Oliver, Perez, Baquet, and others were among those discussed, but so, too, were many of lesser note in critical annals, plus yet others whose names have never appeared in jazz literature. When musicians can clearly recall facts of this sort after a lapse of forty-five years, it is safe to assume that they were familiar with these people and their work. Further, it is a known fact, confirmed by the afore-mentioned gentlemen, that Larry Shields, late clarinetist of the Original Dixieland Jazz Band, was an enthusiastic admirer of Sidney Bechet and his style of clarinet. Thus, on the first white records, made by the Original Dixieland Jazz Band in 1917, a clarinet is heard whose style is based in part upon the work of a Negro musician, a musician fated subsequently to become a stellar performer in popular music far beyond pure New Orleans jazz. Indeed, among white New Orleans musicians it has been said that Shields was virtually the only one who attempted to sound specifically like any other particular musician. Conversely, the Negro musicians of the day were familiar with the work of the white musicians. Both Mutt Carey and Bunk Johnson have commented favorably on the Brunies brothers, in particular, several of whom were important to the Dixieland tradition. The almost legendary white cornetist Lawrence Vega was also regarded favorably by the colored players.

The white jazz of early twentieth-century New Orleans was pretty generally played with the same instruments and repertory that were common to the Negro music. Tunes readily passed between groups, and many of the subsequent harsh words about who "originated" this or that composition seem ludicrous when it is borne in mind that many of the melodies were wandering about nameless for years before any attempt was made to copyright them. There can be no doubt, for example, that such "originals" as *Tiger Rag*, which is claimed by LaRocca and Shields of the Original Dixieland Jazz Band on copyright, were around long before the alleged composers were aware of music. Many of these tunes, or portions of them, had their origins in the folk music of the American Negro. At the same

189

time, it must also be recognized that the Negro musicians used a great deal of white folk and popular material in their playing. Neither the character of the composer nor the date of his work necessarily affects the desirability of his product in jazz.

Recorded examples of the various earlier white musicians' work are not always fully indicative of their style of playing, many of them having made records of a "commercial" nature at the behest of record companies. These bore no true relationship to their "on-the-job" approach. Fortunately, a few groups were well recorded, and some of the older musicians have been captured on wax in more recent time in revival groups that give some indication of their concepts. For the rest, reputations must depend upon the memories of older musicians and listeners, a most unfortunate circumstance in jazz, where the art is found in performance and not on paper.

II   Typical of groups whose full abilities we can never appreciate was Tom Brown's Band from Dixieland, the first white band to leave the Crescent City; it played in Chicago in 1915. Subsequent recordings (released and unreleased) by individual musicians and groups of musicians from this band indicate readily enough the high quality that must have characterized their efforts, but the exact sound of their ensemble cannot be captured by hearing the members individually with other groups. Tom Brown himself, a man now in his seventies, is a trombonist and musician of very considerable ability, still amply capable of playing in the traditional manner. His subtlety of execution makes a simple-sounding passage become fraught with inner significance at every turn, whether he is playing in the long-toned, legato fashion typified by Honoré Dutrey of the King Oliver Band or in the brusque, staccato, "bicycle-horn" style common to the trombonists of the marching bands. Ray Lopez was cornetist in this group, playing excellent jazz lead horn much of the time, but also indulging in some highly unusual solo work, featuring a very punchy attack with a hat-type mute. The clarinetist, Gus Muller, played an unmistakably New Orleans line, notable particularly for a beautiful, organlike tone in the lower register. Pianist Arnold Loyocano was a valuable man because, in addition to his fine rhythmic support at the keyboard, he doubled on string bass when the band would ride about the City of New Orleans and there was no space available on the wagon for a piano. With the help of drummer William Lambert a beat was always maintained that obviated the necessity for additional rhythm support. This five-part instrumentation, identical with the later Original Dixieland Jazz Band's, affords possibilities markedly similar to those of the classic string quartet. Where musicians and material are adequate, artistic creation of the highest type may be known. Conversely, use of improper material or poor musicianship stands out glaringly in such groups, for each part is significant in its own right and a weak melodic line cannot be buried under the lush harmonies of more numerous instruments.

The importance of considering the music of Brown's group lies in a recognition of the contrast it must have offered to the recordings of the Original Dixieland Jazz Band and the subsequent work of the New Orleans Rhythm Kings. A few records made by the latter group with only five pieces may bear a marked resemblance to the style of the Brown band. In general, the Original Dixieland approach was rougher, La Rocca's cornet being somewhat excited as well as "exciting," while Larry Shields's clarinet rarely descended from the upper register, and Eddie Edwards played trombone with considerable firmness of tone and sharp, staccato phrasing. In the case of the New Orleans Rhythm Kings, a fuller band is generally used with added bass and banjo as well as tenor sax. As previously stated, however, the five-piece line-up of cornet, trombone, clarinet, piano, and drums was used on a few of their recordings. On these a strong tonal similarity to the Brown band must have existed, as indicated by comparison of the individual parts. Leon Rappolo, like Gus Muller, favored the lower register far more than did Shields, trombonist George Brunis is said to have studied trombone under Tom Brown, and Paul Mares played a lead style that was probably far closer to Lopez than to La Rocca. Here too there are differences to be noted. Trombonist George Brunis is less staccato than Edwards, but his playing is marked with a forthright power and direct approach. Brown is capable of power but shows a greater degree of subtlety in his phrasing, the contrast between them being similar to that existing between Kid Ory and the milder but decidedly no less convincing style of Honoré Dutrey. Leon Rappolo, on the other hand, provided a highly introspective voice to the New Orleans Rhythm Kings, while Gus Muller of Brown's band, who was not known as "the little bantam rooster" without reason, took a more forthright approach even though much of his work was in lower register. Paul Mares' cornet on record shows quite clearly the influence of King Oliver, who was playing at that time in Chicago, while Ray Lopez reveals a style on records, unfortunately never issued, that is somewhat like that heard later from Sharkey Bonano. This is by no means meant to imply that Bonano "copied" Lopez; rather it is a recognition that they are stylistically similar. Comparisons of the rhythm instruments would be difficult and unfair, unfortunately, as the recording techniques of the era forced the drummers in particular to utilize dynamics in recording different from their normal. Many of the sounds emanating from piano were muffled to a degree that would make comparisons difficult at best.

In general, it may be said of these three groups that the Original Dixieland and the Rhythm Kings represent divergent tendencies, with the Brown band in most respects using an intermediate approach. A high degree of syncopation bordering on straight ragtime is evident in the work of the Original Dixieland Jazz Band, along with a loud, exuberant, at times almost belligerent quality. By contrast, the New Orleans Rhythm Kings used a considerably simpler rhythmic approach. In place of a syncopated common time with marked emphasis on the second and fourth beats, their playing was only moderately syncopated, at times almost "straight," with some tendency toward a four-four time that is only slightly accented. Further, the music was considerably softer much of the time, particularly on later recordings with Santo Pecora on trombone. In general it may be said that this group showed smoothness rather than the emphatic virility found in the style of the Original Dixieland Jazz Band. The music of the Tom Brown band was more strongly syncopated much of the time, yet in dynamics it approached the manner of the Rhythm Kings. This intermediate style is perhaps more typical of Dixieland jazz than the styles of the other two bands as exemplified in their recordings.

The median approach of Brown's band is also to be found on a record made by Johnny Bayersdorffer's Jazzola Novelty Orchestra in 1924. Only two selections were recorded by this group, but many jazz students and enthusiasts consider them among the best examples of Dixieland jazz ever recorded. The tunes, *Waffle Man's Call* and *I Wonder Where My Easy Rider's Riding Now*, are typical multithemed traditional selections played at bright tempos. The over-all sound of the band is decidedly hot. Their rhythm swings somewhat in the manner of the New Orleans Rhythm Kings, but with an aggressive quality in the horn work distinctly reminiscent of the Original Dixieland Jazz Band. Bayersdorffer himself is featured on cornet, while the remainder of the group comprises Nuncio Scaglione, clarinet, Tom Brown, trombone, Johnny Miller, piano,

Alcide "Slow Drag" Pavageau of George Lewis' band.

Members of Paul Barbarin's band. *Left to right:* Bob Thomas, John
Brunious (hidden), Willie Humphrey.

Steve Loyocano, banjo, Chink Martin, tuba, and Leo Adde (or possibly Ray Bauduc), drums. The cornet plays a decidedly hot style, using a partially muted effect to vary the tonal quality of some choruses and breaks. Scaglione's style is markedly similar to that of Larry Shields, although by no means a direct copy. Tom Brown is very much as he usually is, providing a tailgate trombone counterpoint in excellent taste throughout the ensembles. The rhythm is distinctly an improvement over that of most typical white bands of the period outside of New Orleans and is perhaps better than most of the other white New Orleans groups on record as well. Here is an example—there are several others—of a superior group and superior jazz instrumentalists captured only once on record. Bayersdorffer and Scaglione have not been recorded elsewhere, yet obviously they are among the better white jazzmen.

The Halfway House Orchestra is another New Orleans band that deserves greater recognition than it has received. Unfortunately, most of its records were made without the use of trombone, with the added disadvantage that several were made purely for the popular dance trade. One of the records, however, has the full traditional instrumentation with tenor sax added, and this record alone is considered by many as among the best in quality made by a white band from New Orleans. The selections are entitled *Barataria* and *Pussy Cat Rag*. Personnel is not at all certain, but it is believed that Leon Rappolo is doubling clarinet and saxophone, and that Charlie Cordella also is playing reed parts. Further to confuse matters, these men were stylistically similar in many ways, and it is said that they exchanged instruments after playing the first side of the two records. Albert Brunies and an unknown trombonist, rumored to be Joe Loyocano, are also present. This group shows distinct resemblances to the New Orleans Rhythm Kings in rhythm, dynamics, and over-all approach.

An interesting theory sometimes advanced by Dixieland enthusiasts states that the general concept expressed in the music of the New Orleans Rhythm Kings represented in large measure an approach of the numerous Brunies brothers. It is known that Merritt Brunies was intended to be their cornetist, but was replaced by Paul Mares when Brunies decided he did not want to go to Chicago. George Brunis (as noted, he has dropped the "e" from "Brunies") did make the trip as trombonist and performs on most of their records. The records of the Rhythm Kings show a sufficient resemblance in several respects to the records both of the Albert Brunies group and of certain others by Merritt and Henry Brunies to make the theory plausible.

The middle twenties produced one cornetist in particular who has been a potent figure ever since in the realm of New Orleans jazz: trumpeter Sharkey Bonano. Bonano has been recognized by many jazz enthusiasts as one of the hottest white trumpeters of all time, possessing a biting tone and a strong attack that are his trademark. Though he is somewhat more Negroid in his concept than many of the earlier players, there are distinct marks of LaRocca and the Brunies brothers in his styling, indicating not so much a copy of their work as that his is derived from the same sources. It has been said that he was tried by the Wolverines to fill the vacancy left by Beiderbecke, but was rejected, ostensibly because he was not sufficiently seasoned. It is the opinion of many white New Orleans enthusiasts that in reality he set a hotter pace than the Wolverines were able to meet. Bonano has been noted particularly for his work on a record of *Panama* and *Dippermouth Blues* by Johnny Miller and His New Orleans Boys, a band which included the late Sidney Arodin on clarinet. He also made a number of noteworthy records with varied personnel under his own name, in particular a coupling of *High Society* and *I'm Satisfied with My Gal*, featuring trombonist Santo Pecora and the excellent clarinet of Irving Fazola, who was later to become famous with the Bob Crosby band of the 1930's. During the period when white jazz activity was at its lowest ebb, Sharkey Bonano was one of the few musicians who managed to continue playing professionally in the traditional manner, bridging the lean swing-period years with a music that compromised but little with alien types of jazz. While certain suggestions of swing styling are noticeable in his work, it has always maintained a distinctly New Orleans quality, influenced very little, or perhaps not at all, by the Chicagoans or the New Yorkers.

A contemporary of Bonano's, Joseph "Wingy" Manone, made a name for himself during the 1930's more for his comedy than for his jazz, although much of his trumpet work has been very satisfying. His combination of slapstick humor and a genuinely hot horn has brought him a devoted following, many of whom obtained their introduction to jazz through hearing him and his various groups. In addition to playing a good Dixieland lead style, he is noted for an amazing ability to assemble improbable people and make good music with them. It is not at all unusual for Manone to appear with a group containing no musician ever heard of among jazz enthu-

194

siasts and to proceed to play a brand of Dixieland distinctly superior to that purveyed by many a group boasting an all-star personnel.

The major force in maintaining the white Dixieland tradition through the swing era, however, was a surprising "compromise" band. The Bob Crosby band, formed from the remnants of a previous Ben Pollock group, was assembled with the basic idea in mind of playing semitraditional jazz while fulfilling the requirements of the typical commercial dance band or "swing" band of the time. Included in the group were New Orleans musicians Eddie Miller, tenor saxophone, Ray Bauduc, drums, Nappy Lamare, guitar, and subsequently Irving Fazola, clarinet. The Dixieland flavor was somewhat evident in the work of the large band. Perhaps more important was the group within the band called the Bob Cats. This was actually an eight-piece Dixieland band, using the full traditional grouping plus tenor saxophone to play many of the familiar Dixieland tunes. In a period when traditional activity was at its lowest ebb, this group did a great deal to remind audiences of a music that many younger people would not otherwise have known existed. The Bob Cats generally played arrangements, but there was a looseness in them that permitted some improvisation, and if the music was not so warm as that of the New Orleans Rhythm Kings, it at least offered a freshness and a melodic concept that were indications of how much was lacking in the monotonous rhythm-for-rhythm's-sake music of the swing groups.

III   During World War II, a little white jazz was to be heard in New Orleans from groups including Sharkey Bonano, Irving Fazola, and Julian Laine, but it was not until the postwar period that a distinct increase in the tempo of musical activities there became evident. A number of veteran musicians who had played with the Rhythm Kings, the Halfway House Orchestra, and other early New Orleans jazz bands began to join with Fazola and Bonano in weekly jazz concerts. The New Orleans Jazz Club started a program of activities destined to renew audience interest in the home city of the music. Thanks to these efforts, many white musicians who had been all but forgotten again became active in the music. In addition, the encouragement of a growing audience led to the formation of new groups of young musicians bent upon furthering the Dixieland tradition.

Two semiprofessional musicians, men who earn their living in other ways but have an interest in the music that transcends the

195

amateur level, are among those who have done most for the music in New Orleans during recent years. John W. Hyman, a teacher of mechanical drawing, is better known to jazz enthusiasts as Johnny Wiggs, a cornetist combining a taste for Beiderbecke with a Dixieland concept flavored with the New Orleans Negro influence. Dr. Edmond Souchon II, an eminent surgeon, is also eminent in jazz circles for his playing of banjo and guitar. He is one of those unusually gifted individuals who possess both heart and intellect. His intellect finds its jazz role in his vast library of material on traditional jazz and related forms of music, while his warm and generous heart becomes evident in his active participation in jazz performances. A banjoist and guitar player of very considerable ability, he is also a jazz vocalist of incredible power.

Messrs. Souchon and Wiggs have made a number of records that represent the most serious and the most successful attempts of any present-day white groups in New Orleans to play the traditional music as it should be played. Two of these records are of the utmost significance. A full band is featured on one of them, LP recording number MTT-2084 of the Tempo Label, while the second is jazz chamber music in a very real sense, played by cornet, clarinet, guitar, and string bass on Paramount LP number 107. These records possess a significance that will be fully appreciated only when a proper perspective can be attained for judging the musical product of the current era. The full-band record is important both musically and historically, being one of the few examples of trombonist Tom Brown's work recorded in a traditional band. The quartet recordings are true classics in the field, remarkable examples of jazz defined in terms of its stark instrumental essentials. A neophyte hearing his first jazz on these two longplay records would receive an incomparable introduction to jazz values in the tradition.

The Tempo record was made with a band comprising Johnny Wiggs, cornet, Harry Shields, clarinet, Tom Brown, trombone, Ray Bauduc, drums, Edmond Souchon, banjo and guitar, Stanley Mendelson, piano, and Sherwood Mangiapane, string bass. The selections include originals by members of the group, traditional tunes of both Negro and white origin, familiar popular standard tunes, blues, and a most interesting original march on which Tom Brown in particular shines nobly. Throughout the recording date, Brown's very authentic tailgate style is constantly in evidence, tying together the ensembles and occasionally backing a clarinet solo in a most effective manner. His own solo choruses are economically phrased

196

and immensely subtle, boasting the unique rhythmic effects, and the strategic moments of silence broken by sudden thrusts, that are the hallmark of the classic New Orleans trombonist. Despite playing with either false teeth or no teeth, depending upon his mood of the moment, Mr. Brown, a man in his seventies, turns in a performance here that clearly proves him master of the Dixieland trombone. Without ever commandeering more attention than is his due, he is certainly the hero of the session.

Johnny Wiggs, although perhaps somewhat overshadowed on this occasion by Brown, is a musician eminently worthy of attention. His lead possesses a natural vibrato and strictly jazz tone, with never an excessive use of flowery phrasing and never an effort to dominate the ensemble. There can be no doubt of one particular virtue in Mr. Wiggs: he clearly displays an exact knowledge of his instrument's function in the traditional ensemble. No cornet or trumpet player now active among the white musicians in New Orleans is so well grounded in the traditional concept as Wiggs. Certain others may possess greater range or staying power, but in matters of taste he is plainly the master. Others have flash, but Wiggs has depth.

Harry Shields, brother of the Original Dixieland Band's clarinetist, Larry Shields, performs here with the fire that has always differentiated the Dixieland clarinetist of New Orleans from his contemporaries elsewhere. New Orleans musicians of both races have generally been easy to differentiate from jazz musicians of other localities, and nowhere more evidently than in the field of clarinet players. There is a piercing, live quality to their tone and attack that is uniquely their own. Very few players elsewhere come within range of it at any time. The combination of Shields's piercing clarinet, Wiggs's warm-toned cornet lead, and the firm, powerful support of Tom Brown's trombone creates an ensemble that is "authentic" Dixieland in the best sense of the term.

Pianist Stanley Mendelson plays with taste and finesse, whether rendering a well-conceived solo or providing simple but effective background to the wind instruments. In the latter task he is supported by the propulsive but unprepossessing bass of Sherwood Mangiapane and the very two-beat drumming of Ray Bauduc, a New Orleans drummer famed during the swing era for his Dixieland style with the Bob Crosby band. In a period when the hard-pounding "jungle" style of swing drummer Krupa was the fashion, Bauduc was famed for the light, deft touch that is the quality most desired in a Dixieland band. Rounding out the rhythm section of the Wiggs group, Dr. Souchon is responsible in no small part for the strong, steady, well-disciplined rhythm of this unusual session. He is also featured as a vocalist in several selections on the record.

We have alluded to a record made on the Paramount label by Johnny Wiggs, cornet, Ray Burke, clarinet, Edmond Souchon, guitar, and Sherwood Mangiapane, string bass. Groups of this size have recorded before, of course, but usually with a different choice of rhythm instruments. Here, incredibly, are four men with the temerity to think they can sound like a full band—and they do! Their success in so doing is distinctly reminiscent of the Louisiana Five, in which clarinetist-leader Alcide Nunez and his very warm horn, aided by Alfred Laine's trombone, sets the standard for all subsequent jazz "chamber" groups. Apart from a "medley" of badly engineered tapes on part of one side, the Wiggs quartet provides a most unusual and successful example of what clearly is jazz chamber music. Only the addition of a good trombone would be needed to make an excellent performance a perfect one. Its absence is apologized for in many places by bassist Mangiapane or guitarist Souchon, either of whom tastefully "fills in" a trombonistic part in various choruses to achieve balance. Burke and Wiggs improvise freely and beautifully above the surprisingly strong rhythm, their moods varying from the euphoric to the somber, with consistent quality. Most unusual is *When You Wore a Tulip* played in lower key than normal, making for an entirely different mood from that generally created by this selection. The performance is a pleasant vehicle for two soft-toned horns in low register—a most successful experiment. Standout selection is *Mama's Baby Boy*, a rollicking New Orleans stomp, sounding as if at least twice as many musicians are there to drive it down. The rough, shouting vocal chorus of this "lullaby" as provided by Dr. Souchon is clearly unrelated to his bedside manner, serving to stimulate the little group into some of the most exhilarating ensemble choruses of recent time in white New Orleans music.

In this LP it is clearly evident that the interaction of Negro and white music is a continuing factor in New Orleans. Despite Wiggs's preoccupation with Beiderbecke, his style is one of the most Negroid among white New Orleans horns, while Ray Burke shows clearly a fusion of the two sources in his work. Burke and Bob Helm of San Francisco are perhaps the most successful among the white clari-

198

netists who have attempted to play in the manner of the New Orleans Negro.

The determined, optimistic effort of this little foursome is both an indication of the continuing vitality of jazz in the city of its childhood and a lesson to those who are inclined to feel that the tradition has passed away. With numerous musicians still playing it and many younger ones entering the fold, Dixieland jazz can look to a healthy future. Young bands such as the Dukes of Dixieland and the George Girard group, though somewhat tainted by outside influences, are working their way toward the core of the tradition. The day may not be far off when another Halfway House Orchestra or New Orleans Rhythm Kings may be born. Classic bands are not daily creations. The seed, however, is there and ready to grow.

21. Bix Beiderbecke, creative bandsman

1   One of the few names in traditional jazz that need no introduction to a wider audience is that of Leon Bismarck "Bix" Beiderbecke, featured cornetist of the Paul Whiteman and Jean Goldkette
bands in the late 1920's and early 1930's. His spectacular improvi-
sational abilities and his early demise readily lent themselves to the
creation of a modern legend and many have been the hucksters
clambering aboard the band wagon who, if subjected to examination,
could not differentiate between Beiderbecke and Harry James.

Among traditional-jazz lovers, appreciation of Beiderbecke seems
to have run in cycles. There has always been a hard core of admirers who have never been swayed in their admiration. Many
others (including one of the present writers) have blown hot and
cold at different times. During the swing era, his work was considered by virtually everyone, beyond the afore-mentioned hard core,
strictly as a source of hot solos. The growth of interest in Chicago
jazz in the late 1930's began to focus some attention on the band
work of the Wolverines, Beiderbecke's early group. Even here, the
thinking was inclined to accept ensembles solely as a source of additional phrases from Beiderbecke, the genius of the cornet.

Following this period, and more particularly following the publication of *Jazzmen* in 1939, the revival of interest in New Orleans jazz began to get under way in earnest. The growing attention to the work of Negro musicians that preceded this era was now magnified into a reverse-Jim Crowism that engulfed all before it. Many Beiderbecke recordings were sold and auctioned by the afflicted in order to invest in the Louis Armstrong Hot Fives and the Jelly Roll Morton Red Hot Peppers. White music had suddenly become 100 per cent "corn," and those who found substance in it became social pariahs. In the background, however, was a group of enthusiasts whose heads were bloody but unbowed because of an unswerving loyalty to the white Dixieland music of New Orleans. Their numbers have grown steadily, and while many of the ardent reverse-Jim Crowists have plunged into "modern" jazz, the Dixieland enthusiasts have continued to gather strength. Now, at long last, it has become socially acceptable to appreciate and enjoy the Original Dixieland Jazz Band or the New Orleans Rhythm Kings for what they were rather than merely as a stage in transition to something of greater "significance." It is in this frame that Beiderbecke now receives major attention among students of traditional jazz, Beiderbecke and the Wolverines having in large measure descended from this tradition.

The late Harry K. Crawford, one of the foremost students of jazz and an authority on popular recorded music, debunked the concept of Beiderbecke's early style as something totally new or original. While he yielded to no one in his admiration of Beiderbecke, he always maintained that the basic style was not "invented" by Beiderbecke, but was common to many young white cornetists of the period. Crawford referred to it as "Indiana" style and was of the firm opinion that at least some of Beiderbecke's earlier "imitators" were not necessarily aware of Beiderbecke. There seems to be considerable justification for this opinion. Others undoubtedly heard the same early recordings and listened in person to the same musicians as did Beiderbecke. Given substantially similar musical environment and the requisite intellect, there would be every reason to expect similar musical ideas. Too often in jazz circles it is assumed that certain musicians are "copying" others or, conversely, that certain others are almost totally original. The truth is rarely found in large degree in either premise. A classic example is trombonist Jack Teagarden, who has often been accused of copying the Negro trombonist Jimmy Harrison. It has been said by those present at a recording studio on what is believed the first occasion of their hearing each other that they were mutually astonished at their stylistic resemblance. This is not to deny that many musicians did copy Beiderbecke and do so today. It is merely to indicate that he was, in a sense, master rather than originator of his way of playing.

While there is much of musical interest in Beiderbecke's work as hot soloist and section leader in his big band work (including his remarkable ability to put life into Paul Whiteman's elephantine band of the late 1920's), it is as lead voice of the traditional band that we will consider him here. He has often been overlooked in this role because of his significance as a soloist, and some state that his real quality in this area was never apparent because of the "inferiority" of the musicians with whom he was associated, in both the Wolverines and subsequent small groups. He has also been neglected here because the Wolverines' recordings with Beiderbecke playing lead are of the early acoustical variety. Having been made around the same time and in the same place as the King Oliver Creole Jazz Band records, they are similarly difficult to listen to. The continuing improvements in the phonograph, however, are to a marked extent alleviating this difficulty. Failure to give due weight to recorded music because the ear is too lazy to concentrate is a poor excuse to neglect perhaps the most important phase of this artist's career. None of the reasons for the neglect of Beiderbecke, the ensemble leader, appear justified upon careful consideration.

The Wolverines with Beiderbecke and the Bucktown Five with cornetist Francis "Muggsy" Spanier were among the earliest recorded attempts by non-New Orleans white bands to play Dixieland or New Orleans style with any degree of real understanding. They were forerunners of the "Chicago" style, possessing certain characteristics later to be found in the groups associated with clarinetist Frank Teschemacher and guitarist Eddie Condon. Both showed more than a little of the influence of conventional dance bands of the period, but both also owed a considerable debt to the Original Dixieland Jazz Band and the New Orleans Rhythm Kings in style and instrumentation. The Spanier group possessed a somewhat more Negroid approach, due in part to Spanier's keen appreciation of Oliver and Armstrong at the time. Beiderbecke, while also admiring these same instrumentalists, apparently felt a somewhat stronger tie to certain of the white New Orleans horns, as is shown in much of his playing.

There has been much discussion pro and con as to the possible effect that New Orleans white cornetist Emmett Hardy had on

Beiderbecke, Beiderbecke himself supposedly having acknowledged a debt to him. Various musicians who have heard both are inclined to feel that there is some likelihood of this, based upon stylistic resemblances. Others, however, feel that the primary influence was Nick La Rocca of the Original Dixieland Jazz Band. Whatever else may have been his interests, Beiderbecke did have an unfailing devotion to the music of the Original Dixieland group. James Moynihan, a jazz critic and former clarinetist, stated that Beiderbecke knew the parts of the various instruments on that group's records note for note and delighted in playing them with others who were similarly familiar with them. Moynihan recalls having blown duets with Beiderbecke based on these recordings in a New York hotel room while Beiderbecke was with Whiteman, an indication that the interest and influence remained strong throughout his life. A striking proof of this interest is found on the Wolverines' record of *Tiger Rag*, where the solo reserved on the Original Dixieland record for clarinetist Larry Shields is played instead by the cornet of Bix Beiderbecke, following closely the pattern of the Shields solo.

II   The Wolverines, in addition to Bix Beiderbecke on cornet, included Jimmy Hartwell, clarinetist, a disciple of Leon Rappolo of the New Orleans Rhythm Kings, while the group of horns was completed by trombonist Al Gande and George Johnson, tenor saxophone. On several of their recordings, trombone is not included. On one particular date, trombonist George Brunis of the New Orleans Rhythm Kings is present in place of Gande. Rhythm was provided by pianist Dick Voynow, drummer Vic Moore, banjoist Bob Gillette, and tuba player Min Leibrook. This young group was much in demand for work at college dances, fraternity parties, and other activities common to groups of this size at the time. Their style indicates a relationship between traditional jazz and the popular music of the day that was closer than at any time since. Their treatment of then currently popular tunes such as *Big Boy* and *Oh, Baby* was quite in keeping with the typical fox trot renditions of dance bands of the period. However, there was present enough of the jazz intonation and warmth to indicate a subtle difference in spite of a relatively homophonic approach. At the same time, various Dixieland selections are treated in the traditional polyphonic manner. The group attacks both with zest and a total lack of self-consciousness. While the musicians are sometimes guilty of a certain stiff, fussy syncopation common to the era (referred to colloquially as "vo-de-o-do," the onomatopoeic sense of which is readily apparent to those familiar with white music of the era), the occasional appearance of this element is incidental and unimportant in the light of numerous offsetting virtues.

Hearing the Wolverines on *Lazy Daddy* provides a good measure of Beiderbecke's capabilities as a Dixieland ensemble cornetist. This record was one of those on which New Orleans trombonist George Brunis was present, giving Beiderbecke support in what too often is the weakest position in non-New Orleans traditional bands. Gande was considerably better than most trombonists of the period, but he was clearly no match for Brunies in ensemble style. Beiderbecke's phrasing is excellent here, never getting in the way of others, and the ensembles at the start of the piece are close to a good white New Orleans level. There is, however, some tendency to stay closer to the lead on the part of sax and clarinet than would New Orleans natives, with a somewhat greater overt consideration of harmonies notable as well. Although a polyphonic approach is used, the reed parts do not stand out with quite the well-defined clarity that one expects of Larry Shields of the Original Dixieland Jazz Band or, among the Negro musicians of New Orleans, Johnny Dodds of King Oliver's Creole Jazz Band. The over-all ensemble quality remains none the less high. Beiderbecke clearly demonstrates such an affinity for his part that one is led to wonder what might have been his course had he been brought up in New Orleans as a direct participant in the development of the Dixieland style. Too often he, and indeed the Wolverines as a group, have been ignored or condemned by traditional-jazz students because they do not meet all the requirements to permit them to be stamped as a pedigreed New Orleans white band. However, the balance sheet upon final closing would seem to indicate that Beiderbecke had more than a casual grasp of and appreciation for the idiom—that he is a figure to be reckoned with in the Dixieland school on the basis of his work with the Wolverines alone. As an indication of the Wolverines' good taste, listening indicates that George Johnson recorded a true third part in the ensembles of *Lazy Daddy*. Here is one of the very rare examples of an ensemble with both tenor sax and trombone present in which one or the other was not muffled or playing inanities.

Later electric recordings find Beiderbecke playing a lead in the traditional manner in records made under his nominal leadership and others with somewhat larger groups under the leadership of Frankie Trumbauer. These records have frequently been pointed out for their value due to Beiderbecke's lead and solos or because of novel musical circumstances in some instances not related to traditional jazz. In various records made under Beiderbecke's own name, notably *At the Jazz Band Ball,* his beautiful Dixieland lead voicing is particularly worthy of attention. His phrasing in the repeat of the first strain, following the initial rendition of the second, is outstanding. It is an excellent variation, fully in keeping with the tradition and something that would not be at all out of place in a performance by, say, the Halfway House Orchestra or any other Dixieland band in New Orleans. Regrettably, although the remainder of the personnel on this and other related discs is of musical interest, it includes men who do not fully comprehend the type of contrapuntal texture Beiderbecke needed. The lack of a sufficiently powerful trombone is felt most keenly, undoubtedly having a somewhat noticeable effect upon Beiderbecke's own playing. As has been pointed out by the critic Charles Edward Smith, however, Beiderbecke shows a keen resemblance to La Rocca in many of his recordings in this period.

The recordings under the name of Frank Trumbauer were made with basically the traditional instrumentation with two saxophones added to permit the playing of straight homophonic, harmonized dance music. Some of this band's ensemble work falls within the Dixieland idiom, while an equal proportion represents a compromise between the traditional and the commercial dance styles, the remainder being purely straight dance music. Even in the most straightforward of ensembles, there is a rhythmic quality and a feeling of vitality marking Beiderbecke's lead, a good example of the styling that enabled him to "lift" the sound of the large Goldkette and Whiteman bands when he sat in the first-trumpet chair, despite the fact that his horn was but one among many. In this regard, it is interesting to note that Beiderbecke was consistently loyal to the cornet, continuing to use it in preference to the trumpet long after a majority of other instrumentalists had made the change.

III   It is often implied that Beiderbecke "grew" out of the early tradition and was passing on to other things, other interests. Undoubtedly he was a person of very considerable and varied aesthetic capacities, and there seems no reason to believe that widening interests necessarily meant the loss of previous ones. His quasi-modern

205

experiments with the piano and other phases of music quite beyond the scope of the New Orleans tradition apparently did not cause any diminution in his interest in the Dixieland approach, particularly when one notes the statements of Moynihan and others in this regard.

Much has been written about psychological conflicts in Beiderbecke's life and the manner in which they were expressed in his music. Certainly some of this thinking is justified, but other, more mundane considerations explain at least a part of the thwarted feeling present in some of his solo work. Like many other highly sensitive individuals, he may not have been at his best in recording studios; those most familiar with his playing say this is most emphatically true. Also, trying to achieve results with a personnel not fully suited to the concept in view, particularly when the concept is that of a sensitive perfectionist, is not conducive to performances indicating contentment and satisfaction. Particularly trying must have been the inadequacy of the rhythm sections on the Beiderbecke-Trumbauer recordings. In several instances, drums that were hardly adequate and not overstrong piano are the only rhythm instruments, with guitar added on a few performances. Some assistance, however, was offered by bass saxophonist Adrian Rollini, a superb musician who strove valiantly to fulfill the functions of tuba, trombone, and sax all rolled into one.

Beiderbecke was a strong influence on many subsequent white cornetists, notably Loring "Red" Nichols and Jimmy MacPartland, while such men as Doc Evans and Manny Klein and numerous others show the influence as well. Virtually none of the imitators had the fire of Beiderbecke's solo playing, a style in which he was unquestionably supreme, with his superiority manifesting itself even more clearly in his ensemble work. Despite various of his stylicisms and emotional qualities that were partially at variance with the tradition, his work within it is of high quality and significance.

22. Chicago jazz

1   The music played by a number of young white musicians in Chicago during the late 1920's has been often designated "Chicago style" or "Chicago jazz." The term refers somewhat less to a clearly defined manner of playing than it does to the music of the group of musicians with which it is identified. The style is of particular importance because, although it broke in some respects with the tradition, its practitioners ultimately returned in large measure to the tradition in their formal approach. This factor proved of considerable importance in the traditional-jazz renaissance.

The question has often been raised whether or not the Chicago music really constituted an independent style. Its existence as such has been denied by some, including tenor saxophonist Bud Freeman, who was one of the most important members of various groups said to have been typical performers in this style. Occasionally the explanation is offered that it appeared to be "different" only because the New Orleans trombone is missing or because the trombone, when present, does not fulfill its normal traditional function. If this were true, the Chicago groups would have sounded like any New Orleans group that did not have a trombone. The fact that they did not so sound is an indication that they were clearly something different.

Prior to the development of the groups characterizing the Chicago style, white groups such as the Wolverines under cornetist Bix Beiderbecke and the Bucktown Five with Francis "Muggsy" Spanier on cornet established patterns that were later to become increasingly significant to younger Chicago musicians. The Wolverines and the Bucktown Five received their inspiration from the various New Orleans and Dixieland bands that were in and about Chicago in the early 1920's. These same groups plus the efforts of Bix Beiderbecke and Louis Armstrong as individuals were to become principal sources of inspiration to such Chicagoans as clarinetist Frank Teschemacher, considered by many as the foremost exponent of the Chicago style, tenor saxophonist Bud Freeman, sax-clarinetist Milton "Mezz" Mezzrow, banjo-guitarist Eddie Condon, and various others. The Bucktown Five and the Wolverines are distinctly traditional in approach, but both pronouncedly accented their music on the beat and both indicated greater harmonic preoccupation than predecessor groups. This resulted in a reduction of the polyphonic effect of the New Orleans and Dixieland styles.

Beiderbecke never really became a part of the "pure" Chicago group, although he did play on occasion with some of its members. Spanier, on the other hand, was very active in the Chicago-style bands. His personal playing always maintained a large measure of the New Orleans flavor and he himself ultimately was largely responsible for the later emergence of more strongly traditional qualities in the Chicago orbit. In his work with such men as the aforementioned Mezzrow and Teschemacher, however, there emerges a fast-paced band style of more limited syncopation and greater solo emphasis than is found in more purely traditional bands. In the ensembles, little regard is shown for the fulfillment of specific functions by specific instruments. Chicago replaced the economy of New Orleans phrasing with cascading runs and arabesques and a superfluity of notes played in unbroken legato or rapid staccato. Ensembles are blurred considerably, although animation and "excitement" are present in large measure. The Chicago groups in which Jimmy MacPartland is featured on cornet represent an even clearer departure from the strict tradition. His phrasing was considerably less economical than that of either Beiderbecke or Spanier, despite the fact that it was largely inspired by Beiderbecke's style.

Although rather significant structural changes are found in the music of the Chicagoans, including the use of a pronounced four-four rhythm with a lesser degree of syncopation, there remains a considerable measure of feeling that is related clearly to the traditional music. This is much in the manner of later small-band Armstrong recordings where form is changed greatly, but substance only partially. The "hot" qualities in jazz are the goal sought after, with increasing regard shown for the solo as the vehicle of attainment.

II   Chicago music was possessed of many interesting features, a general aura of youthfulness and freshness giving it an exhilarating quality that is often most pleasing in the recorded performances. Its greatest importance, nevertheless, appears to be as a medium that in a measure broadened the traditional base and at the same time stimulated a wider audience. This audience has subsequently discovered the purer traditional style through introduction made possible by appreciation of the structurally less complex music of the Chicago groups. The style's period of life was short in what may be called its "orthodox" form, but its influence was and is considerable. When many of its players migrated to New York, there occurred a merger of this style with the ultrawhite quasi-Dixieland manner of Red Nichols and others, resulting in a style possessing somewhat clearer form but emphasizing the solo increasingly. It is significant to note, as well, that most of these musicians alternated freely between the small jazz bands and large dance orchestras of the day in New York, their jazz work inevitably showing certain effects of this, notably in the use of "cleaner" tonality and a diminution of vibrato. Subsequent developments among the New Yorkers, who are now found primarily in the clique centered in guitarist Eddie Condon, are discussed in the chapter devoted to jazz developments in New York.

Certain of the Chicago-style musicians never left home, including clarinetist Bud Jacobson, alto saxophonist Boyce Brown, and cornetist Carl Rinker. These men and their companions have maintained a style closer to the "pure" Chicago manner than anything to be heard elsewhere. In Chicago as elsewhere, however, the New Orleans renaissance is causing a greater regard for the earlier traditional forms to be in evidence. Pianist Art Hodes, although a native Chicagoan, has been in the forefront of the New Orleansesque activities both in New York and Chicago, while trombonist-leader George Brunis of New Orleans is again leading a band in Chicago, some thirty years after his initial visit with the New Orleans Rhythm Kings.

23. Big bands and the tradition

I   To the educated observer of present-day popular music, the difference between larger groups playing fully harmonized, essentially homophonic arrangements and the typical traditional-jazz groups is quite obvious. In an earlier period, however, a less certain stylistic demarcation was to be found. The jazz "fad" of the 1920's caused all sorts of popular musicians and groups either to play their conception of jazz or to flavor their work in a quasi-jazz fashion. Commercial dance bands of the period were, in general, somewhat smaller than those of later years. In consequence, only minor additions were necessary to convert the traditional instrumentation for the playing of stock dance arrangements. Conversely, moderation or elimination of only one or two parts was all that was needed to permit a dance band at least to simulate a typical jazz band in its instrumentation. The net result of this situation was the existence of numerous bands that were neither fish nor fowl. A few of these groups played music worthy of some attention from the jazz listener, while others were but a sad travesty on the music they attempted to mimic.

In the early years of the 1920's, most of the "compromise" groups were attempting to copy Paul Whiteman, the Original Dixieland

Jazz Band, or both, with at least a few showing clear traces of the King Oliver Creole Jazz Band influence. The results were, at times, startling and in many cases disastrous, particularly so in recorded performances. Later, when more real jazz musicians infiltrated these groups, some improvement occurred, and a little vitality was present in even the early work of some of the colored "commercial" groups.

The early Fletcher Henderson recordings were examples of work by one of the better-known colored bands of the time. A few members of this band were subsequently to become famous as hot soloists. Louis Armstrong was a member of the brass section in 1924. Their records show slight traces of Oliver in the arrangements plus a great amount of the stiff, crudely syncopated brass work usually associated with the early Paul Whiteman efforts. A flash of solo from Armstrong's cornet or Charlie Green's trombone might occasionally add some interest, but the over-all effect is dull.

As for the Whiteman band itself, the records make one wonder what ever possessed anyone to listen a second time to the group. On such "hot" selections as *Until My Luck Comes Rolling Along*, the over-all rhythmic effect would indicate that the desiderated "luck" must have been rolling along in a runaway oxcart on a washboard road. However, discussion of the group's efforts with certain members of the band indicates that the rigidly disciplined recordings were one thing, but the on-the-job performances of a few of the hot men present were quite another. Whiteman and pianist Ferde Grofé were more than adequate "legitimate" musicians, but their understanding of traditional jazz was at best slight. It is said that such men as trombonist Buster Johnson and New Orleans clarinetist Gus Muller would submit to just a certain amount of the heavily becorseted Whiteman arranging and then would rebel, the trombone easing off into tailgate phrasing and a liquid clarinet tempting the rhythm section to loosen up and vitalize the music. Thus it may be seen that the early Whiteman group's appeal to dancers was found in a music that was perhaps more jazzy and less Whiteman than phonograph records indicate.

Whiteman's desire for "respectability," however, led to the considerable enlargement of his group, thus eliminating any possibility of the earlier informality. His clumsily syncopated "jazz" was gradually replaced with ponderous pseudosymphonic harmonies played over dance rhythms, culminating in the concert rendition of Gershwin's *Rhapsody in Blue*, one of the most ludicrous of the popular

211

attempts during the 1920's to merge jazz and "serious" music. In the late 1920's, Whiteman did assemble a group that contained various hot-jazz soloists, including Bix Beiderbecke and Frank Trumbauer. Even in this period there was little of real jazz value produced by the band. A scant few hot solos were the only items of significance.

Among the large bands, in addition to Whiteman and Henderson, a number of other groups possessing some jazz interest made their appearance. One of the most famous, the California Ramblers, made numerous dance recordings using many quasi-traditional ensemble choruses but with a continually growing emphasis on the hot solo. The Dorsey brothers, Red Nichols, Adrian Rollini, and other important popular musicians of the period were to be found in this group, which was typical of the better "compromise" bands of this period. Whatever else may have been lacking, there was at least a degree of vitality in their work that was not to be found in the Whiteman band or its imitators. The white band that was ultimately to bridge the gap between these earlier groups and the swing bands, however, was Glen Gray's Casa Loma Orchestra. This group possessed a high level of musicianship and utilized arrangements that were fast-paced and intricate in their jazz efforts. Here, too, the hot solo was featured to a great extent.

Also making its initial appearance in the late 1920's was the large band of Duke Ellington. This band probably has had a greater influence on popular music styling and big-band jazz or swing music than any comparable organization. The band was known for both the arranging talents of its leader and the heat of its soloists. With the passage of time, however, solo improvisation has been steadily de-emphasized, with jazz interest depreciating almost in direct proportion. The Ellington concept has grown steadily in the direction of "mood" music, with copious arrangements offering assemblages of European ideas coupled with complex passages that are novel and original, but emotionally trivial. The contrast between his recording of *Tiger Rag*, in which many hot solos of fair-to-good quality are heard, and any movement of his later composition entitled *Black, Brown and Beige* clearly indicates the direction of development. Ellington's smoothness and tonal effects are suited to the tastes associated with the popular large dance band. He is considered a "sophisticate" and is therefore admired in the ultraconventional world of the popular musician.

In Kansas City, Bennie Moten during the 1920's led a band that produced many musicians later to become famous in the swing era. Initially, although slightly larger than the orthodox traditional-jazz bands, the group had a decidedly traditional flavor. This was never fully lost until, in the early 1930's, the leader died and control of the group came into the hands of pianist Count Basie. The band had always been notable for the strength of its rhythm, which Basie emphasized above all other considerations. It was this group and the white Benny Goodman band that were to spearhead the swing movement.

II   The Benny Goodman band was the most popular and pretentious of the swing groups. Basing its music in large measure on Fletcher Henderson's arrangements, with hot soloists featured to a maximum degree, it swept the country with its "new" music. Today, of course, it is realized that this music was not particularly different from much of the music preceding it, particularly some work by later groups under the leadership of Fletcher Henderson, groups featuring such hot soloists as tenor saxophonist Coleman Hawkins, trumpeter Bobby Starks, and many others of note in the late 1920's and early 1930's. The more novel qualities in Goodman's work were to be found in his smaller groups, utilizing clarinet and rhythm in music of a light, legato sort having little relationship to the jazz tradition.

Contemporary with the Goodman band were a number of similar large "swing" groups. In a few instances, vestiges of the tradition were still to be found, particularly in the Tommy Dorsey group and the still-popular Glen Gray band mentioned earlier in this chapter. Both of these groups utilized some of the traditional repertoire in big-band "hot" arrangements, their separate records of *Milenberg Joys,* quite by coincidence, being examples of these two bands at their best in this type of effort.

In addition to its full-band work, the Dorsey group utilized an eight-piece segment, known as Tommy Dorsey and His Clambake Seven, which played in a clearly Dixieland manner. Included in both groups at times were such jazz instrumentalists as tenor saxophonist Bud Freeman and drummer Dave Tough, both exponents of the Chicago school. Trumpeters Max Kaminsky and Bunny Berigan also found haven in this group. Dorsey himself always had been a jazz trombonist of the Miff Mole school, playing a jazz style that was virtually a copy of Mole's.

The most significant band of the swing era in traditional-jazz con-

213

tent, however, was the group led by Bob Crosby. In this group were several white musicians from New Orleans, including drummer Ray Bauduc, clarinetist Irving Fazola, tenor sax and clarinet player Eddie Miller, and guitarist Nappy Lamare. While other bands made occasional use of bits of Dixieland, Dixieland playing was a stated policy of this organization. An eight-piece group, forming a traditional instrumental unit, existed within the larger band and was known as Bob Crosby's Bob Cats. This combination played a number of standard jazz tunes, but it was the playing of traditional selections by the full group that was a most unusual feature. Their arrangements included many ensembles in which the clarinet improvised over the rest of the horns, with other similar devices used to impart a quality of freedom. Their spirited, full-band recordings of *Original Dixieland One-Step, King Porter Stomp,* and *Milenberg Joys* are most pleasing—so devoid of commercial qualities that one wonders how they came to be made at all in an era when big-band commercialism was the watchword.

The Crosby band of the swing era broke up early in World War II, its members going in various directions. Many of them have subsequently been active in traditional groups, particularly on the West Coast. In recent time, several have again joined forces with Bob Crosby in a band that is trying with some success to regain the wonderful spirit of its ancestor—a band that caused many a young jazz enthusiast to sneak from his bed and listen to their 2 A.M. broadcasts from the Blackhawk Restaurant in Chicago.

The prewar Crosby band was a far cry from pure traditional jazz, but it did make some pleasant music. It was vitally important to the jazz renaissance because it brought a new audience to at least one phase of the tradition. Instead of smirking at all the music preceding it, the group and its leader spoke and played with respect for such predecessors as the Original Dixieland Jazz Band, Jelly Roll Morton, and others who have been significant contributors to the idiom. It is quite possible that, although a compromise group with much of its music in the commercial dance category, the Crosby band was one of the major causes of the traditional-jazz renaissance.

At best, larger groups have difficulty in trying to play traditional jazz. It is a music of many parts with harmonies used only to support a polyphony. The larger bands, using several trumpets, a number of saxophones, and from two to four trombones are designed for the creation of harmonies. A fluid, three-voiced counterpoint

214

of jazz tonality is something that was never intended for this instrumentation. While some groups have rendered a quasi-jazz of spirit using their full instrumentation, it has never been of the same aesthetic value as the work of good small bands. A single jazz cornetist, even when playing a melody comparatively "straight," will use a little vibrato or slightly alter note value or pitch to accent a phrase. Were he to take such liberties as lead trumpet in a three-man section, he would only muddy the sound of the other horns. Problems such as this are a major reason why traditional jazz is at its best when played by the traditional band.

24. Renaissance

Traditional jazz has been subjected to striking variations in popularity. For a period in the depths of the depression, it seemed that it was becoming part of the past. Few musicians were attempting to play it, and only a small coterie of record collectors showed any continuing interest in the field. Today a much healthier condition exists, with a number of musicians playing or attempting to play in the New Orleans and/or Dixieland styles for audiences as large as or larger than any encountered in the earlier years.

This change is usually explained by the assumption that changing economic circumstances hold a direct relationship to the ebb and flow of the traditional-jazz audience. There is another opinion, however, which seems worthy of consideration, expressing the belief that earlier audiences were less aware of the real content of the music, while a great proportion of today's audience is more fully appreciative of the underlying virtues of the music. If this is true, it is entirely possible that a far smaller number of perceptive people were seriously interested in jazz during the 1920's than is often assumed, thus considerably leveling off the apparent relapse and recovery of the music in the 1930's. This factor may be of more than incidental significance in the interpretation of the continued

216

resurgence of interest. It may well be a clear indication that we are experiencing a traditional-jazz renaissance rather than a mere revival. The revival theory appears unworthy of support, because several abortive attempts made by the entertainment business to stimulate what has seemed a potentially profitable interest of the public have ended in dismal failure, the sponsors invariably stating that the revival was either "over" or "a mistake." In reality, traditional jazz has enjoyed an audience of moderate size continuously, following a resurgence of interest that commenced in the late 1930's. In view of an audience interest covering a period of from ten to fifteen years with every present indication of a continuing enthusiasm, it would seem that audiences are aware of values more lasting than those of a mere popular music fad.

Various persons and various forces have been designated as the originators of the traditional renaissance. As in all things, a number of related causes undoubtedly were responsible. There can be little question that heroic efforts on the part of a small group of musicians and jazz *aficionados* materially hastened its progress, but it is equally true that a latent receptivity existed in the potential audiences for this music.

Perhaps the most remarkable characteristic of this renewed interest was the amount of active participation indulged in by enthusiasts the world over. In the past, traditional jazz received an enthusiastic reception in many countries, but no real attempt was made on the part of any substantial number of musicians overseas to play it. Today it is possible to find bands, ranging from adequate to very good, playing their concepts of traditional jazz in many major European cities, while numerous groups are to be found in Great Britain and Australia, several of them offering performances of considerable interest. A mixture of styles is represented in their playing, with a surprising proportion devoted to the purest New Orleans style. At home, while much of the music has been that of veteran jazzmen, younger musicians again have provided numerous groups, at least one of which, Lu Watters' Yerba Buena Jazz Band, played a vital part in the resuscitation of traditional jazz as a significant factor in our current cultural scene.

The renaissance has found a major source of its strength among the record collectors, but an increasing percentage of direct audience interest is apparent now, as is also an increase in the number of younger musicians motivated by a desire to play in the tradition. It has not yet blossomed out to the proportions of a "craze," much

217

to the regret of various commercial interests, but it seems to be establishing the traditional-jazz band firmly as a basic and continuing medium of expression.

Although traditional jazz is enjoying a period of relative popularity at the present time, it is, of course, not without its detractors. It has all the usual "enemies." It also has too many patronizing "friends" who are quick to state their happiness at seeing a return of the music, but say firmly that it can never possibly attain the level of quality it knew in the past. Even worse, they insist that all who play in the traditional manner are merely "copying" specific bands or performances of the past. Most of those who use the first of these premises are, in effect, maintaining two very questionable propositions: that the old level of quality can be attained only by bands striving for precisely the same goals as did the earlier bands, and that these goals are no longer attainable. As to the second premise, many musicians have had certain earlier groups as their sources of inspiration, but they have rarely contented themselves with mere emulation of a few specific phonograph records. If this had been their intent, their attempts would have been more accurate in achieving the notation and phrasing. The real difficulty in satisfying these patronizing critics is caused by their thinking of musical change in much the same fashion as they think of annual model changes on the automobile mart. The changes in jazz are never so extreme. When extreme changes are made, they almost inevitably end in the creation of a music no longer properly identifiable with the source from which it has ostensibly sprung.

Attempts to trace the beginning of the jazz renaissance are difficult, as a resurgence of interest seems to have occurred in several places at once. New York and San Francisco apparently share major credit for events happening in the late 1930's that led to a resumption of "live" music in the traditional-jazz idiom. New Orleans itself has always managed to keep a little activity in motion even though for long periods it would seem that all was lost until another Mardi Gras would suddenly reveal an enthusiastic audience cheering orthodox jazz sounds emanating from the marching bands. At the same time, a hardy little group in the St. Paul-Minneapolis area was meeting at a club named "Mitch's." This was in effect the equivalent to its cities of what "Nick's" was at the time to New York. In Chicago there was sporadic activity on the part of a handful of the New Orleans and Chicago veterans in town. Somehow, in the period just before World War II, all these points became considerably more

218

active once again, with the number of practicing jazz musicians increasing and a growing audience rising to meet them. While it is not the purpose of this volume to enter the field of jazz history in general, the resurgence of traditional jazz in the period since 1939 deserves more attention as an illustration of its vitality, and also as an indication of why this so-called "popular" music of an earlier period is not merely a revival fad of the moment. It is rather a form of expression as significant in our culture as it was yesterday and as it will be tomorrow. Though the discussion centers in individuals, it does not necessarily indicate their relative significance; indeed, many who are important are not even mentioned. Rather, an attempt is made to illustrate the trend of development through a discussion of the musical activities of several men and groups who seem to have been key figures in shaping the pattern of the development. A few of them are veteran New Orleans jazz musicians who came back from semiretirement, while others are virtually youngsters in the music field. All, however, are men who have been of basic significance in the development of the new traditional-jazz era.

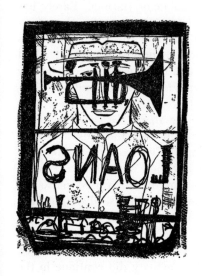

25. Traditional jazz in New York

New York City has always had a number of jazzmen. Rarely has it produced any groups of truly native origin that played successfully within the traditional idiom. Various of the Negro musicians from the big bands spawned in Harlem proved somewhat adept within the traditional frame, but even these groups were largely manned by musicians born elsewhere. Phil Napoleon and his Memphis Five is one of the few groups that were genuinely New York bands during the "golden years," as the 1920's are called by some jazz enthusiasts. It has even been said that the closest certain Brooklyn-born members of the Memphis Five ever got to Memphis was Coney Island. Additionally, Red Nichols and his Five Pennies called New York "home," although most of the varied personnel associated with Nichols came to the city from elsewhere. In jazz, New York has been meeting place more often than birthplace, and at no time was it the scene of such vital activity in the tradition as New Orleans or a somewhat later Chicago. In fairness, however, it may be said that a modicum of jazz activity did continue in the city right through to the beginning of the renaissance.

The reason New York managed to keep a tiny stream of the music flowing was the presence of a large number of the old Chicagoans

220

in the city plus a small but fanatically loyal audience who remained faithful to them through thick and thin. The spark was still smoldering, waiting to resurge when the occasion was ripe. The occasion came at roughly the same time that jazz activities were beginning to show signs of life on the West Coast. A growing coterie of record collectors and others who just liked the music had created a latent audience, and the necessary elements were present to make a revival attempt feasible. At the time, the original Nick's in Greenwich Village was a lone holdout that regularly employed jazz musicians, while slim fare was offered additionally by weekly jam sessions sponsored by the Commodore Music Shop. That there were possibilities of doing something with jazz in a form other than interminable solos or swing banalities had been indicated by the recent success of a group led by cornetist Francis "Muggsy" Spanier and referred to as Muggsy Spanier and His Ragtime Band. This group represented something of a compromise between the Chicago approach and the white New Orleans Dixieland style. The emphasis, despite the presence of tenor sax, was decidedly closer to the latter with distinct overtones of the Negroid New Orleans style as well.

It was undoubtedly the best band that Spanier has been associated with before or since and clearly was one of the best white bands ever recorded. Trombonist George Brunis, formerly of the New Orleans Rhythm Kings, was present and very eager to play in the old way once again, having just escaped with Spanier from the confines of a large commercial band led by Ted Lewis. Rod Cless, a clarinetist who admired the style of the late Chicagoan Frank Teschemacher but similarly appreciated the New Orleans manner employed by Omer Simeon in his work with Morton's Red Hot Peppers and elsewhere, provided an excellent balance for the brass team. It is to Spanier's credit that although his band did use a saxophone, several different tenor men filling the post at one time or another during the band's history, he managed to use men who cluttered up the ensemble sound less than is usual with this instrument. Their 1939 Bluebird recordings, notably *I Wish I Could Shimmy Like My Sister Kate* and *Riverboat Shuffle*, were immediate successes, and the style of the band clearly set a new pace for the Chicago expatriates who were gathered in New York.

When the band disassembled and its members infiltrated the New York group, Brunis was asked to join in the first record date of Commodore in 1940. With his typical New Orleans tailgate style, he set a new ensemble pattern that has marked all the subsequent

221

Chicago efforts as somewhat closer to true Dixieland than most had been before. No other trombonist, with the possible exception of Lou McGarrity, could adequately replace him in ensembles of the renaissance New York groups formed by the Condon clique. Thereafter, at least an attempt was made to find the type of balance that Brunis had introduced.

Two Bostonians, Brad Gowans, a valve-trombonist and clarinetist, and cornetist Bobby Hackett, also had a strong influence at this time. Gowans was an ardent disciple of the Original Dixieland Jazz Band, and his ensemble thinking was along the lines laid down by them. Although his instrument was never quite so satisfactory for the purpose as a slide trombone would have been, he did help considerably in creating a more balanced ensemble. Hackett, also an admirer of the afore-mentioned Dixieland group and a serious student of the Beiderbecke cornet style, provided a lead horn that added further to the strong Dixieland influences at work in the Condon group. Chicago-style clarinetist Charles E. "Pee Wee" Russell fitted neatly into the pattern being established, playing in a strange, sour-toned style somewhat emulating Teschemacher of the Chicago school in solos, but in ensembles reverting to what might be described as a "subconscious" approach that proved unique. It did have some sympathetic relationship to the Dixieland concept. Russell has been perhaps the most utterly controversial figure in jazz. Opinions of his solo work in particular vary from rhapsody to utter denunciation, with few persons having a neutral reaction. In jazz of this sort it is the ensemble effort that is important. Whatever Russell's faults may be, his playing in the late 1930's and early 1940's was infinitely superior for ensemble purposes to the anemic approach of the existing Benny Goodman imitators.

A further shift in emphasis occurred shortly before World War II with the arrival of Chicago trumpeter Wild Bill Davison on the New York scene. Davison possessed at the time a tremendous enthusiasm for the music and a hot, frenzied, somewhat nervous style that many found very "exciting." When he joined forces with George Brunis and Pee Wee Russell, it was the belief of many that, despite a number of obvious faults in taste, a genuinely hot ensemble was achieved that fitted within the tradition. In fairness, it should be pointed out that George Brunis did effect a reasonable degree of discipline in the group. The faults referred to are based on comparison with the highest of traditional standards rather than with those of contemporaneous groups.

222

The Condon clique really hit the "big time" during World War II when Condon was established on a nationwide weekly radio program and received extensive publicity in various magazines. All sorts of jazz and pseudojazz musicians gathered into this huge informal clan, and the resumption of traditional jazz as a live music in New York became an assured fact. In addition to guitarist Condon, Chicago piano player Art Hodes emerged as a focal point toward whom certain individuals gravitated, notably those Chicago expatriates who were more strongly inclined toward the Negroid New Orleans approach. Here one could see a motivation at least partially related to the motivation behind the musicians in San Francisco at the same time.

In 1945, Bunk Johnson visited New York with a band of New Orleans veterans and took the city by storm. The impact upon a growing jazz audience was immense, and the effect upon local jazz musicians was very strong. As usual, many detractors appeared, but even among these were men whose playing was subsequently affected by the fresh approach of this group. Possibly most important of all, this band seemed to serve as an inspiration to more young musicians than any other had before. Only in the period from the time of Johnson's New York visit to the present time has New York produced any substantial number of young newcomers in traditional jazz. A number of groups, such as those led by Bob Wilber and Bob Kuh, attempting to play in the manner of Morton, Oliver, the Armstrong Hot Five, and/or Bunk Johnson's band, suddenly came upon the scene at this time. The Johnson band was important also in that it brought greater attention and popularity to New Orleans musicians already in the area, making it possible for them to play regularly once more in the style of their home town.

While both older and younger jazz musicians in New York were feeling strong New Orleans influences, the younger musicians were also paying considerable attention to the new music of the San Francisco jazzmen. Watters, Murphy, and associates were almost totally ignored by Condon, Hodes, and others from the Chicago era. But the San Francisco style began to have its effect among the younger players, so much so that the principal younger band in New York, the Red Onion Jazz Band, is showing very marked West Coast influence in its approach. As many older New York musicians have become somewhat jaded in their approach or have left the field entirely in more recent time, the growing significance of this group and other younger groups and individuals is having a distinct

223

effect upon the complexion of traditional jazz in the metropolis. Orientation is markedly turning toward New Orleans and San Francisco, the Chicago style influence diminishing in proportion.

In assessing the importance of New York to the renaissance, it appears that its significance was greater as an avenue of communication than as a creative producer of the music. It did produce a market place for the Condon clique, which is still continuing to exploit it in diluted form. Also, it brought attention to such musicians as clarinetist Albert Nicholas, bassist George "Pops" Foster, the afore-mentioned George Brunis, Bunk Johnson, and other New Orleans musicians who were able to achieve popularity through the presence of public relations and communications media in the city as well as recording studios. The recording studios were perhaps the most important single factor of all in reaching the nation-wide jazz public.

Danny Barker.

The Original Dixieland Jazz Band. *Left to right:* Tony Sbarbaro, Eddie "Daddy" Edwards, Nick La Rocca, Larry Shields, Henry Ragas.

26. San Francisco style

1   A focal point of the jazz renaissance from its very beginning
has been the city of San Francisco. Although the area had not
known a very great part of the traditional music in the 1920's as
had Chicago or New York, the mid-1930's found a particularly intense group of record collectors here whose interests were sharply
oriented toward the purest forms of the New Orleans style. Jazz
interests in New York and Chicago were concentrating on the Chicago style, Bix Beiderbecke, Red Nichols, later Armstrong, or soloists in the big bands. The San Francisco enthusiasts were thinking
of King Oliver's Creole Jazz Band, Louis Armstrong in his Hot
Five period, Johnny Dodds, Jelly Roll Morton, and others of the
New Orleans school, with some consideration for the white Dixieland bands of New Orleans, in particular the New Orleans Rhythm
Kings.

The situation was further favored in San Francisco by the presence among jazz enthusiasts of some professional musicians who
were playing primarily in local dance bands. Several of these men
began to gather with regularity after hours to play the early New
Orleans tunes and to learn the traditional manner of playing. One
individual among them, a dynamic, capable cornetist named Lu

225

Watters, emerged from this group as a leader in various efforts to organize a band that would play traditionally for dances and seated audiences. This organization ultimately developed into the group referred to as Lu Watters' Yerba Buena Jazz Band, whose initial recordings aroused a storm of controversy that has as yet shown no signs of diminution. Subsequent work of Watters' groups both before and after World War II has only added to the furor. As in most controversies, there is merit on both sides. Even the strongest detractors must concede, however, that the Yerba Buena Jazz Band and its descendants have been among the major forces in the growth of the traditional-jazz renaissance.

Although some changes in personnel occurred, particularly prior to a temporary cessation of activities while various members were in the armed forces during World War II, the group that remained a unit for the longest period and is the one normally in mind when the band is discussed consisted of the following personnel: Lu Watters, leader and first cornet/trumpet; Bob Scobey, second trumpet; Turk Murphy, trombone; Bob Helm, clarinet; Dick Lammi, tuba; Walter Rose, piano; Harry Mordecai, banjo; Bill Dart, drums. The instrumentation is similar to that of King Oliver's Creole Jazz Band, a group whose concept Watters and his band freely stated was the basis of their own approach. Both repertoire and instrumentation aided in creating the impression of an Oliver imitation. The over-all effort to achieve a New Orleans quality further added to a first impression of the Yerba Buena Jazz Band as a carbon copy of the earlier Oliver group. Certain marked and purposeful distinctions, however, materially differentiated their work. The Watters rhythm section was pronouncedly two-beat in contrast to a predominantly four-four approach of Oliver's. The Watters band differed also in that it made far greater use of the fortissimo attack. Indeed, many seasoned jazz listeners are of the opinion that Watters played the loudest jazz cornet or trumpet they have ever heard and perhaps the loudest of all time, despite the use of a totally unfrenzied horn style. A further difference from Oliver was to be found in the tendency of the Watters group to play fairly regularly on the beat instead of the horns retarding slightly in the typical New Orleans fashion. It may be seen, therefore, that while the Oliver band was unquestionably a principal source of inspiration, other forces also were significant in large measure.

The Yerba Buena Jazz Band has been criticized severely by many for alleged "defects" in its rhythm. It has been conceded by many, including members of the group, that the rhythm as found on their record dates was somewhat "stiff," a quality less marked in normal performance. Too often, however, this criticism is leveled solely because of a lack of "swing." In reality, swing in itself was not a matter of particular moment to this group, at least in the sense in which the word was usually employed in the 1930's and 1940's. They were looking for and often achieved a powerful "rocking" effect in their rhythm, employing a beat and texture utterly alien to the swing bands or the latter-day Chicago or New York quasi-traditional groups. The combination of closely controlled two-beat drums with limited use of cymbals and considerable use of wood blocks, ragtime piano, emphatically two-beat tuba, and tenor banjo varying from a straight four-four to moderate two-beat emphasis, plus a very brassy, powerful, quasi-Oliver horn ensemble, gave the band a characteristic sound clearly its own. Marking it strongly through most of the band's life was the hard-toned, piercing, and very warm clarinet of Bob Helm. Helm's very personal approach to this music, perhaps more than any other single factor, gave the ensembles a unique quality that made the band instantly recognizable to its many devoted listeners.

The band as initially recorded with clarinetist Ellis Horne had a rather pedantic quality that was not prevalent when playing in person. This was undoubtedly ascribable in large measure to initial contact with recording techniques, these often creating an environment calculated to make the uninitiate ill at ease. Despite this, there is much of interest in the records, a few samples of which are at present available on the Good Time Jazz label record LP-8. The remainder are about to be reissued on L-12007. This music, while primarily arranged, was played with some degree of controlled improvisation, all the performances being carefully developed through rehearsal. Reading of music was essential, particularly during the formative period, as the highly industrious musician enthusiasts comprising the band had developed a library of tunes running into the hundreds. The familiar jazz standards formed only one small portion of their repertoire. Various phases of American folk music contributed to their work, as did prejazz music of the United States plus a considerable number of original selections written by Watters and Murphy. Unlike many highly informal jazz groups in other places, the Watters band could play steadily for several nights without ever repeating a selection or resorting to the banal. Further, their playing was marked by an almost total

227

absence of tunes that you could expect to hear commonly elsewhere. As if the band music were not varied enough, pianist Walter Rose could and often did entertain with his remarkably proficient performances of old piano rags, utilizing a superb technique that has made him as notable in European art music circles as in the jazz field. It is highly doubtful that any musician in any phase of popular music can claim a technical facility equal to that of Wally Rose.

When the group reassembled after World War II, it entered into its final period as a unit, a period of almost three years' duration with a very stable personnel as outlined previously. The already large repertoire became truly massive during this time, while the level of musicianship in the group improved continually. These men have been frequently accused of being "amateurs," but nothing could be farther from the truth. All were professional musicians of proved competence in the brass band, concert hall, and dance music fields. Many had proved adept at the playing of loose, jam-session, Chicagoesque jazz. However, for the playing of real New Orleans or, for that matter, Dixieland jazz in the pure sense, they knew that radically different technical equipment was mandatory. The task of adaptation was tackled with humility and perseverance by these men throughout the history of their existence as a band, the same process continuing to this day in descendant groups. The looser, more virile sound to be heard on their postwar recordings is a clear indication of a concept grasped more firmly than when at first attempted, although some stiffness is still to be noted in the rhythm of the group.

The Watters band was of particular significance in the renaissance because of two effects. First, it brought to the ears of many their first experience with a music formally related to the early New Orleans style. Equally important, it broke an existing, almost universal tabu concerning the use of certain techniques and instruments condemned by the swing era as being "corn." In particular, the Lu Watters band brought attention back to the banjo and the tuba as important instruments in the creation of jazz rhythm, while also giving a new lease on life to the style of trombone that is so essential in the creation of a full jazz ensemble. Certainly it was partially responsible for the fading from the traditional-jazz scene of the saxophone, an instrument whose value in jazz has always been open to question, particularly in any group where ensemble playing is emphasized. Even in the presentation of solos, this band achieved a quasi-ensemble quality, the rapport between soloist and rhythm instruments being considerably greater than that of major voice over an anonymous beat. Punctuation of a high order by the rhythm instruments was virtually a trade-mark in this group.

II   When musical and financial complications led to a major change in personnel in 1947, followed ultimately by the dissolution of the Yerba Buena Jazz Band, the San Francisco jazz movement continued onward under various banners. The principal groups are bands led by Bob Scobey and Turk Murphy. For some time, in fact, Scobey played trumpet in the Murphy band, but too wide a gulf in musical ideas led to a separation and continuing developments along somewhat different lines. It is interesting to note, however, that whatever may be the differences, both of these men show very strongly the influences of the Yerba Buena group in the styles of their own bands. While both have made considerable changes in certain facets of their approach, the Murphy band has more consistently followed the line drawn by the Watters band. It may well be considered as virtually a continuation of the earlier group in many senses.

The period since last the Watters band played has been one of constant struggle, study, and practice for trombonist Murphy and those who have gathered around him. With a single-minded devotion to his cause, Murphy has continued in the development of a concept that he and those around him felt was only beginning to flower in the Lu Watters band. Paradoxically, many feel that no subsequent group has measured up to the qualities of the Watters effort. At the same time they point out developments that have wiped out certain aspects of its style not felt to be adequately developed in the Watters group. However, the possibility of assembling another such group of eight gifted, temperamental individuals and forcing them to work in a harmonious relationship over an extended period seems at best remote. There are others, of course, who feel that later Murphy efforts have been infinitely superior to the predecessor, but it cannot be denied that the trumpet or cornet team of Scobey and Watters was a unique feature that it would be almost impossible to replace.

Typical of the Murphy efforts in seeking a perfected ensemble were the drastic steps taken to achieve satisfactory instrumentation and personnel. When it became increasingly clear that certain instruments would be played either improperly or not at all, Turk Murphy did exactly the opposite of what the latter-day pseudo-

Dixieland band leader would do—he eliminated use of the instruments! He shares with the New Orleans musicians of an earlier day the understanding of an instrument's role in the music, and realizes fully that it is the manner in which instruments are used far more than the instruments themselves that gives this music its most significant characteristics. The thought of a jazz band without drums is inconceivable to many, yet for several years Turk Murphy has not, except for a short interval, used drums, in preference to having the beat altered or the ensembles muddied by improper drumming. Drummers of adequate capability in this field, particularly drummers who can read, are hard to find. This band normally uses its library of arrangements primarily to teach the tunes and their harmonies as a basis for controlled improvisation. It is felt here that reading musicians are superior not only because of ability to learn the tunes rapidly, but because of the greater understanding such knowledge can give them of the structure of music and of their role in its creation.

Possibly even more surprising in the Murphy instrumentation was the absence over a lengthy period of a cornet or trumpet. While tuba player Bob Short did occasionally play an ensemble passage on cornet, most of the time the band utilized a "front line" consisting of only trombone and clarinet, with one or the other of these instruments playing lead over a rhythm section consisting of banjo, tuba, and piano. Here, truly, was jazz chamber music. With the exception of the tuba of Bob Short, formerly associated with the Castle Jazz Band of Portland, Oregon, all of this group were alumni of the earlier Yerba Buena Jazz Band, including Turk Murphy, trombone and leader, clarinetist Bob Helm, former tuba player Dick Lammi, who now was playing banjo, and pianist Wally Rose (a man considered by many as the all-time master of ragtime piano in any generation). Before this "economical" instrumentation was effected, Don Kinch, another Castle Jazz Band ex-member, had been with the group, but when nonmusical considerations forced his return to Oregon it was decided to leave the cornet chair vacant rather than fill it with an inferior musician.

Continuance of a rigorous instrumental philosophy is still apparent in the Murphy organization at the time of this writing. The recent increase in travel by the group has forced occasional shifts in personnel. Because nonmusical considerations do not permit Helm and Short to travel extensively, replacements have been carefully selected during travel periods, banjoist Lammi judiciously switching to tuba when personnel changes have made this step advisable or necessary.

It is true that the unique brass team of the Yerba Buena Jazz Band is now a thing of the past and rapidly becoming a legend, but it is equally true that the Murphy band has made solid accomplishments in its own right that are most worthy of recognition. In particular, the rhythm section has shown the results of great effort and considerable experimentation within the idiom. Whether or not the elimination of drums in itself was a most significant move, there can be no doubt that the banjo-tuba-piano combination developed a springiness in its work that was decidedly more satisfactory than the prior efforts of the Watters group. The springiness is still present despite the return of drums to the fold, although this is undoubtedly due in no small part to extreme care in selection of a drummer and close discipline. Of great help also for some time was the presence of Bob Short and his tuba. Short is an instrumentalist of varied and considerable talents, having also played string bass, cornet, and banjo, while at present studying the trombone during a temporary cessation of professional musical activity. His beat was eminently satisfactory and he possessed a stamina sufficient to permit the mobility necessary for occasional creation of highly effective solos on an instrument rarely known in this category for any purpose except fulfilling the role of clown. The greater freedom in pianist Wally Rose's work while with Murphy, though appearing at first as an "improvement" in his playing, actually represents little more than the provision of greater latitude to this part in the planned discipline of the group than was permitted in the Watters band.

In the work of the horns, however, important changes were to be noted. Anyone familiar with clarinetist Bob Helm cannot but be aware of him as a remarkable artist in his idiom, constantly striving for and constantly achieving greater capability and knowledge in his chosen field. He is doubly blessed in being the husband of a highly competent jazz scholar and record collector who has aided no little in maintaining the high degree of courage necessary to progress in a field that is rarely economically rewarding to even its most capable practitioners. His work with the Yerba Buena Jazz Band and the smaller Watters band that succeeded it for a time was interesting and refreshing to an audience wearied of would-be jazz clarinetists who found it necessary to reach a compromise with the Benny Goodman-Artie Shaw school of clarinet. With his unique

231

quasi-Johnny Dodds tone and attack and a tremendous power, he was totally unlike any of the clarinetists who were busiest in the early 1940's. However, it would seem that he really began to reach his present stature only following the Watters period. His subsequent playing with the Castle Jazz Band in Portland with several jazzmen who later were reunited with him in the Turk Murphy band showed certain tonal improvements. This was undoubtedly due in no small part to the lessened need of volume in this smaller group plus a change from a plastic reed to one of the natural variety. The full flowering of his capabilities became most evident during his lengthy association with Turk Murphy. There always existed a strong musical affinity between these two men, either one of them usually sounding better when the other was present. Their unity in the Murphy band cannot but have been of major benefit in their development. During this era, Helm did a huge amount of writing and arranging of traditional music, having in his possession a remarkable library of original material that has been, as yet, little used in public performance, but created for the sheer love of the music by its author. A new band he is now forming will undoubtedly make interesting use of this material.

Helm's natural modesty has prevented many from realizing the full extent of his capabilities. He is one of the very, very few clarinetists who can play the difficult traditional clarinet solo from *High Society*, originated by Creole clarinetist Alphonse Picou in the early days of the jazz bands, without resorting to any form of deceit to pass over various complex passages. More than that, he has "worked out" a harmony part for use in playing the chorus as a duet. Certainly one of the high moments in the jazz renaissance occurred when the Murphy band was in New York in the fall of 1954 and New Orleans clarinetist Tony Parenti joined the group for a few numbers, including an impromptu *High Society* in which Helm played "second clarinet" to Parenti's able rendition of the traditional chorus. In this connection, it is also interesting to observe that Helm has developed a considerable ability at playing second clarinet parts for use on any occasion when another clarinet might be present. This is not a common thing in jazz bands, and perhaps comes nearest to what might be described as being a "new sound" in traditional jazz.

As for Murphy himself, he is perhaps the hardest working individual ever found in this field. His belief in the music borders on the religious, and there is an almost grim purposefulness in every-

232

thing he does to further its cause. He is constantly finding fault with his band and himself, and is constantly seeking for and utilizing various ways and means to improve his work. The drawing board on which he does much of his musical arranging is always set up and ready for action in his home at any hour, and few days pass that do not find him arranging new tunes or making changes in old ones. Together with Wally Rose, ex-Watters pianist with whom he was long associated, he has amassed a huge library of melodies that he feels to be suited to the uses of jazz bands. In preparing them for use, he often rewrites the entire harmonic structure because the original chording was not absolutely correct in relation to the melodic line. This is a phase of musicianship rarely bothered with by other jazz artists. His powerful trombone, amalgamating aspects of the work of New Orleans veterans Roy Palmer, Kid Ory, and Honoré Dutrey, has become virtually the trade-mark of San Francisco jazz. He has a technique that is constantly seeking to better itself within the idiom, much in the manner of the afore-mentioned Bob Helm's.

One particularly notable feature of this group has been the growing use of free-style vocalizing by the band members. There had been some of this in the Yerba Buena group as well, particularly during an early period when ballad-singing banjoist Clancy Hayes was present and virtually coleader with Lu Watters, but never to the extent or in quite the manner the Murphy men subsequently developed. Murphy himself sings many of the old jazz tunes in a hoarse, shouting, baritone style, while Bob Helm often provides solos in what some describe as a "whisky tenor" of a very jazzy nature. Their most significant efforts, however, were achieved in the rendition of duets on various selections, notably spirituals. While singing in harmony, a purposefully loose phrasing was employed that heightened the effect of impromptu performance, adding greatly to the effectiveness of such selections as *Roll, Jordan, Roll.*

The importance of Wally Rose in this band, as well as at times in various groups under the leadership of Bob Scobey, also cannot be overestimated. A superb technician, teacher, and authority on ragtime piano music, his efforts as both musician and musicologist have contributed greatly to the San Francisco jazz scene. At the present time he is leading a band of his own in that city. Don Ewell, a gifted, scholarly pianist who has also been heard with Bunk Johnson (see page 244) and Kid Ory, is filling his spot in the

Murphy band. Rose firmly believes in the use of the classical exercises and disciplines for the development of technique, and equally firmly believes that the jazz pianist must be largely his own instructor in transferring his capabilities into the field of jazz. As a result, although there is strong stylistic resemblance between teacher and jazz pupil, each pupil reveals much in performance that is characteristically his own.

III   While the Murphy band was developing along basically the same lines followed by Lu Watters, Bob Scobey veered off in a somewhat different direction. His groups have had considerably greater variations in personnel, although the instrumentation has remained somewhat consistently more orthodox. His groups have featured tunes of much the same order utilized by the Yerba Buena Jazz Band. He has employed a looser, somewhat Chicagoan ensemble style among the horns, with a rhythmic backing of more conventional mien, in general favoring string bass and somewhat more prominent drums. During certain periods when Wally Rose was his pianist, the Watters flavor was more evident than at other times, and it is still there in some measure. The tempi, however, tend to be a bit more brisk than Watters would accept, and the band has never had a trombonist of any particular ensemble strength, so that the major similarity is found particularly in the leader's forthright horn style, especially on the more emphatically jazz selections. He has also gained no little attention in recent time for the use of ballads of a somewhat more sentimental kind than is usual in traditional-jazz practice, following a little along the lines utilized at present almost exclusively by Bobby Hackett, the popular Eastern musician who is a "graduate" of the New York-Dixieland school and is regarded by many in the commercial and jazz fields as an outstanding "musician's musician." Such performances, however, unlike the present-day Hackett's, are rather more incidental than primary to the Scobey concept.

In common with Murphy, Scobey has resorted to a considerably greater use of vocals than was common with the Watters group, in large measure because of the presence of ex-Watters banjoist Clancy Hayes, a singer combining attributes of the crooner, folklorist, blues shouter, and virtually any other type of major native American vocal style. Hayes possesses a prodigious memory and in the past often astounded jazz audiences and bandsmen alike by calmly stepping to the microphone and singing lengthy choruses

234

on old jazz tunes that no one ever knew as anything but instrumental. Today his talent is somewhat better known, and it is almost a surprise if a tune can be found for which Hayes has not somehow, somewhere found a lyric.

The Scobey group has been bedeviled by numerous major changes in personnel, so that it has not matured stylistically to the extent notable in the Murphy band. While its contributions have been considerable to the San Francisco jazz school, it seems not unlikely that its best days lie ahead. It is a band worth watching in the future.

Whatever may be said of the Yerba Buena Jazz Band and its two principal descendant groups, this much is emphatically certain: Their imprint on the traditional-jazz scene is indelibly stamped on efforts of bands throughout the world. The Castle Jazz Band previously mentioned and various other groups along the West Coast, including the zany but capable Firehouse Five Plus Two of Los Angeles fame, all owe a substantial musical debt to this source. There are and have been Scandinavian, Italian, French, German, and South American groups clearly showing the influence and in many cases attempting to carbon-copy the Yerba Buena coterie. The Graeme Bell band in Australia has shown considerable of the Watters influence in its playing, while the Red Onions in New York, the Dixieland Rhythm Kings of Dayton, Ohio, and another group in that city, the Gin Bottle Seven, similarly reflect this influence. What has too often been painted as a copy of Oliver has pretty clearly proved itself a new synthesis within the traditional idiom. The influences of Oliver, Morton, and early Armstrong are present, but a somewhat different spirit and a unique repertoire have lent themselves to a fusion of elements into a new entity. It is an entity recognized very little by the critics, but very clearly by the other musicians seeking to work creatively within the new area of approach to traditional-jazz music. This cannot be called "Dixieland," because the Dixieland groups, when giving consideration to the past, pretty generally think in terms of earlier Dixieland groups and not Oliver, Morton, or the other colored New Orleans masters. Neither can the style be considered New Orleans, because it is quite different in rhythmic approach. Its acceptance as a style in and of itself is virtually inescapable. Whatever may have been said or written about them, the men of Lu Watters' Yerba Buena Jazz Band created a sound unlike that of any other group before them despite overt resemblances to King Oliver's Creole Jazz Band in various respects

235

and their own stated desire to further the cause of that type of music.

Of more than passing historical importance in the San Francisco jazz movement was the aid and inspiration that these selfsame musicians and some of their more active patrons gave to other traditional players. This group was responsible in no small part for the extended stay of Bunk Johnson in San Francisco during the early part of World War II, giving him an opportunity to be heard and to become better known while playing with several members of the Yerba Buena group. Mutt Carey also received considerable encouragement from these enthusiasts in reaching a decision to resume playing jazz after a lengthy absence from the musical scene. It is not at all unlikely that it was the Yerba Buena efforts that gave Ory the encouragement he needed to establish a band in 1944, a group that has remained active up to the present time with a continuing faithful audience.

There has been considerable speculation as to the reasons for a growth of jazz interest in San Francisco at the time that it occurred, and many have been the opinions expressed in an effort to establish some sort of environmental rationale to cover it. However, Turk Murphy seems to have stated perhaps the main reason clearly in his opinion that it was due simply to the presence of a few like-minded, persistent, and capable individuals who had the courage to play the music and continue their efforts in the face of various adversities. It is his belief that the San Francisco audience is basically no more or less receptive to traditional jazz than audiences elsewhere. What made the whole difference, in Murphy's view, was a willingness to avoid the it-can't-be-done attitude plus the availability of several musicians possessed of leadership qualities. When the full story of the Yerba Buena Jazz Band and its predecessors is finally written, perhaps we shall achieve a better understanding of "why San Francisco." For the present, we can best be grateful to a fair city that played no small part in the birth of the traditional-jazz renaissance.

27. Bunk Johnson, jazz master

1   Unquestionably one of the most important figures ever to appear on the jazz scene is the New Orleans Negro trumpeter and band leader Willie G. "Bunk" Johnson. He was a giant of a musician in traditional jazz who, in a brief flash of glory prior to his death, reminded the world of the creative power existing in a man and a music neglected and forgotten by all but a few for nearly twenty years. His reappearance in 1942 as a vital force, following twelve years away from the horn, is a story too incredible to be good fiction. During his personal renaissance, he utterly demolished an array of concepts that had been coddled over a long period of years by jazz "experts." At the same time he clearly demonstrated the inherent classicism of the traditional form and opened whole new vistas to the attention of the jazz listener. There is no escape from the fact that he and the late Jelly Roll Morton have been largely responsible for the reorientation of thinking anent jazz standards and potentialities that has been in process during the post-World War II period.

Although Bunk Johnson had been earning his living since 1930 in extramusical labors, driving a truck in the rice fields and performing other such chores, something of his early reputation was known to

237

jazz *aficionados* through the stories of other musicians and the book *Jazzmen* (1939). The editors of that book, together with members of the Lu Watters band, were largely responsible for Johnson's acquisition of false teeth and a new trumpet. Their assistance made possible his return to professional activity and participation in the jazz renaissance that was already under way. Johnson, who had been instrumental in the early musical development of the celebrated New Orleans clarinetist Sidney Bechet, was fitted with false teeth by Sidney Bechet's brother Leonard, an outstanding dentist now deceased who was also a jazz trombonist of considerable ability. This was perhaps the most significant set of dentures in the history of American music.

Bunk Johnson's musical career extends from the Buddy Bolden band of the early New Orleans period all the way to the post-World War II era in which he received nationwide recognition prior to his death in 1949 at the age of sixty-nine. Most unfortunately, there are no records of his work as a younger musician, but there is consolation in the fact that a considerable number of recordings were made by him between 1942 and 1947. Although most of these were made under circumstances not fully to his satisfaction, the personnel and surroundings were sufficiently varied to give an insight into his capabilities. His final records attained a quality clearly indicative of what he was striving for. Moreover, his opinions on jazz, or anything else, were expressed freely and forcibly by Johnson to many of his followers (and detractors too, for that matter). One way or another, Bunk Johnson is a fruitful source of information about the capacities of both himself and the traditional jazz of which he was so vital a part.

New Orleans musicians differ among themselves on Johnson's importance in the early New Orleans era, but none has denied him significance. The consensus seems to indicate that he was appreciated by his fellow musicians rather more than by the public. Old-timers recalling his playing state that his phrasing showed some resemblance to that of the present-day white trumpeter Bobby Hackett and that although he was rightfully noted for his ability to "swing" a band, his playing was dynamically restrained. Then, as now, a schism existed within the music world between those favoring power and those preferring a lighter approach. The more obvious appeal of power brought considerably greater public acclaim to such trumpeters or cornetists as Bolden, Keppard, and Oliver than to the musicianly Johnson.

238

The Johnson approach to jazz was basically similar to that of Jelly Roll Morton. This approach is characterized by the use of considerable shading with little recourse to fortissimo passages or use of high registers, and support of the horns by a buoyant but subordinate rhythm. Like Morton, he considered the melody all-important and insisted that the musicians have a full knowledge and understanding of their work and of the leader's concept. Although the major portion of the Johnson recordings was made with musicians who were nonreaders, Johnson vastly preferred those who could and, on occasion, did read. Study of his various records indicates that he was very familiar with the piano scores of most of the pieces played by him. In fact, some of his choruses sound unique, despite the fact that they are very close to the original score, because the ear is used to "simplified" treatments from other horn men. For example, on a recording of *I Ain't Gonna Give Nobody None of My Jelly-Roll*, certain turns of phrase crop up in the trumpet part that are usually elided in the playing of others. The various choruses are phrased interestingly and originally by Johnson, but they clearly show an exact knowledge of the tune structure "as written" that differs markedly from the treatment of a typical jazz musician playing it from casual ear memory.

As often happens with a genuinely creative artist, Bunk Johnson, at his death, left unexpressed much that was in his mind. Numerous plans for a new band and a library of music gathered for its use were sad evidence of thoughts still young and ambitious at the time of his death. A great deal of the work he left behind has not been understood fully, and many of his ideas have been and undoubtedly will be subjected to considerable distortion by many followers of the music. He has the remarkable distinction of having been a vital force in two widely separated eras of an art form and was responsible perhaps more than any other single person for the tremendous surge of interest in New Orleans jazz that has come upon the American cultural scene following World War II. Ironically, the band with which he worked the most and the one that the majority of jazz listeners associate with him was a band that he disliked intensely. This band, however, was fully as important as Johnson himself in spearheading the New Orleans revival. It continues today as the George Lewis band, one of the most popular and respected of the present New Orleans jazz bands. These musicians are primarily "ear" men with whom Johnson claimed he was forced to play in a style different from his desire in order to compensate for certain of their deficiencies.

This band, with which Bunk Johnson played the most after his return to professional activity, included, in addition to his own trumpet, clarinetist George Lewis, trombonist Jim Robinson, banjoist Lawrence Marrero, and Alcide "Slow Drag" Pavageau on the string bass. Warren "Baby" Dodds played drums through much of the era, while the piano, when used, was usually played by Alton Purnell. As previously stated, several of these musicians played entirely by ear, with the over-all concept considerably more inclined to a "powerhouse" approach than Johnson preferred. Whatever Johnson or some others may have considered to be their faults, the band astounded both the critics and the public when it burst upon the scene. No one outside New Orleans had ever heard a group quite like this one. "Wild Bill" Davison, the well-known Chicago-New York cornetist, sat in with the group one night in place of Johnson and played with a degree of fervor and enthusiasm that amazed Davison himself as well as the audience. Upon leaving the stand, he stated that he had never played before with such remarkable rhythm backing up his work. Many other musicians availed themselves of the opportunity to play with these men and agreed in general that whatever their limitations, they possessed a vitality that was both significant and contagious.

The band made numerous records, not all of which have, as yet, been issued. Study of them indicates the basic conflict between Johnson's ideas and the concept of the other musicians, particularly when they are contrasted with recordings by virtually the same group with other trumpet players. It is pretty generally agreed that while this band was fascinating in many ways, both the band and Bunk Johnson are heard to better advantage apart. As a unit, however, the group was nonetheless of great interest. Things happened on their recordings that had never been heard before on record, causing many rapid adjustments in thinking about this music as a result. The habit Johnson had of dropping out of the ensemble for portions of choruses or for whole choruses was, to many, a novel contrast, while occasional brief moments in an ensemble chorus when no wind instrument was to be heard (the continuity being maintained by the rhythm instruments) seemed almost shocking at first. Over-all, there was a thin, hard, somewhat sour or acid quality to the ensembles that defied description, sounding like no other group that ever came out of New Orleans, yet possessed of an incredible power. At times one or the other of the horns is found to be out of tune to an unpleasant extent, but in other instances purposeful dissonances and shadings of note value in varying degrees have been utilized with remarkable effect. There is no better example of the traditional attitude toward harmony as a guide rather than a goal. Indeed, harmony seems here but an incidental by-product in the creation of a polyphony, the logic of which is to be found in other terms.

In speaking of this band, Bunk Johnson stated that he was limited not only in the repertoire that he felt could be utilized, but in the style of horn that he could use himself. Comparison between his work with the group and performances with other groups seems to bear this out clearly. In particular, a comparison with his final recordings, made with highly trained popular musicians in New York, indicates a somewhat more lyrical over-all concept, indicating less preoccupation with rhythmic requirements and a considerable increase in the use of subtle and effective dynamics. The writers will devote further discussion to this group subsequently. Within the limits imposed by the Lewis-Robinson band, however, Johnson created some beautiful examples of the art of phrasing.

An instance of Johnson's capacity for deft phrasing without undue alteration of the melodic line has been pointed out by A. Harold Drob, whose knowledge and understanding of the man and his music are equaled by few and exceeded by none. Mr. Drob points out that Bunk Johnson played *Darktown Strutters' Ball* with the Lewis-Robinson band on two issued records: a twelve-inch American Music record and a ten-inch version on the Victor label. In all, these records include thirteen complete ensemble choruses plus a few incidental solos. The thirteen ensembles reveal, upon study, thirteen distinct variations on the theme. Each gives expression to a variety of thoughts setting the melody in a different mood, yet in no case destroying it or changing it beyond recognition. It has been said by detractors that Johnson played in a simple style, requiring no great technical facility. If thirteen distinct variations on a theme represent simplicity in improvisation, one wonders what these critics would consider complex. Greater complexity would only have tended to destroy the material on which the variations were based, although some present-day musicians and critics evidently feel that it is improper for the underlying melody to be recognizable in any way whatever after an introductory chorus.

The Johnson technique of improvised phrasing offered numerous variant approaches, but can perhaps be most readily understood in choruses where he seems almost to play a melody "as written." In many of these straight choruses, one is almost unaware that a subtle reinterpretation is being created until the recording has been played several times. His way of hitting notes a little late to add power, his use of a short but potent phrase in place of a quarter note or half note possessing not too much significance in itself, his close following of the composer's basic structure with here and there a deft alteration of pitch or application of vibrato, his constant awareness of not only the phrase being played but those to come and those that have passed as well, these were the hallmarks of his phrasing and the hallmarks of a most superior musician.

II   During 1943–44, Bunk Johnson spent some time in San Francisco, taking part in weekly dances with men from the Lu Watters Yerba Buena Jazz Band, a significant white band of the jazz renaissance, which had been temporarily disbanded because several members were in the armed forces. This group made several interesting recordings noted for a peculiar but successful fusion of jazz styles yielding, among other things, the only available example of Bunk Johnson as a vocalist. In an effort to convince Sister Lottie Peavie, the gospel singer, that it would not be a sacrilege to sing *Down by the Riverside* with a jazz band, he recorded a hoarse, throaty rendition with considerable spirit, showing many turns of phrase reminiscent of his own horn work. Also, there is a moving and beautiful rendition of *Careless Love,* featuring the white clarinetist Ellis Horne, and a rollicking, spirited version of *The Girls Go Crazy* which finds Bunk in a happy, vigorous state albeit suffering a bit from lip trouble. These recordings, available on the Good Time Jazz label, have an entirely different sound from those made with the Lewis-Robinson group, the rhythm, phrasing, and dynamics having little in common. The group concept again differed from the personal ideal that Bunk sought. It did, however, permit him to show the listener elements of his capacities not as yet to be perceived elsewhere.

At the same time that the Yerba Buena activities were being carried on, a record date was arranged to utilize a band of New Orleans veterans with Bunk Johnson on trumpet. For some unknown reason, this fell through on the day it was to take place, and Johnson was forced to gather another band in a period of six hours. When the group assembled in the studio, it included Wade Whaley, a

New Orleans clarinetist who had been called from his nonmusical employment to play his instrument for the first time in several months, George "Red" Callendar, a modern bass player who has probably never been found before or since with a group remotely resembling a New Orleans recording band, drummer Lee Young, brother of modern saxophonist Lester Young, Chicago trombonist Floyd O'Brien, who was working in the Hollywood studios at the time, Frank Pasley, guitar, and Fred Washington, piano. That so strange an assemblage could play anything at all on such short notice is in itself amazing. That they succeeded in making several fairly respectable sides (including a previously unrecorded New Orleans number, *Spicy Advice*, which admirably displays the leader's horn style in a manner not previously revealed with other groups) is downright incredible. Johnson's tone is captured here more clearly than on many other records. He is heard in several solos, which were not, for him, a common indulgence.

Although these records, some of which have been released on Brunswick and Decca, are notable in portraying added phases of the Johnson style, his work is limited much as it was on the Yerba Buena records by lip troubles due to the restricted amount of playing he had been doing. As with many other brass musicians, it was necessary for him to play rather steadily to maintain a satisfactory embouchure. The contrast is readily noticeable when certain other record dates are compared with these. It is particularly interesting to note on this session, however, the degree to which the other musicians present subordinated their playing to Johnson's requirements. It is very apparent to those familiar with them that they are playing parts in a somewhat different manner from the styles with which they are normally associated. Most notable in this regard is the tasteful trombone of Floyd O'Brien. While one might wish that it had been more assertive, one cannot but admire a tasteful effort to avoid stylicisms that would have been unfortunate in what was intended to be a New Orleans recording concert. If this group had been together a matter of days instead of perhaps a few short hours prior to recording, it is conceivable that this might have been one of the most significant record dates of all time. As it is, the records are worthy of attention, possessing a unique, almost "studious" quality that is not without charm.

Mention was made previously in this chapter of Bunk Johnson's dissatisfaction with the repertoire of the Lewis-Robinson group. This dissatisfaction would seem strange to many listeners, as the

243

group recorded numerous selections not previously played on records, and utilized in person a repertoire that was infinitely more varied than the public has usually expected from jazz bands. The present-day George Lewis band, which is basically the same group plus trumpeter Avery Howard, has a most interesting and varied repertoire. However, Johnson wanted a group that could not only play virtually everything, but play it in a manner suiting his concepts, having careful regard for each composition as a subject for interpretation, rather than merely as a vehicle for New Orleans improvisation of the freest kind.

III   Ultimately, two sessions were recorded in which the old master did illustrate something of what he had in mind. The first of these was a group of tunes recorded with a trio consisting of piano, drums, and the leader's horn, the thought being that if there was not sufficient backing in the form of a full band of the desired nature, at least there was nothing included that would distract from the message Johnson was attempting to deliver. The second and more successful session, particularly from the standpoint of those concerned with a recording that would fully display Bunk Johnson's capacities, was a group of recordings with New York musicians who worked as a band under him in the fall of 1947. They undoubtedly came closer to meeting his requirements than any other group with which he had been associated since his return to musical activity.

The trio included Alphonse Steele on drums and the white pianist, Don Ewell, a disciple of Jelly Roll Morton's. The three men were playing in the band referred to as the Lewis-Robinson group at the time, the spring of 1947. Included among the selections were *When the Moon Comes Over the Mountain, Where the River Shannon Flows, Ja-Da, Poor Butterfly, Oh, You Beautiful Doll,* and *You've Gotta See Mama Every Night or You Can't See Mama at All.* Most of these are melodies that would not have been attempted with the full group at that time, giving us at least a partial insight into the goals toward which Johnson was striving. The performances are notable for the strong but decidedly unobtrusive drumming and for the uncluttered but effective piano support. Varied dynamics by the horn are very much the order of the day. The variations on *You've Gotta See Mama* are excellent examples of tasteful imagination on the part of a fine New Orleans horn, including interesting forays into the lower register that trumpeters too often neglect. Tasteful, too, is the manner in which the trumpet introduces solos by the piano and resumes the "ensemble" at the conclusion of them. Even here, with only one horn, many passages clearly indicate a rapport between trumpet and piano of a different sort from that of a trumpet in solo flight with a piano tolerated merely to provide supporting harmonies. A basic secret of the whole traditional idiom lies in the meeting of strong individuals on an equal basis in voluntary co-operation. It is forcibly demonstrated here.

The final recordings of Bunk Johnson were fortunately of a very high musical quality. In large measure, they gave dimension to his interpretation of jazz and what a jazz band should be. He firmly believed in jazz as a dance music and wanted a band that included all types of dance music in its repertoire. He felt that a band should be carefully rehearsed, with all members being capable readers of music who would willingly follow the directions of the leader, at all times recognizing the basic significance of each composition's melody. Although this band included musicians of varied interests and origins, and although they were together as a unit for only a few weeks, they exhibited in large measure the Johnson requisites, well illustrated in twelve selections issued on Columbia LP GL-520. Running the gamut of popular music from ragtime to the hit parade, even including a tin-pan-alley rhumba, they clearly justify Bunk Johnson's theory that a good jazz band could play virtually any type of selection, that interpretation is what determines whether or not a performance is jazz.

Although appearing on the Columbia label, they were originally made through the efforts and patronage of Messrs. A. Harold Drob, Robert Stendahl, and William Loughborough. Their high regard for Johnson can be thanked for making it possible to preserve these selections, each a refutation in itself of virtually all the violent criticism that had been previously leveled at his head by "critics" with little knowledge of jazz and less knowledge of Bunk Johnson. Here, at last, he is shown on record at a time when he was in good health, he was at least content with his fellow musicians, and most important, he had been playing sufficiently so that his embouchure was in good order. It has been maintained by some that much of what appeared to be lip trouble on certain of his sessions was rather psychological, the result of an irritated preoccupation with things not done to his musical liking by those around him—not an improbability in a sensitive musician. In the light of his work here, those who had called Johnson a charlatan, an unschooled musician, a tired old man, or simply "corny" seem at best ill informed.

The over-all impression of these performances is one of sprightliness. There is a sound not unlike a good dance band playing for an enthusiastic group of dancing listeners. This effect is heightened by the presence of such dance standards as *Some of These Days, Out of Nowhere, You're Driving Me Crazy, Chloe,* and *Till We Meet Again.* The rhumba *Marie Elena* and the hillbillyesque *Someday You'll Want Me to Want You,* written, ironically, by Johnny Hodges of Duke Ellington fame, add contrast of value. Perhaps the most significant, however, are four well-executed interpretations of rags, including *The Entertainer, The Minstrel Man, Hilarity Rag,* and *Kinklets. That Teasin' Rag,* also present, is a tune of somewhat different rhythmic structure from the true rags. It is worthy of note as a forerunner of the standard jazz piece entitled *Original Dixieland One-Step,* one strain of which is identical with the first strain of *That Teasin' Rag.* It is the only selection in this group that can be even partially identified as a jazz standard in the usual sense of this term.

Throughout these numbers, the Johnson trumpet plays with an easy assurance and an excellence of tone that show clearly what it meant to be with a good band in a good hall doing things right. Too often in the past, there were sessions where the trumpet was lost in a bad hall on worse recording equipment with too little time, uninterested engineers, and unsatisfactory accompaniment. Here at last were compatible circumstances, and they were not wasted. The horn spoke once more with the eloquence that brought it fame in an earlier day back home. This was no old man fighting false teeth and mealy-mouthed critics with cellophane-wrapped, chromium-plated musical "standards"—this was King Buddy Bolden's boy Bunk, giving more than a few of these selections the best interpretation they have ever known or are likely to know on record. At long last the time had come when what was fast turning into hazy legend might yet be shown to be concrete fact. In three short recording sessions on December 23, 24, and 26, 1947, made with a deceptive speed and smoothness that astonished all who had taken part in other jazz recording activities, it was done. Mr. Willie Geary Johnson, aged sixty-seven, had proved himself a master creator of American popular dance music in the New Orleans manner. There is honesty here, and humor. Beauty is present, fused with the exhilarating qualities constituting "heat" in "hot" jazz. There are pleasantries to delight the casual not overmusical listener, yet at the same time there are subtleties thrilling to the most sophisticated student

246

of jazz. One almost feels oneself dancing at the Waldorf, cover charge and all, when some of the standard fox trots are being played, and some of the rags sound most reminiscent of a brass band of the Sousa caliber playing in a bandstand on a village green for a springtime Sunday evening concert. The trumpet solo on *Hilarity Rag* gives particular expression to this mood. It is "hot," yes, but there is also a certain quality of dignity and importance emanating from it. Bunk Johnson's Original Superior Brass Band must well have known these characteristics in its leader in years past.

As with the recordings by King Oliver's Creole Jazz Band, repeated listening to these sides is most rewarding. The band is admittedly not quite of the caliber of the superlative Oliver group, but beyond question its leader is on the Oliver band level.

Many anecdotes have been recorded concerning the colorful personality of Bunk Johnson. There can be little doubt that in days to come they will prove the source of biographic effort. It is a strong temptation to indulge in some of these anecdotes here. One of them, concerning an event at the final record session, might not be inappropriate, illustrating as it does some of the leadership qualities Johnson possessed. At one point in the recording, heated discussion began to develop among several of those present. They had been working hard at music that was rather complex, the rags particularly so. The strain began to show at this point. Suddenly the leader opened a case and pulled out sheet music for the *Sugar Blues*. This confounded all concerned, who wanted to know what this was for—why were they concerned with a tune they were not to record? Johnson did not answer their questions directly, but insisted that they run it through. The number was played once, twice, Johnson still dissatisfied. After the third playing, he picked up the music without comment, stowed it away, and the band proceeded into the next tune they were to record. The point? Good, simple psychology. After the third rendition of *Sugar Blues*, not only was the issue of the heated discussion forgotten, but even the fact of its occurrence was history, and the necessary tranquillity re-established for good performance. There is more to being a musician and a leader than rapidity of instrumental execution. What it took, Bunk Johnson had.

Fully as important as the preservation of Bunk Johnson's music was the successful interpretation by a band of a number of beautiful and complex ragtime selections. The writers know of no other

247

similarly successful attempt to date by any band to interpret this music on record utilizing the full resources of a jazz band rather than a piano solo with or without rhythm accompaniment. They are played here as written in the famous old *Red Back Book of Rags,* which had been favored equipment among the New Orleans bands of the past. With their complex rhythms, multiple strains, and changes of key, they represent a challenge to any band. However, careful attention to a good band rendition of rags, such as these, makes an understanding of the rag as a piano solo much easier for the listener to achieve. It may be noted in passing that here, perhaps, is the answer to those who dogmatically state that jazz can never be written.

When Bunk Johnson was told that there was a young musician attempting to copy his style at the time he was in New York with the Lewis-Robinson group, he replied that this was quite all right, for he had seven styles and he would simply discontinue the use of the one copied. As with many other things he said, this statement contained as large an element of truth as it did of humor. Comparison of the various performances of selections on the Columbia LP indicates considerable ability at stylistic variation, while comparison with other recorded work shows it with still greater clarity. The Bunk Johnson of the Lewis-Robinson recordings or the Yerba Buena Jazz Band session sounds quite different from the soloist on *Marie Elena* and *Till We Meet Again* in the final recordings. The first of these is an excellent example of the wry Johnson humor. It is a sweet, enticing, seductive, light performance through to a sudden ribald, crashing dénouement in the last two bars, with a sharp tonal change from cajolery to conquest that is tremendously effective. The second is a beautiful variation of a theme not usually considered a jazz vehicle, particularly noteworthy for a very simple but effective opening. It is played in four-four time with the first three notes of the melody just sufficiently retarded from the natural beat to create a remarkable sensation of "lift." This is indeed dance music of a high order.

The full measure of Bunk Johnson's importance to jazz, and more particularly to the jazz renaissance, can only be measured in the course of time. There can be no doubt that his coming to New York in 1945 was an event that rocked the jazz world in its orbit. Many jazz musicians, some of them not young, were greatly influenced by him and his groups in their playing thereafter. The fantastic popularity of the old spiritual, *When the Saints Go Marching In,*

248

is almost certainly ascribable to the band's revival of the number as a popular selection during the New York performance. It was a number the band played with vigor, and it has known no rest since. Nor have others played it with as much respect for its religious connotations. Important, too, was the effect of the records and of Johnson's visit to the West Coast in 1943–44. Young musicians already interested in this type of music learned a great deal about it through playing with Bunk Johnson or through hearing him in person.

Although Johnson received considerable support from some of the few really knowledgeable jazz critics, he was severely panned by several of the more "modern" writers as well as a few of the New Orleans-minded who were still unable to comprehend what was to them a new and strange approach to the music they knew and loved. Despite adverse criticism, however, a number of bands were formed by young musicians attempting to capture the sound of the Johnson-Lewis-Robinson group, not alone in the United States, but in other areas as well. Great Britain, in particular, shows this band's influence markedly in the playing of several younger groups. Actually, it is unfair to consider Bunk Johnson's music in the 1940's as merely a "revival." In all verity, even though the idiom and much of the repertoire were from another time, the sound was like nothing previously heard outside New Orleans, and perhaps heard not too frequently there. Bunk Johnson was an important guiding force in the earlier period of jazz, yes, but it may well be that his later work was destined to be his most important and significant achievement. As a partial consequence of that achievement, there is today a growing awareness of traditional jazz and of the variety of the music that can be produced within its formal and substantive framework.

28. Kid Ory and his bands

1   Edward "Kid" Ory shares with Bunk Johnson the distinction of having been a vital force in New Orleans jazz through both its classic era and its present renaissance. Considered by many as the typical New Orleans trombonist and perhaps the best of them, he has an importance equally apparent in his activities as a band leader. He has played at various times with a large proportion of the most famous of early New Orleans jazzmen and either heard or competed with most of the rest. Fortunately, his recording activities cover a wide and varied number of bands in the period from 1923 to the present. The first record ever made by a Negro jazz band was, in fact, a record of *Ory's Creole Trombone* and *Society Blues* as played by Kid Ory's Sunshine Band in 1921.

The Ory bands were very popular in New Orleans prior to the time of his departure in 1919. Many of the best of the New Orleans jazzmen were in his employ at various times, including cornetists King Oliver, Louis Armstrong, and Kid Rena and clarinetists Johnny Dodds, Jimmy Noone, Wade Whaley, and George Lewis. Musicians have spoken of his music during this period with considerable favor, the band being consistently popular regardless of the personnel Ory might be using at any specific time. Bob Thomas, cur-

250

rently playing trombone with Paul Barbarin's band, vividly recalls attending dances where Ory's band was the featured attraction.

After leaving New Orleans, Ory was active as a leader on the West Coast and subsequently went to Chicago, where he participated in the numerous recordings made by Louis Armstrong and his Hot Five, a number of Jelly Roll Morton records, and several made by King Oliver's Dixie Syncopators, with whom he played regularly as well. Eventually he returned to Los Angeles, where his musical activities diminished, coming virtually to a halt during the depression. Prior to giving up music, he had been playing string bass and alto sax instead of the trombone with which jazz enthusiasts identify him.

When the jazz renaissance got under way in the late 1930's and early 40's, various collectors and critics urged Ory to resume his musical career. The year 1944 found him doubling bass and trombone with a quartet. In March of that year, he appeared with a full New Orleans seven-piece band on the Orson Welles radio program, receiving a tremendous ovation and national publicity in *Time* magazine. Thus encouraged, Ory decided that the time was ripe for resuming his band-leading career, and Kid Ory's Creole Jazz Band has been on the scene ever since. The initial personnel included, besides the leader, Thomas "Mutt" Carey, trumpet, Jimmy Noone, clarinet, Ed Garland, string bass, Buster Wilson, piano, Bud Scott, guitar, and Minor Hall, drums. Tragically, Jimmy Noone, a New Orleans clarinetist who was admired not only in his own field but by modern clarinetists as well, died shortly after this, ultimately being replaced by Joe Darensbourg, who remained with Ory over an extended period. Death has subsequently claimed Carey, Wilson, and Scott as well, but Garland and Hall are still with Ory. The basic concepts governing the 1944 band still apply to the present group, and Ory insists that these concepts are no different from those of his bands in New Orleans.

The continuity of Ory's music may be further noted from his consistency in selection of personnel. Mutt Carey and Ed Garland were on the 1921 recording made by Ory, while Bud Scott and Minor Hall also were with him frequently in that period and Jimmy Noone played with him in New Orleans.

With the exception of Noone, the 1944 personnel recorded a number of selections now available on Good Time Jazz LPs GTJ L-10 and L-11. On some of these, Omer Simeon (recorded with Ory in 1926 under the leadership of Jelly Roll Morton) plays clarinet. Subsequent recordings were made for Columbia, Decca, and other labels with clarinetists Darnell Howard and Joe Darensbourg. Since the death of Mutt Carey there have been additional LPs, but the level of good taste achieved by Carey has not yet been equaled by subsequent trumpets in this band. On records, the group seems to have given the best account of itself with the basic 1944 personnel, especially in the performances with clarinetist Joe Darensbourg. As is so often true of jazz bands, records do not always succeed in capturing the full capabilities of the group.

Although Ory has been the leader of this group, many who have been close to the band state that Mutt Carey exerted at least as strong an influence over most phases of the purely musical activity. "Papa Mutt," as he was affectionately known, was a quiet, intelligent, dignified person, admired by musicians and enthusiasts alike. Like Ory, he had a keen sense of dynamics, and the subtleties of shading they achieved together were a source of constant amazement to a generation who expected nothing more than they had been hearing from the quasi-Dixieland bands of the period. Carey was a very capable vocalist, as were others in the group, with the result that many and varied solo and group vocals were used to spice performances of the unit. When Mutt finally left the group several months before his death, Ory was hard pressed to find a suitable replacement. Of several who have subsequently been with him, only Al Alcorn, a younger New Orleans trumpeter, seems to have come reasonably close to meeting the full requirements. Mutt Carey, like Bunk Johnson, was a master of phrasing and could lay down a lead that would inspire any group in which he played. The writer recalls hearing him one night not long before he died, sitting in for Bunk Johnson in the last group with which Johnson played and recorded (see Chapter 16). He was playing truly remarkable lead despite a bad lip, a strange horn, and no opportunity to warm up. He played a version of *Panama,* using a clipped, terse, economical phrasing that conveyed great vitality, capping the climax by playing *Till We Meet Again* at a moderate tempo, purposefully hitting notes very hard just behind the beat. As a concluding number for the evening's performance, it seemed much more effective than the usual mad-dash-to-the-showers sort of thing that is now too commonly used.

The Carey-Ory combination, although an excellent one, was often disturbed by the type of difficulties that can occur where a close group understanding of a subtle concept is necessary. This was

252

particularly borne out after the loss of Jimmy Noone. While the average New York Dixieland band can undergo a total change of personnel during the playing of a selection with no important difference noticeable in the level of playing, the change of a clarinet in the Ory group would result in a letdown until the new member became fully educated to what the band was doing and the nature of his function in it. They had an approach that a musician could not acquire overnight, partly because improvisation within a loose framework was the basis of the group's playing. With a superb and subdued rhythm section fulfilling its assignment most adequately, mere rhythmic phrasing of a type often indulged in by jazz clarinetists, or "noodling" as it is sometimes called, would seem both ridiculous and ineffective. A musician without a good imagination would be totally lost in such an organization.

The rhythm section in itself bears note. All the men in the section were veterans who had played together off and on for many years, and the result was a rapport that was well-nigh incredible. Minor Hall, the drummer, considered by many to be the best jazz drummer extant, provides a perfectly steady beat, with the traps used solely for occasional brief punctuation. Buster Wilson was a pianist comparable in style and ability to Jelly Roll Morton. Ed Garland, the bassist, and guitarist-vocalist Bud Scott fulfilled their rhythmic-harmonic part with the metronomic accuracy yet sense of motion that characterize Hall's neat drumming. It was a most unusual and satisfactory unit. Just how satisfactory may be ascertained by a comparison of those 1944 records on which drummer Alton Redd performs with the remainder of these records, featuring Minor Hall. While Redd is an at least adequate drummer, the contrast is strong because of the unique requirements of the band and Hall's perfect understanding of them.

II   The factor that particularly sets this band apart is the high level of musicianship that it requires and that it achieved in no small measure after its formation. Ory has said and still maintains that there are far more elements in the jazz picture than most people realize. In his own playing, both past and present, he has forcibly demonstrated this again and again. Indeed, many of the selections he has played and the dynamics he has used which have seemed modern are elements that he states were used commonly in his bands forty years ago. Paul Barbarin, the New Orleans leader-drummer, told the writers that the varied dynamics utilized by Ory

253

were typical as well of Oliver's Creole Jazz Band in person. As Oliver was Ory's cornetist in an earlier period, it is not inconceivable that Ory's approach shows its effect indirectly here as well.

As with most good New Orleans bands, the emphasis in the Ory group has been consistently directed toward the achievement of effective ensembles. Ory himself, while sometimes very interesting as a soloist, is primarily bent toward ensemble playing, an art at which he is certainly one of the most adept. It is doubtful whether any other recorded trombonist has shown himself Ory's master in this regard, although there are several older New Orleans musicians who state that the late Zue Robertson was unquestionably the best performer on this instrument in New Orleans. Others declare that Honoré Dutrey, whose style was radically different in a number of important respects, was at least Ory's equal in the New Orleans idiom. Ory himself is known to have admired Dutrey's playing. The group concept expressed here, in any case, requires nothing better than Ory can offer. Few other groups, for example, would essay a fast selection in which the dynamics would soften for closing ensembles rather than go "all out" in power style for a smashing climax. Yet, much of the time, this is just what the Kid Ory band has done, as illustrated on the Exner record of *High Society*.

Comparison of the Ory band with the Bunk Johnson-George Lewis-Jim Robinson band at the same period provides an enlightening contrast between two radically different schools of New Orleans jazz. While the contrast is between two "revival period" bands, it is none the less fairly representative of a schism that existed in the earlier period as well. With the exception of Bunk Johnson himself, whose personal tastes more closely parallel those of Ory, this band was, and today under Lewis's leadership is, primarily of the New Orleans street brass band type. The Ory band and the type of band that Bunk Johnson was seeking were primarily bands more closely disciplined in the European sense, having a greater regard for harmonies. Conversely, a rough, powerful sound with some variance in pitch and a measure of purposeful dissonance characterizes the Lewis band. While technical musicianship certainly is pointedly superior in the Ory group, the Lewis-Robinson band shows qualities that are vital and refreshing, with an inner exuberance that is delightful and significant. Both bands represent styles that are clearly New Orleans, symbolic of the myriad approaches possible within the limitations of this music.

In the matter of repertoire, the Ory band has been notable for

254

its willingness and ability to play virtually all types of dance music. On dance jobs they have played waltzes and the various Latin tempos, yet still managed to utilize methods clearly indicating that it was a New Orleans jazz band doing the playing. Although their recorded repertoire has been somewhat more orthodox, they have added selections to the record catalogues from New Orleans music that had not previously been recorded. These include such numbers as *Get out of Here and Go on Home,* the selection with which Buddy Bolden ended his evening performances. Because of the highly diversified talents of the group, their capacities for sustaining interest through a lengthy program are most satisfying. Not the least of their talents is the presentation of various Creole selections which Ory sings in the patois of the New Orleans Creole. This band's value in fostering the continuance of traditional jazz as a vital force has been inestimable.

Ory himself, of course, is one of the most important individual musicians in New Orleans jazz. He is considered by many as the definitive example of "tailgate" trombone, although in more recent time his playing has shown more of the Dutrey manner than on recorded examples in the past. However, on various records made with the Louis Armstrong Hot Five, circa 1925–26, notably his own tune *Muskrat Ramble* (see Columbia LP CL 851, "The Louis Armstrong Story, Volume 1"), his playing is very much in the tailgate idiom. Older musicians hearing these records state also that his style here is distinctly similar to that of trombonists in the prejazz ragtime and cakewalk bands. Actually, the line of demarcation between jazz bands and ragtime bands is a difficult one to locate, but it is interesting to note that this style may date back even farther than is usually assumed.

Perhaps the best recorded examples of Ory's playing, however, are to be found on the spectacular recordings of Jelly Roll Morton and his Red Hot Peppers made in 1926–27. While the Armstrong recordings were highly informal, to the point of being occasionally sloppy despite their heat, the Morton sessions were primarily examples of top-notch jazz musicianship. Further information concerning these is supplied in the chapter on Jelly Roll Morton.

29. Renaissance jazz groups

1   We have devoted consideration to the Lu Watters band and its successor groups led by Turk Murphy and Bob Scobey; but there are other renaissance groups and personalities elsewhere who were or are of similar significance. A few developed parallel to the San Francisco school, while another and larger number appeared a little later and were, in some cases, strongly influenced by the Watters band and its successors.

Doc Evans, the popular Middle Western cornetist, is one of the musicians who became active in the very beginning of the renaissance movement of the middle 1930's. From that time until very recently, he has led various groups whose general character included elements of Chicago style within a basically Dixieland concept. The twin cities of St. Paul and Minneapolis have usually been the scene of his activities, with occasional periods of work in Chicago and elsewhere. While his groups have been primarily "white" in style, the Negroid influence has increased in his work with the passage of time. More of the older traditional selections appeared in the Evans repertoire in recent years, and as a result, listeners in the Middle West were introduced to elements of the tradition that they could previously hear only on record. Although numerous

256

The Johnny Wiggs Band. *Left to right:* Edmond Souchon, Ray Bauduc, Harry Shields, Stanley Mendelson, Johnny Wiggs, Tom Brown, Sherwood Mangiapane.

Left to right: Dick Lammi and Burt Bales, traditionalists in the San Francisco style.

Turk Murphy.

Lu Watters' Yerba Buena Jazz Band. *Standing, left to right:* Turk Murphy, Lu Watters, Bob Scobey, Bob Helm. *Seated, left to right:* Harry Mordecai, Bill Dart, Clancy Hayes, Wally Rose.

solos are featured by Evans, he has placed an increasing emphasis on ensemble style, striving for a neatly harmonized counterpoint. His own cornet playing seems to combine various aspects of Bix Beiderbecke and Muggsy Spanier, with other influences also apparent. A clean attack in the middle register is characteristic both of his personal horn work and of the over-all sound of the bands he has led.

Evans has been the best-known nationally of a group of jazz musicians in the Twin Cities. Others, including clarinetist and leader Harry Blons, have tended to develop along similar lines. Unfortunately, little attention is given these groups because this area does not offer the opportunities of New York or Chicago for publicizing performances. It is only through the issuance of occasional records by independent producers that these musicians become known to the jazz enthusiast.

Banjoist Monte Ballou of Portland, Oregon, was leader for several years of the Castle Jazz Band, a group that recorded for the now defunct Castle label during the 1940's. Ballou's concept was primarily Dixieland, becoming heavily infiltrated with the Lu Watters approach in the course of time. Cornetist Don Kinch, tuba player Bob Short, pianist Freddie Crewes, and, following the Castle band's dissolution, Monte Ballou himself have played with Turk Murphy during various periods. Conversely, clarinetist Bob Helm went to the Castle band after leaving Lu Watters during the later portion of the Castle group's career. Trombonist George Bruns of the Castle group further complicated this picture by subsequently playing tuba for a period with Murphy. It can be seen from these shifts of personnel that the San Franciscans and the Castle Jazz Band had much in common, personally as well as musically.

Although the Castle records were issued by a small independent label, they were relatively well distributed around the United States, the band being popular and well liked among jazz enthusiasts. It possessed a liveliness and enthusiasm that were infectious, in no small part the result of the keen enthusiasm of the band's members for the type of music they were playing.

One of the most unusual of the more recent jazz bands is the semiprofessional Firehouse Five Plus Two of Los Angeles. With the exception of criminologist Danny Alguire, a fine Dixieland cornetist, most of this group's membership finds its employment in the Walt Disney studios, where their activities are devoted to the production of a variety of extraordinary motion pictures. Leader Ward

257

Kimball, in addition to playing tailgate trombone of a high order, is also keenly interested in antique automobiles and railroad locomotives. It is one of the great mysteries in jazz to all who have encountered this phenomenon, but there seem to be a considerable number of jazz enthusiasts who share deep interests in railroading and antique or classic automobiles. While few have the good fortune to own an ancient fire engine, a fleet of antique cars, and a genuine full-sized steam railroad as does Mr. Kimball, the number who share such interests is sufficient to be worthy of serious study. One of your writers, in fact, falls in this category. The Firehouse Five Plus Two first became known upon the issuance of their initial records, a good-humored group of selections played with a light heart, but played well. In addition to Kimball and Alguire, such men as banjoist Harper Goff, clarinetist Clarke Mallery, pianist Frank Thomas, drummer Monte Mountjoy, and bass sax and tuba player Ed Penner have done much to give meaning to the name of the record company on whose label they appear—Good Time Jazz.

The band does not work regularly at its music, but plays occasional dates as suits the fancy of its members, in addition to making records or just playing for its own pleasure. Because of the occasional use of fire bells, sirens, etc., it has been compared to the strictly comedy band of Spike Jones. In reality, the jazz content of their work is more considerable and of better quality than many overserious record reviewers are willing to recognize. Their recording of *Lonesome Mama Blues,* for example, is a very pleasing, relaxed, medium-tempo performance that any open-minded traditional-jazz enthusiast would find most satisfying. The same is true of their *Fire Chief Rag* and numerous other selections. Contrary to the allegations of some critics, this group does not play continually with tongue in cheek. In both tone and energy, better records of the group show a distinct resemblance stylistically to the Original Dixieland Jazz Band, while other facets of their work clearly derive from the Lu Watters-Turk Murphy school. Like the Castle Jazz Band, the crew from the firehouse have always enjoyed friendly relations with their San Francisco "neighbors."

The Frisco Jazz Band was another group that sprang up for a period in the latter part of the 1940's. Their playing was very much in the Dixieland manner, the clarinet style of Jack Crook most particularly so. Crook's good-natured instrumental belligerence gave a quality to their ensembles that was emphatically traditional. Any of their records on the Pacific label or subsequent Trylon recordings

258

that featured Crook with Bob Scobey's band are good samplings of his capabilities. A particularly satisfying example is found on the Pacific record of *You've Gotta See Mama Every Night*. Crook's fiery ensemble playing here is an utter delight to the listener, while the brash thrust with which he enters into a solo following cornetist Red Gillham's vocal is in excellent taste, fully in keeping with the mood, selection, and style.

Pianist Ray Jahnigen, who has also played with Lu Watters, provides strong accompaniment and a number of satisfying solos on the Frisco Jazz Band records, assisted by the neat drumming of Gordon Edwards and string bass by Pat Patton. Cornetist Red Gillham plays a firm, clear, rhythmic lead style, driving the melody hard and wasting no effort on pointless embellishments or inane displays of technique. Jack Buck, who has since played trombone and piano with Bob Scobey, is the band's trombonist, providing an adequately phrased but dynamically weak part. Buck is at times very interesting, but he should be somewhat more assertive. Although stronger in his playing than the typical Chicago-style trombonist, he is not quite up to the level of the "tailgate" stylists commonly desired in bands of this nature. Where both clarinet and cornet are played as here in an outspoken manner, it is of considerable aid to the balance if the trombonist uses comparable force.

This band also made records on which Clancy Hayes plays guitar and provides vocal choruses. On their final session with Hayes, cornetist Gillham was replaced by Eddie Smith. Smith's playing was a little more Chicago or New York in type than Gillham's, but not to an extent that injured the group concept. His strong, interestingly phrased lead on *I Ain't Gonna Give Nobody None of My Jelly-Roll* is quite satisfying.

In Los Angeles, where the huge Hollywood Bowl is filled by jazz lovers once each year for a Dixieland Jubilee, a number of bands have been active. Pete Daily, a cornetist of no little ability, and clarinetist-arranger Rosey McHargue have played together or have led separate groups playing in the Dixieland manner for some time in this region. Also active here have been groups led by various members of the old Bob Crosby band, including trombonist Warren Smith, guitarist Nappy Lamare, tenor saxophonist Eddie Miller, and various others. While a few of these groups have been of some merit, their personnel has been most fluid. Too often their playing is merely uncontrolled improvised ensembles with innumerable solos in the vein all too common to New York and Chicago.

II   Further support for the Turk Murphy thesis that a good jazz band may spring up wherever a few capable players will devote their energies to it is found in the Dayton-Cincinnati area. In this vicinity there are now two active traditional-style bands, the Dixieland Rhythm Kings and its virtual offspring, the Gin Bottle Seven. The former of these has existed for close to ten years, during which time it has contributed young musicians to several other groups and has been the parent of at least two additional bands. The "D.R.K.," as it is affectionately known to its devoted fans, is a young band led by tuba player Gene Mayl, an ardent disciple of Lu Watters and the San Francisco style who is similarly devoted to New Orleans playing. His onetime drummer, Bob Thompson, now leads the Red Onion Jazz Band, a traditional group of somewhat similar concept, in New York. Hank Ross, the Red Onion band's pianist, also has played with the D.R.K. Ex-cornetist Carl Halen, ex-banjoist Jan Carroll, and ex-drummer Tom Hyer of the D.R.K. are the impetus behind the afore-mentioned Gin Bottle Seven. Bob Mielke's Bear Cats of Oakland, California, include leader-trombonist Mielke and banjoist-cornetist Dick Oxtot, both of whom have been members of the D.R.K.

The Dixieland Rhythm Kings, at the time the band first became known beyond its home territory, included cornetist Carl Halen, trombonist Charles Sonnanstine, clarinetist Jim Campbell, drummer Tom Hyer, banjoist Jan Carroll, and tuba player and leader Gene Mayl. For some time the group used no piano, but after numerous personnel shifts the rhythm section now features a piano but no drums. The group's ensemble style was relaxed, loose, and brassy, with trombonist Sonnanstine's very simple, broadly phrased approach readily identifying the band. Today's group finds little change in manner of playing, although only Mayl and Sonnanstine remain from the earlier personnel. Cornetist Bob Hodes, who played for a time with Sonnanstine in the aforementioned Red Onion Jazz Band, a group initially formed by Hodes, is now in Halen's place. The clarinet chair, which had also been occupied by Ory's ex-clarinetist, Creole Joe Darensbourg, is now assigned to Ted Biehlefeld, a disciple of Johnny Dodds and Bob Helm. Robin Wetterau, a saloon-style pianist and student of ragtime, gives a unique sound to the rhythm section, while banjoist Jack Vastine rounds out the group with his playing and frog-toned vocalizing. Vastine, like predecessor Jan Carroll, plays an energetic style, yet never muffles the work of other players.

260

This band has been accused of being "utterly unmusical" by some critics and has been castigated for a lack of technique, taste, or any other virtue. At the same time, it has been defended with equal fervor by others. It is true that certain members of the group are restricted somewhat in instrumental dexterity, and it is also true that this is not a band of "sight readers." On the other hand, their technical limitations are largely phases of music that are of least importance to their personal concept. Though not sight readers, all have a sound knowledge of music theory, and many of their selections utilize involved and well-conceived polyphonic and harmonic structures played with no apparent strain. Indeed, several items in their repertoire are originals by members of the band. Those who criticize their technique are invariably thinking in terms of different goals from the ones sought here. Their detractors in general feel that they do not sound sufficiently like an Eddie Condon group, perhaps, or Duke Ellington. As these are groups that the D.R.K. musically shuns, this is readily understandable. The traditional critic might well take Messrs. Condon and Ellington to task for their technical and intellectual inability to emulate the Lu Watters or George Lewis bands, if one must judge musicians by their failure to sound like the very music they wish to avoid.

A more recent group, the Gin Bottle Seven, includes the outstanding cornetist-trumpeter Carl Halen, whose conservatory training provides a superb technique that has fortunately not mottled his taste in the idiom. Pianist Fred Gary, a graduate student at the Cincinnati College of Music, is an ex-D.R.K. member of similar capacities. Banjoist Jan Carroll is perhaps the best of the post-World War II generation of banjo players. His ability has been amply demonstrated in this group and previously in the D.R.K. Trombonist George Stell, a most proficient instrumentalist, and drummer Tom Hyer, whose playing leans to the West Coast or San Francisco style, are also old D.R.K. veterans. Clarinetist Martin Kollstedt is a well-known musical instructor with highly diversified playing experience. The tuba player, Johnnie Pollock, has had brass band, dance band, and concert experience. In all, regardless of whose nominal standards apply, it would be difficult to accuse these men of being "unmusical." They are that most unusual combination in traditional jazz, a group possessing eclectic tastes and also unity. There is a very strong flavor of New Orleans about much of their playing, and it is readily apparent that the inspiration of Lu Watters and a memory of the D.R.K. are here. At the same time, however,

261

one finds the influence of Bix Beiderbecke, something of Red Nichols, a spicing of Chicago, and a hint of the better aspects of larger bands. Listening to "Volume II—The Gin Bottle Seven" (Empirical LP EM-104) is an elevating experience for those still holding the mistaken belief that the renaissance has produced no music of quality similar to that of various groups of the 1920's. In simple truth, much of this is better jazz than many of the so-called "golden age" recordings by some of the most famous names in jazz.

Among this band's more notable features is the careful placement and use of solos to build a performance instead of merely to add variety. Valuable also is the capacity shown by tuba-player Pollock for occasionally filling in a harmonic part in the polyphony of the horns without, at the same time, abandoning his responsibilities in the rhythm section. In so doing, he provides the occasional harmonic enrichment that several bands have achieved using tenor saxophone, yet has eliminated the muddying effect the saxophone too often creates in ensembles. Pollock provides a steady, rhythmic bass most of the time, but his periodic sustained notes and phrases behind portions of solos or in a few suitable ensembles are a decided asset to the group. Similarly sensitive good taste is shown by Carl Halen, a Nichols-Watters-Beiderbecke-New Orleans student, who uses both cornet and trumpet, choosing between these instruments as his taste dictates a need for the subtle variation of tone thus afforded.

The Red Onion Jazz Band is a group located in New York that is musically unrelated to the various elements previously characteristic of most New York efforts at traditional jazz. As leader-drummer Bob Thompson has aptly put it, it is a "structured" band, a term applicable as well to the D.R.K., the Gin Bottle Seven, and the spiritual ancestor of these groups, Lu Watters' Yerba Buena Jazz Band. Although obviously related to the other groups in this "family," it has today a sound distinctly its own, a quality not yet captured adequately on record. Records made by the group thus far have used radically different personnel from that of the present group, although cornetist Jim Heanue (pronounced "Hey-new"), pianist Hank Ross, and Thompson are present on the band's initial Empirical LP.

As trombonist Sonnanstine clearly marks the D.R.K. style, the cornet of Jim Heanue is the identifying characteristic of the Red Onions. There are traces of Bunk Johnson in much of his playing and not a little of other Negro players from New Orleans. The strongest influence, however, is the white Dixieland school as exemplified by the New Orleans Rhythm Kings, the New Orleans Owls, the Halfway House Orchestra, and similar groups. Heanue is markedly similar in his lead style to Abbie Brunies, depending for drive upon well-constructed phrasing rather than undue volume or nerve-racking excursions into the upper registers. He is an already interesting and capable jazz artist who shows indications of an even greater productivity in the future. With him are clarinetist Eric Heysteck and tailgate trombonist Steve Knight, who succeeds in sounding typical of the idiom but unlike any specific earlier player. Their dynamically controlled, well-integrated ensembles indicate that clear-thinking individuals can play jazz as well today as it has ever been played, given the necessary instrumental dexterity.

Thompson himself and pianist Hank Ross, however, are no small reason for the growing prowess of the "front line." Both are ardent students of traditional jazz, and both have played and practiced diligently with all sorts of jazz groups, from the best to the worst. As a team, they have developed into a highly satisfactory rhythm section, aided by a promising young banjoist, Paul Goodman.

Thompson firmly subordinates the role of drums to its proper supporting position, while adding texture and punctuation carefully as needed, including an occasional shot at a large cowbell—a happy reminder of the humorous side of this music. He is quite adept in his use of wood blocks, a favorite device of many traditional drummers, but one not always used by others with good taste.

Ross combines in his playing various characteristics of such diverse predecessors as Chicagoan Joe Sullivan, the New Orleans pianist Jelly Roll Morton, New Yorker James P. Johnson, and San Francisco ragtime artist Wally Rose. Like all the afore-mentioned pianists, Ross plays a true accompaniment style instead of the simple "one-two" rhythmic chording affected by many early pianists. He is also a noted performer of piano rags, a field in which only Wally Rose is recognizably his superior. Ross is a devoted "fan" of Rose, who he feels is unquestionably the best jazz pianist of the renaissance and perhaps of all time. The Hank Ross style, however, is somewhat different, showing clearly the sensitive yet strong individualism of this gifted personality.

We have already made reference to Bob Mielke and his Bear Cats. While trombonist-leader Mielke and banjoist-cornetist Oxtot have played with the D.R.K., virtually none of that group's character is evident in the Bear Cats. Together with cornetist Pete

263

Stanton, clarinetist Bunky Coleman, and a rhythm section, this group makes a most satisfactory attempt at the playing of strictly New Orleans-style jazz. Mielke first captured attention in the Bob Wilber group of 1947, a very young band that was perhaps the first of the "new" bands in the post-World War II period to win recognition. He has continued to develop in the idiom since, showing steady progress but seemingly a little self-conscious in his playing until recently. A similar attitude has been characteristic of many jazz newcomers and was true also of some of the musicians now associated with him. However, a growing self-assurance and additional playing experience have developed Mielke into one of the most interesting young bandsmen on the jazz scene. No less can be said of clarinetist Bunky Coleman, whose style is very much in the New Orleans manner, or of similarly disposed cornetist Pete Stanton. An interesting feature of their playing is found in the occasional instrumental exchanges, Pete Stanton shifting to banjo while banjoist Oxtot plays cornet as he did when he and Coleman had a band known as Dick Oxtot's Polecats. A unique feature of this band is that, while the musicians are white, they are playing a largely Negro music in a night club catering in large measure to an enthusiastic Negro audience. This is doubly amazing when it is realized that Negro audiences have generally viewed the jazz renaissance with apathy.

In addition to various other groups too numerous for discussion, there have been several "traditional" bands that have attempted to cash in on the jazz renaissance with music varying from caricature to utter degradation of the idiom. In some instances, sincere individuals have entered the field with an insufficient knowledge of the music and simply were not fully aware of what they were doing to it. Others obviously realized the shortcomings of their efforts but were unconcerned because they were making money despite their musical banality. Similarly irresponsible critics and promoters have not hesitated to present such groups in Carnegie Hall, on television, and elsewhere, complete with silly hats, comic masks, and all the bad features of the worst pseudo jazz bands of the early 1920's. A little comparison of ensemble styles soon separates such chaff from the wheat for the interested listener.

III   Elsewhere in the world, a high level of traditional-jazz activity has been found in several areas. Australia, France, and Great Britain have notably contributed to this music. Australia has had several interesting traditional-style bands, Graeme Bell's group, the Southern Jazz Group, Frank Johnson's Dixielanders, and a number of others having created much music of interest in a movement that is still growing. There have also been groups led by a strangely assorted, highly gifted instrumentalist who has also been a vital member of the Bell band and the Southern Jazz Group, Mr. Ade Monsburgh, known to his associates as "Lazy Ade." Among his many accomplishments, he may be found playing valve trombone, slide trombone, cornet, trumpet, alto sax, and clarinet. There is little doubt that he will also provide a passable performance on other instruments in the traditional field. In addition, he has been known to render vocals on various jazz selections, but it must be admitted that the effect of a good Australian accent on material designed for Basin Street consumption is, to say the least, rather startling. Such Australian musicians as trombonist Dave Dallwitz, clarinetists "Pixie" Roberts and Bruce Grey, cornetist Roger Bell, and many more have shown that worth-while jazz in the tradition is not a monopoly of any locality or people. A particularly notable factor in Australian jazz is the presence of considerable San Francisco influence in addition to that of the New Orleans stylists. In both playing and repertoire, several of the Australians have shown a distinct awareness of Lu Watters, Turk Murphy, *et al.*

France has produced several interesting groups, that of clarinetist Claude Luter being particularly so. This group studiously copied the King Oliver Creole Jazz Band, Luter himself having more than a little resemblance in his style to clarinetist Johnny Dodds of that group. While a little stiff rhythmically and at times faltering in attack, a fine spirit is shown on the Luter band's records, the cornet team of Pierre Merlin and Claude Rabanit acquitting itself nobly on several recordings released in the United States. Their performance of *Gate Mouth*, an old New Orleans standard that was never recorded by Oliver, is a driving, happy rendition of this fine stomp tune in much the manner that Oliver would undoubtedly have played it. The entire piece is given ensemble treatment, a solo being only approximated in one chorus which finds a muted cornet playing a free-flowing but simple improvisation that stands out only slightly from the continuing, driving ensemble of the other instruments. Luter himself and trombonist Maurice Jospin complete a most satisfying display of jazz counterpoint over a rhythm section including Claude Phillippe, banjo, Christian Azzi, piano, and Michel Pacou, drums.

265

The British Isles in the post-World War II period have been literally ringing to the sound of traditional jazz. In addition to visits by the Graeme Bell band and various American players, their own groups have been most numerous. Humphrey Lyttleton, a member of the peerage and descendant of Richard the Lion-Hearted, is the best known of their many jazzmen. A gifted cornetist, he has also proved adept on alto sax and clarinet. In conjunction with clarinetist Wally Fawkes, he has continually played with interesting groups, showing a remarkable perspective in the field. His admirers world-wide are legion—Turk Murphy has used his recordings to cover intermissions for his band on more than one occasion in San Francisco. Close on Lyttleton's heels, however, are a vast number of groups such as the Yorkshire Jazz Band, the Saints Jazz Band, Freddie Randall's band, the Crane River Jazz Band, and an astonishing number of others. All too few of these have been well recorded or recorded at all. Many, however, are worthy of attention. Although British dance bands have usually seemed almost pathetic to American ears (with the emphatic exception of Ray Noble's band of the mid-1930's), their recent efforts to play "pure" jazz have been infinitely more successful.

Whatever else may be said of the renaissance groups, one fact is particularly apparent: a steady flow of new talent is continuing to enter the jazz scene. Though many are discouraged and others lack capacity, a number continue onward with the long, difficult study and practice necessary to the creation of good jazz musicians and good bands. Men such as the gifted pianist Don Ewell, who has played with Bunk Johnson and Kid Ory, appear upon the scene infrequently, but with a strange regularity. Washington, D. C.'s tailgate trombonist, Pete Hart, is another such example. Although it is true that jazz was easier to learn in New Orleans circa 1910 when the very walls rang with it, it is similarly true that those who are studying it today as their chosen art are probably aware of a deeper meaning and greater worth than was perceived by many or most of the early players.

30. The jazz amateur

One of the most intriguing aspects of this peculiarly American art form is the growing degree of active participation by jazz enthusiasts. While amateur orchestras or string quartets, many of them possessed of admirable competence, are not uncommon in European art music, the average lover of such music is normally resigned to the role of auditor. Traditional jazz, however, is a music of relatively small groups, offering considerable ego satisfaction to its participants because of the individualism-within-ensemble creativity that is practiced by each participant. As our understanding of this music has grown, enthusiasts have become more fully aware that they themselves can become a part of the music they love through creative participation in groups attempting to play within the traditional idiom.

In reality, this music has always been the scene of much amateur or semiprofessional activity. Students of the music have rarely given very much attention to the nonmusical activities of many performers. As a result, they have not always realized that playing jazz has frequently been of secondary economic importance in the lives of various musicians. Many if not most of the early New Orleans jazzmen had other occupations. Even Buddy Bolden, the almost legend-

267

ary cornetist who led the earliest recognized New Orleans-style band, was a barber by day who also found time to be "Editor & Publisher" of a scandal sheet called *The Cricket*. Others were known to pursue all sorts of employment, the emphasis on music varying with the economic circumstances. This has remained consistently true, with a large proportion of present-day New Orleans musicians earning a major portion of their income in nonmusical pursuits.

It was otherwise with young New York and Chicago musicians. The early 1920's found most of the "name" musicians employed pretty consistently in jazz bands or popular dance bands without recourse to other types of work. It is by no means unlikely that this had a strong effect upon their jazz playing, particularly for those who moved freely between jazz bands and music of other types. The musician who plays jazz when the circumstances permit but derives his major income from totally unrelated fields is perhaps less likely to dilute the idiom than is the man playing other types of music much of the time.

During the swing era, musical professionalism came fully into its own. Increasing emphasis was placed upon technique. Instrumental dexterity replaced creative emotion in the standards of critics and performers alike. The ideal musician was the one who could develop a feeling of "swing" while playing something "difficult," at all times being careful to avoid the element derided as "corn," i.e. anything that had been played elsewhere more than six months prior to the performance of the moment. This peculiar attitude became the basis for continually changing fashions in music. It seems to be rapidly approaching its imbecilic climax in much of the current "modern" jazz as well as in the writings thereon in so-called professional magazines catering to popular musicians and the younger elements in their audiences.

At present, there is arising a growing realization that traditional jazz is not essentially and solely a music that must be performed by professionals. Instead, a cult of amateurs, the writers not excluded, and semiprofessionals have been taking an active part in jazz, with every indication that such activity will continue to increase in significance as time passes. The possibilities offered for evolution within the tradition by capable individuals in this category are of the utmost significance.

It has been said that American culture and American art have been limited because we have not yet developed any degree of leisure in our lives. In recent time, however, more leisure has been created through technical, economic, and social advances, with still greater advances clearly on the horizon. Is it not conceivable that the growth of amateur jazz musicianship is one indication of what our recently increasing leisure is leading to? Recognition of this phenomenon does not, of course, necessarily suggest acceptance of the assumption that our American culture is so limited as some European intellectuals would have us believe. While we as a nation are perhaps less culture-conscious than our European contemporaries, it must not be forgotten that America, both as a nation and as a cultural complex, is the result of a revolution that overthrew a European colonial civilization and replaced it with one that is still new and by no means as yet fully comprehended in European thought. Our standards of value differ in many important respects from traditional European standards, while the sharp European distinctions between classes of mental activity, or, indeed, classes of people, are decidedly less finely drawn in this country. The American who is a specialist in his daily work may be quite the reverse in his myriad extracurricular activities, expressing himself in highly diversified avocations that overlap in a way somewhat alien to conventional old-world thought. In retrospect, it may well be found in the future that our positive cultural contributions have been far greater than realized up to this time.

The renewed interest of traditional-jazz amateurs is of vital significance for a number of reasons. Perhaps most important, it means that the continued existence of the music as a living entity is assured in the foreseeable future. Important, too, is the greater appreciation and understanding both of the form itself and of the earlier music in the form that the participant may achieve through his activities. The achievement of even a minor degree of competence in the field is sufficient to demonstrate to the participant how much greater is the scope of the music than the portion generally recognized by the casual listener or by most "critics." Among many lessons that the neophyte jazz instrumentalists will learn is the fact that playing techniques differ somewhat from those of both the conservatory and the commercial dance band. Many musicians can read the most difficult of scores fluently but are totally incapable of jazz improvisation. Others can improvise on the basis of personal techniques permitting them to play any idea that comes to mind, yet their playing is uninteresting in solos and improper in ensemble passages. It may be seen, therefore, that instrumental dexterity and a knowledge of music theory are only a part of jazz.

269

Both of these attributes may be of value to a good traditional player, but these in themselves are not sufficient for good jazz playing.

The amateur, if he is not self-schooled, will find his way beset by mental blocks of his teacher's making. The trumpet teacher is invariably striving to give his student the tone and clarity of Raphael Mendez, a foremost player of European art music. When the student is thinking, instead, of the sound of Freddie Keppard or King Oliver and their powerful but smoky New Orleans intonation, it is obvious that student and teacher will face problems that are dire for at least one of them, perhaps both. Similarly, the clarinet instructor who quite possibly views Goodman as his idol will be horrified at the playing goals of a student inspired by Johnny Dodds, whose style was of an order of beauty radically different from the Goodman concept. It has been said that a proper embouchure for jazz clarinet is quite different from the so-called "legitimate" position of the instrument.

Whatever the hazards of learning an instrument, the jazz amateur will find the experience rewarding. He will learn, for example, that many seemingly difficult passages are but simple fakery, while other "easy"-sounding phrases require the utmost physical and mental dexterity. He will learn, too, that all the instrumental technique he may acquire is worthless unless his taste and his knowledge of the elements of traditional jazz are sound. Equally important, he will soon find that playing even adequately in the tradition requires a sharp ear, fast thinking, and a high level of self-discipline. The casual, free-and-easy, every-man-for-himself approach exemplified by the post-World War II efforts of the Condon clique in New York represents a different order of mental activity from the creation of a real traditional ensemble. Veteran New Orleans instrumentalists who have also played in large bands using written parts state that the big band with the arrangements offers easier work, but the jazz band is more fun. This is a thesis with which the competent amateur will find himself in full agreement.

31. The jazz audience

1   Only a small proportion of the persons who attend "classical" concerts are as intimately learned or as expertly critical with respect to "serious" music as the typical New Orleans-jazz *aficionado* with respect to the music he loves. He knows the musical history of dozens of composer-performers, how they derived and developed their respective styles, and with what sorts of fellow musicians they can best perform. He knows the traditional solos by heart and sternly rejects a performance of one of them in which the soloist evades any of its technical difficulties. He recognizes the tastefulness, impudence, or indiscipline of a musician's personal departure from prior styles and methods. He is quick to detect a lapse into lifelessness, however skillfully it may be disguised by technical competence or by rhythmic and dynamic emphasis. In short, he is an exacting listener but one who responds sensitively and enthusiastically to genuine merit.

There are also much less learned and less critical traditional-jazz lovers, who look upon the music primarily as a stimulant to gaiety and excitement. This segment of the audience applauds with equal vehemence the fine jazz bands and the worst of the pseudo-tradi-

Notes to this chapter begin on page 306.

tional bands. Sometimes, where such listeners predominate, jazz musicians are inclined to play "down" to them. One often finds this situation, for example, in a hall in New York where weekly jam sessions are held, featuring, in the main, "pickup" bands that play unrehearsed and careless improvisations on a limited repertoire in which many of the musicians have lost all interest. The music is usually wild, tense, loud, and utterly lacking in the emotional content and intellectual stimulation that characterize good jazz. Ensemble efforts are muddy; solos are featured out of all proper proportion, partly because of the entrepreneurs' eagerness to bring the "stars" conspicuously to the audience's attention. The contrast between good and bad jazz becomes especially striking on those nights when a genuine, integrated traditional-jazz band plays alternately with one of these random collections of musicians, however famous.

It is seen, from the foregoing, that a traditional-jazz audience is likely to exercise a greater and more immediate effect, whether favorable or unfavorable, upon the music performed for it than an audience exercises upon the music performed at a "classical" concert. The fact that the traditional-jazz musicians are improvising to some extent, composing in the presence of the audience, adds to their responsiveness to the audience's taste and understanding. Again, the audience's influence is enhanced by the intimacy of the usual surroundings—often a small night club—in which the music is heard and by the freedom with which persons in the audience address the performers. As a rule, some members of the audience are personal acquaintances of some of the performers, who chat with them, and sometimes with persons they have never seen before, during the intervals between sets.

Traditional jazz is often played for a dancing audience, which generally exercises a favorable effect on the music. When jazz is played for an audience that is watching the band, some musicians are inclined to indulge in antic gestures and posturing. Under this condition, it is more difficult for them to achieve the natural, relaxed manner in which the best jazz performances are usually produced. In their effort to create a favorable visual impression, they may fail to concentrate adequately on the music. Furthermore, the mutual rhythmic participation of musicians and dancers adds to the rapport between performers and audience. The dancers indicate in their movements some sense of the adequacy of the music and may thus affect the performance itself. A sort of beneficent circle is set up, in which the dancers, reacting to the music, stimu-

272

late the musicians to perform still better, with consequently favorable effects, in turn, upon the dancers. Also, the discipline imposed upon the band by the needs of a dancing audience tends to discourage the use of frenetic tempi and bizarre dynamics.

Perhaps the ideal place in which to hear traditional jazz is a reasonably small establishment in which the patrons both dance and dine. Food tends not only to reduce the effects of liquor—a drunken audience is an undiscerning audience, which will generally accept mediocre music—but also, like dancing, to divert the audience's visual attention from the band and thus to discourage kinetic showmanship.

In a seated traditional-jazz audience there are always some—not necessarily the *aficionados*—who beat time noisily with feet or hands or who rock in time to the music. This conduct is characteristic also of audiences listening to a swing band or to the rock-and-roll music currently so favored by the less promising of our adolescents. It undoubtedly has psychological significance, with which the present writers are not competent to deal. One psychiatrist has suggested that the rockers and stompers are persons who need to establish firmer relationships with their human environment and are seeking to do this in a primitive or childish manner. In any case, their conduct is not especially characteristic of the traditional-jazz lover as distinguished from persons who prefer other notably rhythmic types of jazz.

II   Some lovers of "modern" or "progressive" jazz possess detailed knowledge, within this field, comparable to that of the most learned traditional-jazz *aficionado* in his field. Some of them know and respect the developments—in swing, in Ellington, and even in Louis Armstrong or some of the Chicago-style jazzmen—that led to "modern" jazz. But most of the "modern"-jazz *aficionados* are interested primarily and almost exclusively in the latest thing. "The audience for no other art form," says Nat Hentoff, "is so cruel and so generally unaware of the importance of a living tradition as the jazz audience. . . . It turns on the older men in the field with the most punishing weapon an audience can wield—apathy." [1] (The context, indeed the passage itself, makes it clear that Mr. Hentoff's cruel jazz audience does not include the audience for traditional jazz.)

Mr. Hentoff links "this shallowness of the jazz audience" with the age of the persons constituting the audience. Lovers of "modern" jazz are younger, on the average, than lovers of traditional jazz, and there is certainly a tendency on the part of shallow listeners to prefer the kind of music that is (or was) current or new during their period of adolescence. Many of them uncritically continue to prefer this music for the rest of their lives. Surely some of the middle-aged persons who enjoy traditional jazz have never really chosen it, but have had it thrust upon their other-directed tastes by their early musical environment. They are, in truth, very close to the current crop of youths who prefer "modern" jazz not by virtue of the application of personal standards of selection but merely because it is "the music of today."

Like traditional jazz, "modern" jazz is often played in intimate surroundings. Dancing to this music is uncommon and in many cases virtually impossible. Although playing to a seated audience, most of the performers eschew showmanship. If anything, they go to the other extreme, manifesting detachment and almost a sort of asceticism. The audience, in tune with the performers, often assumes an appearance of lifelessness—"sitting there," said one observer of the patrons of a New York "modern"-jazz center, "like so many Buster Keatons side by side." The influence of the audience is felt but perhaps less so than in traditional jazz, not only because the audience, on the whole, is likely to be less learned and more readily taken in by novelty, but also because some "modern" jazzmen associate their music with independent self-expression, which would be inconsistent with audience-dependence. In determining to emphasize the communication of its musical expression to the audience, the Modern Jazz Quartet took a step, doubtless a wholesome one, specifically away from the tendency of much "modern" jazz.

Some of the more reflective among "modern" jazzmen regard their new jazz as part of a new way of life, shared by the more understanding and devoted of their followers. This way of life embraces the rejection of established values, even including vitality as ordinarily conceived, and a sort of integrity associated with the avoidance of pretense and of presumption. Although a man of religion in the conventional sense, or indeed any person not "hip" (i.e. in the know) in the field of "modern" jazz, might find profoundly presumptuous the very effort to create something valuable out of oneself or one's group in disregard of man's accumulated wisdom and means of grace, a "modern" jazzman who shows signs of presumption on a more superficial level is likely to be told by his fellows to "come down." The ultimate criterion of merit, in music and elsewhere, appears to be represented by the question, "Does it swing?" So far as this can be paraphrased, perhaps it may be taken to mean, "Does it have a movement and inner logic of its own?" With such a criterion, the "modern"-jazz way of life establishes a large area of tolerance for persons and conduct which, by ordinary standards, might be considered censurable. There is, in this whole approach to life and to music, an implied relativism and rejection of what is thought unauthentic that suggests the influence of existentialism.

Two persons, one of whom prefers traditional jazz because it was the music with which he grew up and the other of whom prefers "modern" jazz because it is the latest thing, are, as already suggested, very close to each other in their musical taste or, more precisely, in their lack of genuine taste. A person who likes all types of jazz equally provided they are equally well performed is, as indicated in the introduction to this book, suspect of judging music without reference to its content and therefore of reaching purely "musical" judgments rather than judgments based upon human values. He is judging as an aesthete rather than as a man. What remains to be considered is the nature of the distinctions between persons who have different preferences among types of jazz and who appear to have acquired their preferences *critically,* not in consequence of such fortuitous circumstances as age.

III   Three hundred ten individuals responded to a questionnaire listing the names of five composers, three jazz bands, and four types of music. Because of the likelihood that a subject would greatly prefer some instances of a type of music to others, the words "at its best" followed the designation of each of the types of music. The subject was to grade the twelve categories, except those with which he was "unfamiliar," according to the degree to which he liked the music represented by each. The highest grade was 10; the lowest, 0. Word equivalents for the grades were given—10 superb, 9 excellent, 8 very good, 7 good, 6 fair, etc. One of the bands was unfamiliar to most of the subjects. The other eleven categories are shown in Tables I and II.

Each subject was asked also to indicate his age and formal education, and to state whether he was a professional musician, an amateur musician, or no musician at all. He was asked also to grade, on the 0-to-10 scale, each of two religious figures, Norman Vincent Peale and Albert Schweitzer, on the basis of his admiration for them, and each of two television comedians, George Gobel and Jackie Gleason, on the basis of his enjoyment of them. This somewhat unorthodox device was intended to provide an indication of the quality of a subject's general taste and judgment.

More than half of the subjects were associated in some way—as students, teachers, or administrators—with New York University. All of them resided or worked in the New York metropolitan area. The effect of these limitations upon the significance of the results of the study may be somewhat mitigated by the primary purpose of the inquiry, which is to determine not the popularity of the various bands, etc., but the likelihood of correlations between people's jazz preferences and certain other characteristics, including their preferences in "serious" music.

Because of the claims to musical respectability asserted by proponents of various types of jazz, an effort was made to segregate the musically elite among the subjects. A comparison of their jazz preferences with those of the other subjects, the nonelite, would presumably be significant. In reliance on the judgment of musical authorities in general, subjects who showed a marked preference for Bach over Tschaikowsky and Debussy were selected for the elite category. (Only those were included who preferred Bach to both of these other composers by an aggregate preference margin of at least four points.) There were twenty-nine such subjects. They were conspicuous also for their love of Haydn, whom they gave an average rating of 8.1, substantially higher than the average 6.8 given to Haydn by all other subjects. They may therefore be thought to like classical music, in the most precise sense of the term, more than the other subjects in general do. The twenty-nine appear to be distinguished as an elite in other respects as well. Nineteen of them were college graduates; eight of the remaining ten were undergraduate students. Twelve had postgraduate degrees. Thirteen were amateur or professional musicians. Their grades for the religious and television celebrities, when compared with the grades given by the other subjects, suggest that the twenty-nine constitute an elite in taste and critical judgment; but allowance must be made in the case of their Schweitzer grade for the likelihood that some lovers of Bach admire him more for his Bach scholarship and performances than for his achievements as a humanitarian and man of religion.

Because the average age of this elite was thirty, well above the 22.5 average age of all the subjects, an effort was made to minimize the effects of mere age by comparison of the elite with the other

276

subjects (numbering sixty-five) of age twenty-four or more. The average age of these "old" nonelite subjects also was thirty. (The median age of the elite group was twenty-nine; of the "old" nonelite, twenty-six.) In addition to their average grading of Bach and Haydn well below Debussy and Tschaikowsky, their grading of the four religious and television celebrities showed much less discerning judgment than that of the elite. Also, a much smaller percentage of the "old" nonelite were college graduates (31 per cent compared to 66 per cent for the elite), had postgraduate degrees (18 per cent to 41 per cent), and were musicians (29 per cent compared to 45 per cent). If the eight elite under twenty-four years of age were eliminated, the three percentages for the elite would rise to 90 per cent (college graduates), 57 per cent (postgraduate degrees), and 48 per cent (musicians). In all the respects indicated, the broader group of the nonelite—everyone other than the twenty-nine elite—was inferior even to the "old" nonelite group, which is included within it. There is virtually no doubt, then, about the superiority of the elite over both the nonelite and the "old" nonelite. The average grades given by each of the three groups are shown in Table I.

Table I

Average grades given to designated composers, bands, types of music, and celebrities, by (A) the elite, (B) the nonelite, and (C) the nonelite of age 24 or more

Grade Scale: 0 to 10

	A	B	C
J. S. Bach	9.7	7.0	7.4
Haydn	8.1	6.8	6.9
Tschaikowsky	6.3	7.9	8.4
Debussy	7.1	7.2	7.75
Negro New Orleans jazz	7.6	7.6	7.4
Gershwin	7.1	8.8	8.5
Sweet dance music	6.2	8.6	8.1
Duke Ellington's band	7.4	7.5	7.1
Bongo drum music	6.9	5.4	4.8
Dave Brubeck's group	6.3	7.3	6.9
"Modern" or "progressive" jazz	6.6	6.8	5.8
Norman Vincent Peale	3.5	6.7	6.9
Albert Schweitzer	9.1	8.7	8.7
George Gobel	6.5	7.0	6.8
Jackie Gleason	4.1	6.9	6.3

The elite and the "old" nonelite group gave the same over-all average grade to composers, bands, and types of music: 7.2. The broader nonelite class, with the enthusiasm of youth, gave an average grade of 7.4.

Certain probabilities immediately suggest themselves. For one thing, the "highbrow" pretensions made on behalf of Gershwin and Brubeck, respectively, are not supported by the comparatively modest grades given to these by the elite. The nonelite, both "old" and general, ranked Gershwin above all the other composers and above all the types of music in the questionnaire. The elite ranked his music below several other categories, including New Orleans jazz.

The judgment of the elite on sweet dance music was sternly adverse. They ranked it below both "modern" and New Orleans jazz. The nonelite preferred it to both of these.

The elite ranked New Orleans jazz above all the other musical categories except Bach and Haydn. They preferred it to "modern" jazz by a margin slightly higher than that indicated by the general nonelite. This casts doubt on the proposition, so often stated or implied, that "modern" jazz is more advanced and more acceptable to a competent listener than New Orleans jazz. The fact that the "old" nonelite ranked "modern" jazz considerably lower, both relatively and absolutely, than the general nonelite doubtless reflects the element of age. This element was probably far less effective in the case of the comparatively self-determining elite, but it nevertheless beclouds somewhat the interpretation of the differences in margins of preference of New Orleans over "modern" jazz.

Grades were averaged for the forty-six subjects who indicated a preference of two points or more for "modern" over New Orleans jazz and, separately, for the 104 subjects who indicated a preference of two points or more for New Orleans jazz over "modern" jazz. The averages are set forth in Table II.

As might have been expected, group D gave Brubeck and bongo drum music much higher grades than group E did. More interesting is the higher grade given by group D to Duke Ellington's band. Whether or not Wilder Hobson is justified in calling Ellington's music "the best jazz,"[2] most of his music is surely much closer in content to "modern" than to New Orleans jazz.

Disparagement of the taste of persons who prefer New Orleans to "modern" jazz may be discouraged by the fact that the grades

278

Table II

Average grades given to designated composers, bands, types of music, and celebrities, by (*D*) persons who markedly prefer "modern" jazz to New Orleans jazz and by (*E*) persons who markedly prefer New Orleans jazz to "modern" jazz

Grade Scale: 0 to 10

	D	E
J. S. Bach	7.3	6.9
Haydn	6.9	6.5
Tschaikowsky	7.9	7.6
Debussy	7.0	6.9
Negro New Orleans jazz	5.3	8.3
Gershwin	8.5	8.4
Sweet dance music	8.5	7.9
Duke Ellington's band	8.0	7.2
Bongo drum music	6.8	4.9
Dave Brubeck's group	8.7	6.0
"Modern" or "progressive" jazz	8.8	4.5
Norman Vincent Peale	7.4	5.7
Albert Schweitzer	8.4	8.7
George Gobel	7.5	7.2
Jackie Gleason	7.0	6.7

given by group *E*, composed of such persons, are a little closer, on the average, than those of group *D* (persons who prefer "modern" jazz) to the grades given by the elite.

IV   A psychiatrist, writing in 1951, observed that traditional-jazz *aficionados* fall generally into three categories: intellectuals, Negroes ("but an increasingly small number of them"), and adolescents. "Each of these groups," he remarked, "consists of individuals who, consciously or unconsciously, regard themselves as outside the accepted cultural framework and as unbound by many of its conventions." [3] At the present writing, many adolescents of college age and some intellectuals, especially Negro intellectuals, are embracing one type or another of "modern" jazz. There is, indeed, always an advance guard eager to adopt a loyalty that will distinguish it from the generality of mankind, whether it finds the object of its loyalty in a supposedly new movement or in a return to old styles and ideals antagonistic to those currently accepted. At the same time, a larger audience—the "ever-novelty-seeking public," as Sammy Kaye

279

calls it in commenting on the many types of dance (and dance music) that have been popular for short periods—seeks something new on a less pretentious level.

But psychological emphasis and mass observation must not blind one to the fact that listeners tend to seek music, as well as literature, theater, etc., that reflects their own values and ideals. The quest of such music is pursued by many persons whose primary interest is neither in novelty nor in differentiation from the generality of mankind. Just as one may turn to, say, certain Renaissance music not in order to be "different" or rebellious but because it expresses what one wishes to hear expressed, so for the same reason one may turn to a type of jazz other than the types currently most popular. Nor is it always necessary to account for a musical preference on the basis of assumed psychological drives, unless spiritual needs are believed to be mere reflections of such drives.

To inquire further into the values sought by individuals in jazz, one of the present writers interviewed a number of persons who had evidenced an interest in jazz. The nature of the questions asked will appear in the following summaries of the interviews with four individuals who, although exceptionally articulate and superior in other respects, are nevertheless roughly representative of significant categories of jazz listeners.

A. Born and resides in Brooklyn; age twenty-one. A college senior. Owns about two hundred and fifty jazz records. Likes both traditional jazz and "modern" because "good jazz is good jazz no matter what the style." Does not care much for sweet dance music or for rock-and-roll except, in the latter case, when some of the old blues singers (like Joe Turner) are heard. Within the field of traditional jazz, prefers the "original New Orleans men," likes the "sincerity" of their music. Asked what he thought their music expressed, he replied that it "comes from within them" and is "more emotional than other types of jazz." Asked whether other types of jazz expressed the same thing as New Orleans jazz, he differentiated them only on the basis of the degree of emotion. Loves Charlie Parker's music, which is "very emotional." Thinks the Modern Jazz Quartet is best of the "modern" groups. Says that Brubeck sometimes plays chords that have little meaning, and that Desmond's alto saxophone tone is too smooth. In "classical" music, which he does not go out of his way to hear, he generally prefers the "earlier stuff" to romantic music. Used to like Tschaikowsky but now finds him "too sweet." Tried to organize a jazz club among college students, but became discouraged when he found that many students wanted to exclude traditional jazz. Two of these students said that they could not listen to traditional jazz, it made them sick. Found that the haters of traditional jazz say they like Armstrong, but that they do this merely because the critics have extolled him; they haven't even heard the Armstrong Hot Five or Hot Seven records. Asked how one might characterize the haters of traditional jazz, he said that they generally were persons who used bop talk and who admired performers who played "way out," i.e., in a very "progressive" style. He rarely reads fiction; occasionally reads biography. Has made photography a hobby.

The subject whose responses have just been outlined may be considered representative of intelligent, alert, somewhat artistically inclined jazz *aficionados* who are not especially observant of or critically interested in the nature of the content of music. Consequently they sometimes like highly diverse (with respect to emotional attitude) types of jazz.

His observations on haters of traditional jazz are significant. The hatred that some of them feel seems to approach the pathological. It brings to mind the fact that a group of "modern"-jazz lovers came repeatedly to an establishment where an older musician was performing, just to jeer at him. In part of the "modern"-jazz audience, the desire to reject certain values represented by traditional jazz (and perhaps to reject older persons) sometimes inspires a cruelty and a frenzy that are not likely to make for the enjoyment of music which is either morally or humanistically acceptable.

B. Born in up-state New York; has lived in several cities in the eastern United States and abroad; age twenty-eight. College graduate. Businessman. Plays jazz clarinet. Does not like musicians who are technically inadequate and rejects several New Orleans jazzmen for this reason. Has greatest "emotional response" to Chicago-style Dixieland. It is "spontaneous" music, expressing "individuality, whimsy, defiance, sometimes cynicism." He has the next greatest response to swing, as summed up by Benny Goodman, whose music in the late 1930's expressed chiefly "open enthusiasm." Just as the Chicago-style musicians added an intellectual element to New Orleans jazz, so some of the "moderns" have added an intellectual element to swing. In both the Chicagoans and "moderns" there is "a dissatisfied probing, a looking for something"; the Chicago men think they have found it and proceed to state it, but the "moderns" are more tentative. "Moderns" are less humorous than Chicagoans and sometimes "smart alecky" or "cute." However, B understands what they are trying to do and sometimes gets "an emotional kick" from their music. Among "classical" composers, prefers Bach, with perhaps Stravinsky and Bartok next and then, possibly, Sibelius. However, he has "very limited powers of concentration" in listening to "classical" music. Feels about Debussy as he does about Victor Herbert or mood music: he finds it pleasant as a backdrop against which he can concentrate on *other* things. "I can accept some pretty bad music on this basis"—for example, Kostelanetz playing Gershwin. Doesn't read much, but has read poetry and books on aesthetics and philosophy.

This intellectual and artistically sensitive subject thinks in terms of both content and musicality, giving perhaps equal emphasis to each. Like many persons who seek to state in words the content of jazz, he is far more explicit about the content of the traditional jazz he likes than about that of "modern" jazz. One may attribute this either to an ineffable content or to a thinness in the content of "modern" jazz; the latter, in most cases, is more probable. B appears to prefer Chicago-style jazz to New Orleans jazz both because the content of the former is very attractive to him (it actually corresponds to observable features of his personality) and because he considers the Chicago jazz musically more advanced.

C. Born in New York City and has resided there most of her life; has lived also in Boston and abroad; age eighteen. First-year college student. Plays "classical" recordings a great deal, much more than jazz recordings. Bach is, "without a doubt," her favorite composer. Beethoven, in whose music she is taking a noncredit course, comes next; she likes especially the second movement of his Seventh Symphony; prefers his early quartets to later ones. Also likes Haydn and Mozart. Does not like Italian opera. Likes very little modern "classical" music. Strongly dislikes the recording of *Vendôme* by the Modern Jazz Quartet because of what it does to Bach. Can't stand "modern" jazz when it borrows from the classics. When it doesn't, she likes some of it, but not the ultramodern jazz. Likes to play Brubeck's music when she needs background for doing something else (like homework), because it's not distracting, doesn't demand attention; it is more "down to earth" than a lot of other "modern" jazz. Brubeck often expresses "melancholy." Charlie Parker's music is "empty." She doesn't usually like hit-parade music, but it's sometimes a good background. Likes Paul Barbarin's band very much; its music expresses "a gusto, enjoyment of life, almost a fearlessness of life," but not a "devil-may-care attitude." It expresses "an under-lying cheerfulness and sincerity." A band she heard at Nick's (either Pee Wee Erwin's or Phil Napoleon's) did not "put as much into it" as Barbarin's band. The band at Nick's "gave you a sudden joyful feeling" but not so deep a feeling as Barbarin's band, more a "tem-porary" thing. Barbarin expressed a "deeper, more lasting emo-tion." Maugham is her favorite author, Robert Frost her favorite poet. Likes Rembrandt; also some medieval religious painting, which is "ornate in a simple sort of way." When in a "light, floating mood," she likes Renoir who, like Brubeck, is "pleasantly unobtru-sive." Dislikes nonobjective art.

The criterion used by this extraordinarily perceptive young lady is primarily one of content. In this respect she is still farther re-moved from A's point of view than B is. Her preference in content leads her chiefly to traditional jazz, especially to New Orleans jazz. There is a basically classical, although by no means snobbish, ori-entation to her taste in both "serious" music and jazz, and, to some extent, in the other arts. Like B, she makes a distinction between music to which she likes to listen and music to be used merely as a background.

D. Born in Pennsylvania; lived almost entire life in New York; age thirty-eight. Has received Ph.D. degree in history. Now a col-lege professor. Mother was trained to be a concert pianist. He began to study music at age of five. Had a dance band, in which he played piano, from about 1933 to 1940. Does not listen to music very much because of other demands on his time. Prefers the light classics such as Debussy's *Clair de Lune*, because he can use them as back-ground. He does not want music that will distract him; Bach and Wagner demand too much attention. In popular music, prefers show music—e.g. by Kern or Rodgers—because it has more to a melody than just repetition of a four-bar phrase. Liked Larry Clinton's orchestra; also Casa Loma. Is intrigued by clever arrange-ments. Neither traditional nor "modern" jazz has made a strong impression on him. He enjoys Dixieland and rather likes Garner and Shearing, but would not go out of his way to hear them. Has very little time for reading apart from his work; if he had time, he would probably read biographies.

This subject's tastes and attitudes indicate that musical skill and training do not necessarily entail an intense or profound interest in music. Like B and C, he distinguishes between music to be listened to attentively and mere background music. Unlike them, he finds only the latter acceptable. Even if the demands on his time were less intense, one gets the impression that he would become neither a traditional-jazz lover nor a "modern"-jazz *aficionado*. For him, the content of music is secondary in importance to the "musical" interest of its melody and arrangement but, even in this area, music is apparently not an important part of his life. His attitude toward "classical" music, it may be noted, is thoroughly consistent with his attitude toward jazz.

The four interviews that have been outlined serve to indicate some of the major characteristics of and lines of distinction among jazz listeners. There appear to be two principal lines along which listeners may be classified: (1) interest and preference in content and (2) "musical" interest. Acuteness in perception of content and critical interest in content vary greatly from listener to listener. The listener who has comparatively little concern about the nature of content, but who is musically alert and perceptive, tends to like traditional and "modern" jazz equally. As his interest in content increases, he becomes more selective, his preferences depending upon his character and ideals. The sort of character that leads a listener to be very observant and critical of content often leads him to prefer the type of content found in traditional jazz.

With respect to individuals who are highly responsive to music, their tastes in "classical" music are likely to be consonant with their tastes in jazz. The consonance often extends also to their taste in the extramusical arts. In the last analysis, questions of jazz taste are seen to be questions of artistic judgment, which, when not merely aesthetic, depend largely upon the content of the art products. Finally, the desirability of the content of an art product depends upon judgments of desirability and undesirability in spiritual and emotional attitudes. Conflicts of taste in jazz run deeper than is sometimes supposed.

32. The jazz record collector

The importance of the phonograph to jazz can hardly be over-stated. In perhaps no other medium has it been of comparable significance. Not only is it the principal source of music today for traditional-jazz listeners, but during the lull of the mid-1930's it was virtually the only means of communication between this art and its audience. Fortunately, the renaissance of traditional jazz has brought at least a little of the music to listeners in person. Appearances of various bands at night clubs, at concerts, or on radio and television have created an audience of considerable proportions for the "live" music. In large measure, however, this audience consists of people who are also record collectors. Constant improvements in the phonograph and in recordings, as well as the opportunity afforded to hear the type of music desired at any time, make the phonograph virtually a necessity for the serious enthusiast. Traditional jazz of the best quality remains somewhat rare in other media, and in many communities even the most popular of jazz artists are not to be heard save through the phonograph record.

Record collectors of various kinds have existed virtually as long as the phonograph. The collecting of jazz records undoubtedly started with the issuance of the first records by the Original Dixieland Jazz Band. Although serious collectors were to be found throughout the history of the music on record, their real significance first became apparent in the 1930's. Prior to that time, it had not been particularly difficult for anyone interested to obtain records by jazz artists that were made over a period of several years. However, the demise of several record companies and changes in catalogue by remaining producers created a situation of scarcity. Human nature promptly asserted itself. Where scarcity exists, man finds that value exists. Overnight the existing small coterie of collectors found their ranks swelling perceptibly. There can be little doubt that this growing ardent body of record collectors supplied the inspiration for the return of many musicians to activity in the jazz tradition. Indeed, several such musicians were themselves collectors, while a number of collectors have ultimately become jazz musicians.

Collecting jazz records is an activity that recognizes no social or professional barriers. Included among the most active and interested members of the collecting fraternity are names to be found in *Who's Who in America,* in *Burke's Peerage,* and in the files of various police departments. Collectors vary greatly in motive. Some have only a secondary interest in the music itself.

Many tales have been told of collectors' persistent efforts to obtain the records they seek. Door-to-door solicitation of promising neighborhoods was not uncommon at one time. The shuffling of thousands of records in junkshops was virtually a routine spare-time occupation for the enthusiast. There are those among them who have been in junkshops of every major city of the United States but have seen nothing else in their travels. In this category, perhaps the classic instance is that of a record dealer-collector who toured the southeast with a large truck seeking valuable stock for resale to individual collectors. What made his safari unusual, however, was not his own activity, but that of a similar dealer-collector who also sought large quantities of collectors' stock. As the first of these men was traveling the highways, he was totally unaware that the second was furtively shadowing him at a discreet visual distance with another huge van.

A brief review of some of the major types of jazz record collectors, in roughly ascending order of musicality, might prove of some interest. At the bottom is the small but energetic group of record historians or antiquarians who engage in record collecting much as others go in for stamp collecting. They are interested primarily in the rarity of records made by artists of some reputation

286

in the field. The issuance of a work on different labels or changes in the catalogue numbers are matters of the greatest significance to them. So are the issuance of second masters (performances of selections in addition to the performances initially issued by an artist from the same recording date; occasionally there is a significant difference) or changes in names of artists, titles of selections, etc. It is not an uncommon thing for such a collector to possess all the known records made by a famous jazz artist, but no phonograph and no interest in hearing the music that has been so carefully collected. Of course, many antiquarian-collectors are deeply interested in the music as well, but those who collect solely for the sake of collecting are by no means uncommon. Certain of these collectors are better acquainted with records by their master numbers than by title or artist.

Related to the above group, but with somewhat greater interest in the actual music, are certain highly specialized collectors. Perhaps the most typical are the "tune collectors." Such a collector may seek, for example, to acquire a copy of every known recording (no matter how bad) of *Tiger Rag* and will seek to obtain a copy of every new recording released. Carrying his interest one step farther, he may try to acquire all the records of tunes borrowed from *Tiger Rag*. As the trio strain of *Tiger Rag* has formed the substructure of a large number of tunes, both jazz and nonjazz, this can turn into a substantial undertaking.

In addition to the more avid brands of collectors, there is, of course, a comparatively casual group interested in the music but with no particular concern as to the performing artist, the particular style, or the record itself. Little need be said of these collectors; their behavior and capacity are neither more nor less than is found among dilettantes in other areas. At best, they provide a modicum of financial support to the medium and offer occasional converts to the circle of more deeply appreciative jazz listeners. At worst, they are responsible for the existence of diluted or pseudo-jazz bands that pander to their limited understanding and faddist attitude. These are the listeners who are the most susceptible to the "progress" thesis. Thus, although they find traditional jazz somewhat to their liking in contrast, perhaps, to "progressive" jazz, they are nonetheless quickly impressed by anyone claiming "improvements" upon the idiom. In the past, these were the followers of Gershwin, Whiteman, etc. Today, the approach is somewhat more subtle. They are wooed, instead, by displaced swing musicians who no longer can find big-band employment. These are the men whose Dixieland bands consist of musicians still playing with phrasing, intonation, and attack as they did in the swing era, unhappy in a music they consider "backward." Their work is frequently flavored with traces of light European art music, be-bop, and other elements, utilizing numerous solos to avoid undue attention to ensemble passages that are either lackluster or frantic. This is the "new" New Orleans music merchandised by malcontent "professionals" who state that Morton and Oliver would undoubtedly have "improved" in this manner if they were alive today. At the same time, they sneer at the efforts of those who are sincerely trying to play the music as the New Orleans pioneers and their followers have shown it should be played. There is always room for new material in a valid music, but not for elements obviously hostile to it. It is unfortunate that so many still fall victim to this type of rationalization. This is obviously based upon the same logic that convinces such people that next year's Cadillac automobile will automatically be the most beautiful machine ever created, to be similarly displaced by the following year's Cadillac, ad infinitum. The saddest fact about these spurious semi-traditional bands is that here and there one finds a real jazz musician whose presence is an indicator of validity to the ignorant, although he himself is unhappy with what is being done and plays in such a group for purely economic reasons. Neophyte jazz enthusiasts are often impressed by the technique and execution of such groups. To the serious jazz lover, the sound of such a band racing through the *Milenberg Joys* in a manner suggestive of a progressive group imitating the Hoosier Hot Shots is execution indeed, but execution of a different sort.

The more keenly interested listener in the jazz record collecting fraternity may have little or no interest in the rarity, label, or other antiquarian aspects of the record, but is concerned almost solely with the music. The advent of high fidelity recording and playing equipment in recent times has swelled the numbers of these people, particularly because of the salutary effect that such material has had upon the sound of records made by the old masters. The old records themselves sound considerably better on high fidelity equipment, and reissues of them reprocessed by modern recording laboratories have elements of quality not to be discerned in the original copies.

This latter group of collectors represents the hard core of jazz enthusiasm. They, above all others, have made it possible for tra-

288

Wally Rose.

Bob Helm.

ditional-jazz musicians once again to find an audience after the black days of the mid-1930's. Many of these collectors gave encouragement to the music not only by their collecting but through direct contact with the musicians as well. The Hot Club of Newark, New Jersey and similar modest-sized but ardent fan organizations hired jazz musicians whenever they could in order to hear the music and encourage those still able to play it. Constantly growing pressure of such people led to reissue programs by record companies and the slow return of jazz as an attraction in various places of entertainment.

The listening collectors are divided into a number of allegiances within traditional jazz, many of them overlapping into other areas as well. There are even a number of highly eclectic individuals who are equally intrigued by the music of the "moderns," finding in the two mediums widely divergent bodies of emotion, both of which are expressions of ideas holding meaning and interest to them. Other somewhat similar individuals find traditional jazz to be but one expression of the over-all field of American popular music, in which they take a broad general interest. Related too are some of the swing enthusiasts, although in this instance there is a somewhat closer connection through the diluted tradition found in some of the big bands. Strictly within the tradition, however, there are considerable variations in interest. The Chicago style, for example, is avidly sought on record by many who either are indifferent to or actually dislike New Orleans music, while many New Orleans or Dixieland enthusiasts view the Chicago product or the pseudo-Dixieland of many New York and Los Angeles bands that descended from the Chicago style as a weak travesty on "real" jazz. Somewhat less numerous but notable are the San Francisco-style collectors, whose world is limited to the production of Lu Watters, Turk Murphy, Bob Scobey, and those closely allied to them. Other groups are found favoring purely vocal jazz or piano jazz, while another category of some significance confines its listening to those performances and performers most closely related to the pure "folk music" category. These categories are representative of major groupings to be found today among record listeners and purchasers. It should be noted that various combinations of these categories are also to be found, with many collectors expressing interest in several phases or all phases of music that can be described as traditional jazz. Usually, however, collectors tend more to express interest in specific facets of the music than undifferentiated equal interest in all its parts. Despite the allegations of "sameness" thrown at this music by many critics, there are such vast gulfs separating the approaches of different schools as to make it difficult for a sensitive person to bridge them all.

The classification of collectors according to "schools" of traditional jazz is sometimes further subdivided by differentiating those interested solely in specific bands or even artists. Such collectors are declining in significance, although still numerous. Whatever may be the merits of a particular group or artist, the listener, if he reaches a true understanding of the idiom, will be attracted by others stylistically similar. A typical case is Louis Armstrong. Many collectors have sought every possible record containing even the briefest examples of his work, finding in him an appeal of great magnitude. As Armstrong has been admired for years by both musicians and collectors, this is readily understandable. Eventually, almost unavoidably a listener will find that many of the qualities admired in Armstrong are not peculiar to him. What seemed to be his invention is found to be in large measure at one with the New Orleans tradition. Men who seemed to be imitators are suddenly found to be similar because of their common musical heritage, not because of imitation. Armstrong has had many imitators, but upon close observation the common notion once held that "all jazz trumpeters are imitating Louis" is found ridiculous. The same is true of virtually any of the better-known musicians who have been idolized by the public or other musicians. There is ample reason to favor certain musicians or groups, but there seems little justification for listening to them to the exclusion of all else that their idiom has to offer.

Historically, the collector became a potent factor in the early 1930's, at which time the major interest of those who collected seemed to have been the solo efforts of various "hot" musicians. A very small minority was interested in traditional jazz as such, *in toto*. Its meaning was all but lost to the man who listened only to hear the direct message of an individual musician. Emphasis of the swing bands and of remnants of the Chicago jazz groups upon solo style undoubtedly was a major factor in the creation of this attitude. Many of those who began to collect were primarily interested in the swing music of the time and considered jazz records as merely a precursor of swing. This was the period when collectors would "suffer" through the records of the Louis Armstrong Hot Five to hear the Armstrong horn, believing that the other men present were playing in a "corny" fashion. It is interesting to note that the pendulum has now swung so far on its return stroke that many consider these records more significant because of the presence of clarinetist Johnny Dodds than because of the playing of Armstrong. Indeed, some feel that substantially this same group sounded better on records with George Mitchell rather than Armstrong on cornet. In effect, collectors had to learn afresh the meaning of jazz ensemble music. As they listened to older records to hear such soloists as Armstrong, Beiderbecke, blues singer Bessie Smith, and others, their attention was drawn forcibly to a manner of playing that they had ignored or overlooked. For the younger collectors, it was a totally new experience. With the passage of time, interest in ensemble playing has increased steadily. As a result, both collectors and jazz musicians are giving at least as much attention to it as to solo work. Once more the solo is being recognized for what it properly should be, a decoration or addition rather than the basic goal of the music.

Initial attention of the collector group to soloists led subsequently to a concentration of interest in a handful of personalities during the 1930's, with major emphasis placed upon the Chicago musicians and Negro groups featuring various "hot" solo artists. The early big-band work of Henderson and Ellington received much attention because these bands offered an array of such individuals on record. Ensemble capabilities were totally ignored by most collectors, and even certain instruments were viewed with little interest. The trombone was accorded respect only when played in the manner of Jack Teagarden or perhaps Miff Mole. The New Orleans and Dixieland stylists were viewed almost with horror save by a small coterie who had not been affected in their thinking by the "improvements" of the late 1920's and the early swing period. Indeed, Kid Ory was considered somewhat of an outcast until the slow awakening that got under way late in the 1930's began to reveal that this music was possessed of virtues more important than mere excitement.

The period that began before World War II, however, found the followers of New Orleans jazz becoming both more outspoken and more numerous. As we have noted elsewhere, the Muggsy Spanier Ragtime Band, Lu Watters' Yerba Buena Jazz Band, and the group of Chicago expatriates in New York all began to show signs of life at this time. Their activities and those of a few others, including the Bob Crosby band, helped spark the growing jazz movement. Their widely divergent approaches to the existing tradition offered a renewal of old ideas and several whole new concepts of the tradition

291

as well. Not only did they do much to increase the interest and activity of the record collectors in jazz, but they also stimulated in addition a host of aesthetic battles within the field that have continued unabated ever since.

Whatever disagreements already existed, however, were magnified a hundredfold with the advent of the renaissance of several old-time New Orleans jazz musicians. Music as played by the Bunk Johnson and Kid Ory bands proved to be quite different from anything the collectors had known in their previous listening experience. A whole new conception of what this music was and could be emerged in their performances. Followers of the other styles were astounded and either immensely pleased or utterly horrified by what they heard. Beyond any question of doubt, it was the effort of these groups that brought the already growing traditional-jazz renaissance to full flower. In so doing, it coincidentally brought renewed interest to other phases of the tradition as well.

Traditional-jazz enthusiasts, as a result of the diversity of concepts expressed by the aforementioned factions, are themselves divided in their musical preferences. The world of commercial popular music has taken little or no cognizance of these divisions, and the "moderns" and "progressives" as well as the publications that speak for them have recognized but one division: a sheep-and-goats classification of those traditional-jazz musicians who represent a compromise with "progressive" jazz and "popular" music and are therefore "good," and those who prefer to continue their development within an evolving tradition and are thus "bad." As a result, the commercial and "progressive" musicians, enthusiasts, and writers tend to create some very strange categories indeed when evaluating traditional-jazz musicians or performances. It is by no means an uncommon thing for them to group men together who find one another's music revolting, while viewing other traditional players as being in worlds apart despite deep personal and musical sympathies existing between them.

Those whose musical interests are oriented to the jazz tradition, however, tend to show marked preferences for one or another of the schools of the renaissance. Some, of course, feel that none of the renaissance music has been worthy of attention, or that at best it represents but a shadow of the music recorded in the early 1920's or perhaps in a period extending into the early 1930's. In this group as well, however, a similar categorization of interest among earlier jazz stylists is normally found.

292

The various concepts of traditional jazz all seem worthy of a measure of attention on the part of the *aficionado*. It is inevitable, nonetheless, that the same differences of personality and philosophy that cause differing approaches by musicians will cause differing aesthetic standards among their listeners. This discrimination is sharpened when the record collector is forced by economics to choose carefully from the large and varied selection of recordings now on the market. However wide his interests, this factor alone must cause some degree of specialization for all save the wealthiest of purchasers. The close relationship of the jazz record collector and the musician also plays a part in this, the collectors' opinions reflecting those of their favorite musicians in far greater degree than in many other types of music.

Among serious collectors, it is virtually axiomatic that the lover of Chicago jazz in its present-day version (the clarinetist Pee Wee Russell and various members of the Eddie Condon clique typifying this music) has little or no regard for the music of the San Francisco school, while the strictly New Orleans-style collector considers both invalid when contrasted to Bunk Johnson, Kid Ory, Paul Barbarin, and their bands. As for the San Francisco enthusiasts, they too are sometimes guilty of a cultism that recognizes no jazz music save the San Francisco style. To such collectors, jazz was invented by Lu Watters at the Big Bear Roadhouse in the late 1930's. When jazz "pioneers" are mentioned, they assume you refer to musicians such as cornetist Al Zohn, drummer Gordon Edwards, or the remarkably talented pianist Paul Lingle, men who were very active in San Francisco jazz at that time. In view of the strong ties to the New Orleans style professed by most of the San Francisco jazz musicians, this provincialism on the part of some of their following is a strange anomaly.

Even within the various collecting schools there exist numerous schisms, as is to be expected in an art whose history has been one of constant strife. There are dogged New Orleans enthusiasts who refuse utterly to believe that the renaissance styles of various groups from that city bear any qualitative relationship to King Oliver and his contemporaries. Conversely, many New Orleans enthusiasts insist that records of the better contemporary New Orleans bands have more clearly demonstrated Oliver's approach than his own early records did. It is certainly true that better recording techniques permit a more natural balance than could be employed on the early records, while the basic traditional style would seem to have been well preserved in a home city whose strongly musical environment continues to give in some degree the necessary sustenance. Too many earlier critical beliefs about this music were based upon a priori reasoning after listening to a handful of records made by a small number of musicians. The unexpected resurgence of "live" New Orleans music has made necessary a complete revaluation of this vital force—a revaluation by no means yet completed. Questions of relative quality notwithstanding, recent bands led by Bunk Johnson, George Lewis, Kid Ory, Paul Barbarin, Oscar Celestin, and others have in fact enhanced interest in the earlier groups because of the more complete understanding they have given us of this music.

A schism between followers of earlier and later Chicago-style music also exists. The greater degree of continuity in the making of records by this school, however, tends to make this division less clear. For some of the affected collectors, all interest is lost if any record more recent than the 1930's is played. Others find the greatest of interest in the music of the Condon clique and those surrounding it during the late 1930's and the early portion of the next decade. An additional group is blithely unaware of anything created prior to World War I and seems to have little or no realization of the relationship between the Chicago style and the New York brand of jam sessionesque quasi-Dixieland that they enjoy.

With the contrariness of mind that one eventually takes for granted among jazz enthusiasts, the San Franciscans are less vociferous in their preferences; yet theirs is a style representing the most emphatic rejection of the jazz dilutions of the depression period. The San Francisco musicians picked up jazz where they believed the pioneers had left off, totally oblivious of Chicago, the swing music of Benny Goodman, and the light Dixieland of Red Nichols, Phil Napoleon, and others of their period. They felt that popular music and jazz itself had taken a wrong turn somewhere in the 1920's. Their music represented not only a resurgence of interest in the purer forms of traditional jazz, but also a clear-cut break with trends to which others had resigned themselves. They have been labeled in many quarters as an unsuccessful attempt to emulate early New Orleans-style recordings. In reality, theirs was a new synthesis, combining many aspects of the New Orleans style with elements purely their own. Consciously or unconsciously, it was a manner of playing in which polish for its own sake and extreme rhythmic liquidity were rejected as facets of Chicago-cum-Swing decadence. The buoyancy characteristic of pure New Orleans is present in some measure—more notably so in later recordings—but this resurgence has not been at the expense of other rhythmic qualities or of ensemble clarity through unduly legato styling by the horns. Such tunes as *Sage Hen Strut, Annie Street Rock,* or *Antigua Blues,* written by San Franciscan Lu Watters, are clearly related to the tradition, yet are obviously a thing apart in several respects. The degrees of difference and similarity are such that New Orleans jazz lovers tend eagerly to accept or violently to reject the music, according to what it is they seek and find in the mother-music itself. San Francisco-style jazz is a music enthusiast's love or hate. The moderate like or distaste some listeners indicate for Chicago style is rarely found in reference to the music of the Bay City. Any readers of the major popular music magazines, magazines whose thinking is governed by their New York-Chicago environment and a yen for "progress," are aware of the hate reaction. One would obviously expect rejection of this music by writers whose journals cater to schools of music that are constantly compromising with one another. In listening to some of the modern mood music in the "progressive" vein, a music they frequently favor, it is impossible not to observe a very strong resemblance to certain efforts of the "schmaltz" or "Mickey Mouse" bands so frequently spoofed by these same publications during the swing era.

Although the phonograph record has been of the utmost significance in the development and continuity of jazz as a living music, a true understanding must be based at least in part upon some degree of personal contact as well. It has often been said that jazz bands are very rarely found at their best in recording studios. In addition, too many of the finest musicians have been recorded very little, very badly, or not at all. Many bands have been poorly displayed because of the whims of recording "directors" who were sure that they knew more about the music than its creators. On the other hand, certain rather lackluster, irresponsible players have managed to make records indicating great potentialities, only to prove utterly disappointing whenever heard in person. One need only think of a few New Orleans musicians who have never been recorded in satisfactory circumstances—men such as the Dixieland clarinetist "Pinky" Vidacovich, or perhaps trombonist Ernie Foster—to realize that listening to records alone will never yield a full picture of this music and its constituent elements. Record collecting is almost an essential activity of the jazz student or enthusiast; but for a full understanding it is still advisable for Mohammed to go to the mountain. Hearing the music played "live" by really satisfactory musicians brings a whole new meaning to the recorded performances.

Conclusion

In New Orleans jazz and, to a somewhat lesser degree, in other types of traditional jazz, the United States has produced and continues to produce a music characterized, in the hands of skilled composer-performers who understand its traditional content, by a sort of humanistic balance between expression and restraint and, more deeply, by a synthesis of Christian feeling and robust vitality. Its content is therefore comparable to that of eighteenth-century classical music and, again more deeply, to that of Bach.

Within the area of New Orleans jazz or of traditional jazz, as within the area of baroque-classical music, considerable variety may nevertheless be achieved, because the underlying world view or attitude stimulates individuality and inventiveness in the approach to basic truth. This variety includes the simplicity of George Lewis, the precision and muscularity of Morton, the busy high spirits of Brunis, the forthright heartiness of the Watters group, and so on. It includes also individual styles yet unheard and individual points of view yet unexpressed in the medium. That such variety should be possible within a highly disciplined music, closely bound by tradition, will be paradoxical only to persons who have not yet

Note to this chapter is on page 306.

come to understand that a sound tradition is as necessary to genuine artistic freedom as it is to political freedom.

Recognition of the value of the New Orleans tradition does not imply rejection of experimentation in jazz. Nothing can be more misguided and ultimately futile than a protest against newness or change, and the authors of the present volume make no such protest. But they consider it axiomatic that the new is desirable only if it represents genuine progress, which is not to be confused with novelty. Toynbee's definition of progress as a "cumulative increase in the means of grace at the disposal of each soul in this world" [1] may serve as a guide. The use of the word "cumulative" is especially significant in the present context. It suggests that if new jazz can provide additional means for the attainment of grace, it is acceptable even if the additional means are not superior to the old. It suggests also that New Orleans jazz or other traditional jazz, if it helps to provide means of grace, must not be rejected merely because more novel types of jazz are found to do the same thing. And in determining which of two types of jazz is the more progressive, the criterion will be not novelty or complexity but efficacy in promoting movement toward the only ultimately desirable goal. By this measure, New Orleans jazz is seen to be more progressive than virtually all the jazz currently called modern or progressive.

The development of jazz away from its norm, and of European art music away from Bach and the classical norm, was dominated by romanticism, secularization, and in time, thanks partly to these two influences, by the inferior taste of the egocentric, expansive man (mass-man) who has forgotten the great heritage represented by the humanism and, still more, by the vital, spiritual synthesis that inform the classics in both cases. These tendencies have led, again in both cases, to the effeteness of "modern" music and ultimately to reaction.

This reaction presents one of today's chief problems in both jazz and "serious" music. So accustomed to running away from the norm, and now running away from that toward which he ran, the "modern" composer must forgive those of his critics who suspect that he has got lost. Turning to old forms and methods of expression, he may still eschew the content associated with them. This may be true not only of a "classical" composer but also of a "modern" jazzman who looks outside jazz to those forms and methods, as some have done within the past few years. If he turns to jazz tradition, he may still fear, or fail to recognize, the out-and-out religiousness and hearty vitality of the norm and may therefore stop at an intermediate level where he will find mediocrity and frustration.

"Modern"-jazz musicians have complained that traditional jazz is a musical cul-de-sac because of its formal limitations. Departing from it, they have got themselves instead into an emotional cul-de-sac. Some of them are now turning back to find the point at which they went astray. Perhaps the most helpful suggestion that can be made to the more energetic of them is that they seek the point at which Western music, whether "serious" or jazz, left the mainstream of spiritual wisdom that inspired its greatest products. If they associate themselves with that wisdom, their problems of expression, form, and originality will become more manageable. For their principal difficulty is one not of method or technique or personal competence, but of spiritual orientation. The exertions required for achievement in this direction may be quite as strenuous as the efforts now required to drag inspiration and novelty out of a disoriented, harried subconscious, but they will prove more fruitful.

Notes

INTRODUCTION

[1] *Politics*, Rackham's translation, p. 661.
[2] See Edward Podolsky, editor, *Music Therapy.*
[3] *Down Beat*, August 24, 1955.
[4] *Ibid.*, p. 22.
[5] Written in 1923, quoted in Rudi Blesh, *Shining Trumpets*, p. 330.
[6] *Ibid.*, p. 40.
[7] *The Real Jazz*, pp. 6, 8.
[8] *Jazz: From the Congo to the Metropolitan*, p. 42.
[9] *Spanish Character and Other Essays*, p. 66.
[10] *Republic*, Jowett's translation, *The Dialogues of Plato*, Vol. III, p. 98.
[11] "The Capurso Study," *Music and Your Emotions* (prepared for the Music Research Foundation), pp. 56–86.
[12] F. S. Marvin, editor, *Progress and History*, p. 243.

CHAPTER 1

[1] Hugues Panassié, *The Real Jazz*, pp. 3, 11.
[2] *A History of Jazz in America*, p. 7.
[3] *Ibid.*, pp. 7–8.
[4] Ernest Giardina. See Frederic Ramsey, Jr., and Charles Edward Smith, editors, *Jazzmen*, p. 41.

301

CHAPTER 2

[1] Alan Lomax, *Mister Jelly Roll*, p. 63.
[2] Barry Ulanov, *Duke Ellington*, p. 22.

CHAPTER 3

[1] Preface, p. xii, to Albert Schweitzer, *J. S. Bach*.
[2] See Max Graf, *Composer and Critic*, p. 311.
[3] *The History of Music*, p. 23.
[4] *Beethoven and His Nine Symphonies*, p. 384.
[5] *Composer and Critic*, p. 24.
[6] *The Arts and the Art of Criticism*, pp. 62, 71, 272, 283 ff.
[7] Charles T. Smith, *Music and Reason*, p. 44.
[8] Theodore M. Greene, *The Arts and the Art of Criticism*, pp. 271–72.
[9] *Ibid.*, p. 43.
[10] *J. S. Bach*, p. 338.
[11] *Ibid.*, p. 339.
[12] Theodore M. Greene, *The Arts and the Art of Criticism*, pp. 283–84.
[13] P. 103.
[14] *The History of Music*, p. 23.
[15] See Charles T. Smith, *Music and Reason*, p. 42.

CHAPTER 4

[1] William S. Hannam, *Notes on the Church Cantatas of John Sebastian Bach*, p. 53.
[2] *Ibid.*
[3] *Ibid.*, p. 52.
[4] Frederic Ramsey, Jr., and Charles Edward Smith, editors, *Jazzmen*, p. 89.
[5] *Ibid.*
[6] *Ibid.*, p. 91.
[7] Alan Lomax, *Mister Jelly Roll*, p. 252.
[8] Louis Armstrong, *Satchmo: My Life in New Orleans*, p. 11.
[9] H. E. Krehbiel, *Afro-American Folksongs*, p. 48.
[10] Dorothy Scarborough, *On the Trail of Negro Folk-Songs*.
[11] See Rex Harris, *Jazz*, p. 47.
[12] James Weldon Johnson, *The Book of American Negro Spirituals*, p. 20.
[13] Cecil Gray, *The History of Music* (second edition), p. 12.
[14] Salomon Reinach, *A Short History of Christianity*, p. 44.
[15] Hugo Leichtentritt, *Music, History, and Ideas*, p. 33.
[16] *Ibid.*
[17] H. E. Krehbiel, *Afro-American Folksongs*, p. 45.
[18] *Ibid.*, p. 46.
[19] *Ibid.*, p. 47.

[20] This has been observed by a number of writers. See, for example, Joachim E. Berendt, *Das Jazzbuch*, p. 41; Hugues Panassié, *The Real Jazz*, p. 9.

CHAPTER 5

[1] W. C. Handy, *Father of the Blues*, p. 10.
[2] Okeh 41538.
[3] Decca 2230.
[4] Robert Goffin, *Horn of Plenty*, p. 157.
[5] Nat Shapiro and Nat Hentoff, editors, *Hear Me Talkin' to Ya*, p. 51.
[6] Sidney Finkelstein, *Jazz: A People's Music*, p. 45.
[7] James Weldon Johnson, *Along This Way*, p. 378.
[8] Charles Edward Smith, *The Record Book*, p. 120. Cf. Rudi Blesh, *Shining Trumpets*, p. 187.
[9] Nat Shapiro and Nat Hentoff, editors, *Hear Me Talkin' to Ya*, p. 35.
[10] *Ibid.*, p. 36.
[11] *Ibid.*, p. 37.
[12] Wingy Manone and Paul Vandervoort II, *Trumpet on the Wing*, p. 40 and *passim*.

CHAPTER 6

[1] Eddie Condon and Thomas Sugrue, *We Called It Music*, p. 104.
[2] *Ibid.*, p. 27.
[3] *Supra*, p. 67.
[4] Alan Lomax, *Mister Jelly Roll*, p. 43.
[5] *Frontiers of Jazz*, p. 67.
[6] Robert Goffin, *Jazz: From the Congo to the Metropolitan*, p. 47.
[7] See Chapter 7.
[8] See Chapters 4 and 5.
[9] Robert Haven Schauffler, *Beethoven: The Man Who Freed Music*, p. 69.
[10] Esther L. Gatewood, "An Experimental Study of the Nature of Musical Enjoyment," in Max Schoen, editor, *The Effects of Music*, p. 114.

CHAPTER 7

[1] Winthrop Sargeant, *Jazz: Hot and Hybrid*, pp. 254–55.
[2] *Shaw on Music*, p. 19.
[3] *The New Laokoon*, pp. 159–72.
[4] For example, Rudi Blesh, *Shining Trumpets*, p. 18; Lois von Haupt, *Jazz: An Historical and Analytical Study* (thesis), p. 24; Jake Trussell, "Dostoyevsky on Jazz," *Jazz Quarterly*, Vol. 2, No. 2 (Summer, 1944), p. 28.
[5] *The Second Line*, March–April, 1955, p. 6.

[6] Sidney Finkelstein, *Jazz: A People's Music,* p. 28. See also Barry Ulanov, *Duke Ellington,* p. 276.
[7] Rudi Blesh, *Shining Trumpets,* p. 148.
[8] *The Appeal of Jazz,* p. 186.
[9] *Jazz: Hot and Hybrid,* p. 266.

CHAPTER 8

[1] *Shining Trumpets,* p. 188.
[2] Percy A. Scholes, *The Oxford Companion to Music,* article on United States.
[3] Alan Lomax, *Mister Jelly Roll,* p. 99.
[4] *Ibid.,* p. 100.
[5] "On a Negro Orchestra," *Revue Romande,* October 15, 1919.
[6] *Random Studies in the Romantic Chaos,* p. 209.
[7] *J. S. Bach,* p. 166.
[8] *The Evolution of the Art of Music,* pp. 231, 234.
[9] *J. S. Bach,* p. 369.
[10] *Ibid.,* p. 166.
[11] Preface, p. xii, to Albert Schweitzer, *J. S. Bach.*
[12] *Music, History, and Ideas,* p. 147.

CHAPTER 9

[1] Columbia CL 851 and CL 852.
[2] *Horn of Plenty,* p. 283.
[3] *The Real Jazz,* p. 68.
[4] See Robert Goffin, *Horn of Plenty,* p. 301.
[5] *Record Changer,* July–August, 1950, p. 22.
[6] *Modern Music Quarterly,* May–June, 1936; quoted in Rex Harris, *Jazz,* p. 122.
[7] *Jazz Panorama,* p. 60.
[8] *Jazz,* p. 122.
[9] *A History of Jazz in America,* p. 70.
[10] Quoted in Barry Ulanov, *A History of Jazz in America,* p. 158.
[11] Ralph de Toledano, editor, *Frontiers of Jazz,* p. 154.

CHAPTER 10

[1] Anatole Broyard, "A Portrait of the Hipster," *Partisan Review,* June, 1948, p. 725.
[2] Charles M. Fair, in William Phillips and Philip Rahv, editors, *Modern Writing,* pp. 270, 278.
[3] Jean-Louis, "Jazz of the Beat Generation," *New Modern Writing,* p. 14.

[4] Nat Hentoff notes the "fierce passion" of one of Kenton's soloists. *Down Beat,* July 27, 1955, p. 17.
[5] *Down Beat,* Sept. 21, 1955, p. 14.

CHAPTER 11

[1] Albert Schweitzer, *J. S. Bach,* pp. 227-28.
[2] Barry Ulanov, *A History of Jazz in America,* p. 70.
[3] Nat Shapiro and Nat Hentoff, editors, *Hear Me Talkin' to Ya,* p. 403.
[4] *Ibid.*
[5] See Howard Taubman in *The New York Times,* September 27, 1955, p. 40.
[6] *Modern Music,* Vol. III, No. 3 (March–April, 1926), p. 26.
[7] Nat Shapiro and Nat Hentoff, editors, *Hear Me Talkin' to Ya,* p. 403.
[8] *Time,* November 8, 1954, p. 76.
[9] *Ibid.*
[10] William Phillips and Philip Rahv, editors, *Modern Writing,* p. 278.
[11] Mr. Kershaw has written an article along much the same line. A. L. Kershaw, "Religion and Jazz," *The Intercollegian,* Vol. 73, No. 3 (November, 1955), p. 9.
[12] Irving Babbitt, *The New Laokoon,* p. 111.
[13] Hugo Leichtentritt, *Music, History, and Ideas,* p. 264.
[14] Frederic Ramsey, Jr., *A Guide to Longplay Records,* p. 37.
[15] *Music for the Multitude,* p. 361.

CHAPTER 12

[1] Ortega y Gasset, *The Revolt of the Masses* (Mentor Books), p. 41.
[2] Ibid., p. 42.
[3] *Random Studies in the Romantic Chaos,* p. 208.
[4] Notes on Columbia CL 851.
[5] Barry Ulanov, *Duke Ellington,* pp. 22–23.
[6] *Ibid.,* pp. 27, 224.
[7] *Ibid.,* p. 94. See also p. 110.
[8] *Ibid.,* p. 35.
[9] *Ibid.,* p. 234.
[10] *Ibid.,* p. 18.
[11] *Ibid.,* p. 165.
[12] For example, *ibid.,* p. 155.
[13] *Ibid.,* p. 240.
[14] *The New Yorker,* April 2, 1955, p. 135.
[15] *Music, History, and Ideas,* p. 264.
[16] Merle Armitage, editor, *Schoenberg,* p. 256.

CHAPTER 31

[1] *Down Beat,* July 13, 1955, p. 12.
[2] Ralph de Toledano, editor, *Frontiers of Jazz,* p. 138.
[3] Aaron H. Esman, "Jazz—A Study in Cultural Conflict," *American Imago,* Vol. 8, No. 2.

CONCLUSION

[1] Arnold Toynbee, *Civilization on Trial,* pp. 262–63.

Index

307

309

311

313

314